D0834108

The Special Education Team

Stuart M. Losen, Ph.D.

Clinical Psychologist
Formerly Coordinator of Special Services
New Canaan, CT Public Schools

Joyce Garskof Losen, Ed. M.

Assistant to Superintendent
Westport, CT Public Schools

Allyn and Bacon, Inc.

Boston   London   Sydney   Toronto

Copyright © 1985 by Allyn and Bacon, Inc.
7 Wells Avenue, Newton, Massachusetts 02159

Library of Congress Cataloging in Publication Data

Losen, Stuart M.
  The special education team.

  Bibliography: p.
  Includes index.
  1. Handicapped children—Education.   2. Teaching teams.
I. Losen, Joyce Garskof.   II. Title.
LC4019.L67   1985   371.9   84-12417
ISBN 0-205-08203-3

Printed in the United States of America

10 9 8 7 6 5 4 3 2 1 89 88 87 86 85 84

To our children,
Laurie and Daniel Losen,
who are very special to us

And to all the special children

Contents

Chapter 4
Leadership in Team Meetings

Chapter 5
Effectively Involving Parents in Decision Making

Chapter 6
Coping with Unusual Team Problems

Chapter 7
Parents' Rights

Chapter 8
Training School Staff for Working in Teams

Chapter 9
Relations with School Boards

Preface

Our interest in writing about the special education team stems from the conviction, based upon many years of experience in the public schools, that the team concept works! We believe that the advantages derived from interdisciplinary problem solving and the active inclusion of parents in decision making far outweigh the drawbacks often cited, e.g., the danger of sharing prematurely formulated biases or of being unduly influenced by political or budgetary considerations.

In our experience, the careful development of effective teamwork requires the utilization of knowledge derived from group dynamics, communications theory, and leadership training. We have, therefore, drawn upon some of the basic research findings in those areas for major portions of this book. We also have experienced personally the limitations inherent in applying theory to practice in the schools. Consequently, we have tempered our suggestions for more effective teamwork by practical knowledge of what may or may not be feasible, given the daily pressures and realities of public school existence. Nevertheless, we remain convinced that the team approach is the best way to make decisions about children's special needs, because the team process lends itself to the checks and balances that bring us back to our superordinate goal: to serve children and to provide each child with the best available support services and special educational programs to help that child realize his or her potential for learning.

We have tried, whenever possible, to present our discussions of team meetings in an informal, case-illustrated format. Although all the material in the examples is based upon actual case records, it is organized and presented in composite form. Therefore, no illustration represents a complete, single case or situation. No real names of parents, children, or staff members are used, and all potentially identifying characteristics of individuals have been obscured to protect privacy and preserve anonymity.

The decision as to which gender pronoun to use when making general references to the parent or the child or to a staff member becomes no easier with each subsequent book. In most instances we have rejected the unwieldy he/she and we have never used the distracting and not yet standard s/he. For the most part we have tried either to use case material that specifically refers to a particular child by name or to use plural constructions so that we may duck the question by using "they" and "their." In unavoidable cases we have used "he or she."

This book presents opinions, convictions, knowledge, and insights gained, to a great extent, from personal experience. Therefore, the use of the personal pronoun was often unavoidable; since the book is a collaborative effort, we have used the plural.

We wish to thank our many friends and colleagues in the Westport and New Canaan public schools for their encouragement and support and interest in our efforts and activities. We wish especially to thank our typists, Dorothy Ahearn, Ann Cerretani, Dorothy Kerrigan and Nancy Miller, who, at various times, have had to struggle to decipher our various and seemingly endless rough drafts.

Finally, we thank one another for making it through the process of a joint writing venture which entailed the difficult task of melding two very different work styles, and often required us to relinquish our special attachment to our own particular words.

Joyce and Stuart Losen

1

The Changing Scene

The changed relationship between schools and parents brought about by the passage of the Education for All Handicapped Children Act of 1975 (PL 94-142) may prove to be a great boon to public education in unexpected ways. Thus far, in response to its mandates, special educators have developed new structures for providing options for children with special needs, for assigning youngsters to special education programs, and particularly for involving parents in the determination of their children's school programs.

The major vehicle for interaction between parents and staff for the determination of delivery of services to children, the multidisciplinary team established by federal law, is the subject of this book. And, although we will discuss briefly the views of practitioners who doubt the validity of the team approach to decision making about children's programs, we will not dwell on those views at length. It is our firm position that the involvement of a team of professionals, who bring different skills and differing perspectives to decision making, coupled with the active inclusion of the parents can result in more careful attention to a child's individual needs and more effective placement decisions.

This chapter will present a brief historical overview of the special education team (along with some speculation about future directions) and review the basic provisions of PL 94-142.

For the sake of variety, and because the team is called by different names in different places, we may use various designations throughout the book. But, whatever we call it, we refer to the multidisciplinary team established by law.

1

The passage of the Education for All Handicapped Children Act of 1975 (PL 94-142) wrought great changes in special education and generally set public schools on a new path with respect to handicapped youngsters.

But for many school personnel the law was, if not an actual bureaucratic nightmare, at least a very bad dream. It tangled them and parents in red tape and nearly stifled them in cumbersome legal procedures. These procedural problems notwithstanding, the law's overall effect was, is, and will continue to be positive. Regardless of future shifts and changes in detail, the law established basic precedents regarding the education of handicapped children that are unlikely to be reversed. On the contrary, we may well see the day when some of the special considerations now given to handicapped children may be extended to all children. When that occurs, the multidisciplinary team will be even more important than it now is, as it will have an impact on everyone's education.

Among the provisions of the law, two are basic: the law requires schools to provide comprehensive services for all "exceptional" children, (i.e., children who need special education), and it further requires that decisions about recommendations for those services be made by a professional team that is multidisciplinary. This double mandate was welcomed by the parents of handicapped youngsters; they, to some extent justifiably, saw it as the result of their vigorous and persistent lobbying, which had contributed significantly to the law's passage. The efforts of the parents resulted also in another aspect of the law, one unparalleled in laws relating to education, and in general educational practices: the requirement that parents be *formally* involved in decision making about their children's educational programs and placements.

The features of PL 94-142 that are of greatest significance for a discussion of special education teams, and the subject matter of this book, are the following:

1. It stipulates that all handicapped children determined to need special education must be provided with special education and related services.
2. The law calls for the identification of handicapped children as early as possible, even before they are of school age.
3. PL 94-142 requires regular consultation with parents or guardians and provides for detailed appeal procedures (referred to as "due process") in instances when parents do not concur with decisions about their children's identification, program, or placement.

4. Most important, and most directly related to the concept of decision making by professional teams, PL 94-142 also introduced the concept of the development of a written individual educational program (known as an IEP) for every handicapped child. The law required the program to be designed initially in consultation with the child's parents or guardian and reviewed at legally determined intervals.

In most states this written program must be developed by an interdisciplinary team whose functions include evaluation of the child, determination that the child is in need of a special educational program (referred to as "identification" of the child), specification of *what* the program should be, and determination of what placement is most appropriate for the child. The IEP must state specific goals and must include procedures and timelines for meeting them.

Considering the magnitude of the law's implications and the enormity of change it presaged for the educational establishment, public school educators should be admired for their responses to it. In many places, they moved with commendable speed to offer required services to handicapped children. They also generally acquiesced in the participation of parents and worked to comply with the spirit as well as the letter of the law.

As experience with the law has accumulated, government agencies have changed (and will undoubtedly continue to change) regulations and requirements to reduce the burden of paperwork and define limits of a school district's financial responsibility for special education services. But the basic precedent has been established. Given the essential humane intentions of the law, given the fact that services for handicapped children were long overdue, and given the strength and organization of the parental and professional lobby groups, it is unlikely that the basic concept of PL 94-142 will be reversed, regardless of specific changes in the near or more distant future.

Early in the law's existence, while most school systems attempted to comply voluntarily, some school systems chose to wait to implement the law until they were pressed by lawsuits or subject to state or federal pressure. These school systems may persist in dilatory tactics, particularly in light of some uncertainty about the degree to which federal regulations may be changed and funding allocations maintained. But even as specific regulations change, few now deny the law's inevitability. All will increasingly comply, and all will need assistance in forging the new relationship between the school system and the parents that the law requires and the times demand.

That there would have been some reluctance and widespread anxiety is not surprising. Even setting aside financial considerations, the philosophical changes required by this approach to handicapped education are significant.

Traditionally, parents' responsibility for educational decisions had been limited to sending their children to school. Parents may have been more directly involved in specific decision making in private schools, although for many the basic decision they make is to send their children to private school, presumably after having examined the programs and philosophies of several before choosing one, or after opting for a parochial school education. In some private schools, parents have little real say in decisions about curriculum or about their own children's specific programs, as requirements may be somewhat rigid.

At any rate, parents who sent their children to public schools had heretofore had little direct impact on their children's programs. The public schools have had literally unilateral authority regarding programs and placement so long as they adhered to basic state regulations and did not violate any of their own written policies in making a placement. Since most parents lack the financial means to choose private schools, and since in only a few districts is there an open enrollment policy where parents have the right to transfer children to other schools if they are not satisfied with the one to which their children are assigned, parents do not really have the means to "vote with their feet." Therefore, the public schools' power to place children and determine program had been largely unchallenged. Obviously, in many school systems active, interested, and inquiring parents have been permitted some influence on decisions about their children. Many a principal has yielded to demanding parents' insistence that their child be placed with a particular teacher, or not placed with someone they do not like. But the ultimate authority to decide what children shall study, which class they shall be in, and what outcomes are expected had been vested in the school system. And the schools had the power to offer, expand, or withhold parents' opportunity to participate.

This traditional "ownership of power" had certainly seemed to be satisfactory and convenient for the schools and for many parents. It was not, after all, the professional educators who strove to change that status quo or to share their power, or the parents of children in the educational mainstream who demanded a changed relationship. But the situation was very unsatisfactory for many parents, and it may well be that the lopsidedness of this division of authority, which made parents feel impotent to bring about change either in their own children's program or in the system as a whole, contributed to the public disaffection with the schools in the 1970s that was evidenced in opinion polls and "sensed" by many educators. For when people feel powerless to affect an institution upon which they are supremely dependent, they may be inclined to blame that institution for a wide range of problems, including problems which have their genesis outside the institution.

Thus, as drug and alcohol abuse increased among school-aged youngsters in the late 1960s and early 1970s, for example, it became "de rigeur" to blame the schools, rather than to view the problems (that then manifested themselves in school-related difficulties) as symptomatic of a wider societal malaise. Further experience with these problems eventually produced a more balanced perspective, but the schools took a great deal of the early heat.

The law that changed the relationship between schools and parents may serve to prevent such reactions in the future. However, even as late as 1982 many educators sensed that although objective measures clearly produced evidence that the public schools were improving in performance of their mission, the general public still had a negative view of education. The very title of the 1983 report of the President's Commission on Excellence in Education, *A Nation at Risk*, reinforces this attitude. As the lay community becomes more directly involved in education and more knowledgeable about what the schools are supposed to be doing—and are doing—and about what the schools are doing well, the gap between the schools' actual performance and the public's perception of that performance may begin to close.

Bringing parents into the decision-making process (and hence into the schools) also gives them some sense of responsibility for educational outcomes, and for ownership of problems if they exist. They are no longer the outsiders, judging, accusing, avoiding responsibility, and blaming. They are part of the team dealing with the problems, large and small.

PL 94-142 is currently applicable only to the educational programs of "exceptional" children (who, their parents feel, had heretofore been educationally neglected). But given the precedent of this law, it is possible that parents of "normal" children as well may bring increasing pressure for greater involvement in decisions affecting their children's education. As a matter of fact, it would not be at all surprising if this pressure came first from parents of handicapped children who have normal offspring as well. Once having shared authority with the schools regarding their *handicapped* children, these parents may desire the same degree of active involvement in decisions about the education of their own "normal" children. Soon after passage of PL 94-142, for example, educators became aware of stepped-up pressure from the parents of gifted children who, though not handicapped, might certainly be considered "exceptional" in a positive way and who even fall within the legal definition of "exceptional" in some states.

Broadening of the requirements for all parents' involvement may be inevitable. This direction is healthy and desirable and could result in increased public support for education as more and more individuals become formally involved. Some professional educators may initially see parent participation as troublesome, and parents, heady with the new influence, may initially be overly intrusive. Public education may go through a period of confusion and agitation until educators and parents at all levels learn how to deal with each other equitably. But when that happens, the increased support and interest may rescue education from some of the decline it has been suffering from the unhappy combination of falling enrollments nationwide and general public disaffection in many places.

It is possible that future laws may require involvement of parents of many other children and may require the provision of individualized programs of instruction to bring them up to standard, similar to the individualized programs (IEPs) now required for handicapped students.

Other educators also appear to detect this trend, and not all are happy about it. Their discomfort, however, stems not from an unwillingness to admit parents into the process, but from some skepticism about how well the team approach would work when applied to all children.

Watras (1981), for example, cautions that the team approach may not be effective because he sees it as "diffusing authority for the teaching act" (p. 143). He also is concerned that it may encourage the use of drill and repetition for normal children found to be deficient in particular skills, and that the team may consider the child's deficiencies without giving appropriate consideration to the context in which the deficiencies occur. His major concern is that, with a team approach, no one individual assumes responsibility for the child's learning.

While his concerns are certainly worthy of consideration, it is our position that these inherent dangers in the team approach are not in and of themselves sufficient reason for abandoning it with handicapped children or for not trying it with others. We will discuss models of team functioning that require one member of the team to assume the primary coordinating function for each child so that there is appropriate liaison and contact between the team and the classroom teachers at all times.

We do not quarrel with Watras's assertion that specialists should not attempt to be instructional experts but should serve as advisors to the teacher, nor do we deny his point that goals must be flexible enough to permit the teacher to use professional judgment and thereby assume responsibility for the results.

Even before the notion of the team is applied to all children, it is even more likely that some form of evaluation-and-program-development team similar to the special education team will be required to serve students whose learning deficiencies are not severe enough to warrant their designation as "exceptional" or "handicapped" or "learning disabled" but who, nevertheless, have for generations been referred to as "slow learners" within the mainstream of education. Consequently the team, which in its special education function is already regarded in some states as having quasi-legal status and hence greater power in decision making in some instances than the Board of Education itself, may assume an even greater mandate in the future.

But whether or not the expansion of role occurs, there is now an urgent need for techniques of effective cooperation between parents and schools, and for new kinds of professional relationships among staff members from various disciplines.

In every state the law now requires identification of children with special needs and development of appropriate programs for them. The major vehicle for interaction between the parents and the staff *written into the law* is the special education multi-disciplinary *team* referred to in some states as the core evaluation team, and in others under a variety of titles such as the child evaluation, child study, child management, or planning and placement team. This team, whatever its title, has created new patterns of group responsibility. In addition, the special education team has already begun to capture interest as the prototype for the evaluation process which is likely to be needed to follow up proficiency testing for *all* public school students, a procedure which is being established increasingly by state laws. In many states, the demand for minimum standards of competency in basic skills is coupled with the requirement for formal identification of students falling short of minimum expectations, despite the fact that they do not fit the definition of students in need of "special education" as that concept is now commonly understood. However, should the thrust for minimum competency standards continue and grow, and should more states require identification and remedial programs for students falling below these standards, the special education team or a group very much like it may well be formalized for planning programs for such children.

The special education team can provide the greatest opportunity for mutual problem solving. It can promote gratifying constructive relationships among all those concerned about children's growth and development in schools. But not only has its potential not yet been realized in most places, but rather it has often become one of the most common sources of confusion, antagonism, mutual distrust, anxiety, and potentially adversarial relationships that school systems have ever experienced.

As a result, there are differences of opinion in some professional circles regarding the real value of teams. In the view of Trachtman (1981, 156), "In a cooperative setting, roles evolve with clarity; each specialist focuses on those competencies which are unique to the setting, overlap is minimal and accompanied by a steady flow of communication, and the pupil personnel staff provides optimum services." He cautions, however, that in a competitive setting, "providers of different services attempt to perform similar functions, strive for ascendancy, establish territoriality and usually provide much less effective service to the school." Thus he sees both the enormous potential that we have noted and the possibility of great difficulties.

Tolor (1978), however, takes a less optimistic view, stressing the negative potential. He asserts that teams simply duplicate effort, waste time, and reinforce shared ignorance. Tolor also believes that the decisions made in the groups are really dictated by emerging patterns of dominance and submissiveness and that it is often illusory to think that unbiased child assessments are, or might be, made by teams.

If Tolor's harsh judgment has any basis, it can probably be applied to all decisions about children, and all consultations, whether between two specialists or between a principal and one of his or her support staff members. Inaccurate assessments and bad judgments undoubtedly are made, and they are made not only in school systems but also in child guidance clinics, hospitals, private schools, and private practices. Most would acknowledge that professional judgment is imperfect; errors are made, and human factors unrelated to the problem under study may enter into judgments and decisions. But to acknowledge imperfection is still not reason enough to condemn a team approach or give up on it, any more than it is reason to condemn or give up any means of assessment and any effort to give children the special treatment or special school programs they may need. It does not profit us to throw up our hands—and do nothing!

In this regard, we share the position of Trachtman (1981) and others that negative thinking about the value of teams may possibly block the necessary efforts to improve the team process, which we, along with Pfeiffer (1981) and others, feel *can* be improved, and which we feel can be extremely useful and desirable. Indeed, the basic subject matter of this book deals with means of making teams more effective and guarding against the errors and abuses that can creep into team deliberations for extraneous reasons.

It must be acknowledged that Tolor's is not the only indictment of the value of teams for decision making. Ysseldyke and Mirkin (1982) cite a series of investigations by researchers at the University of Minnesota, that underscores their impression that those making placement decisions frequently base their decisions on results of technically inadequate test data. They also assert that assessment decisions are systematically biased as a function of characteristics of students, such as sex, socioeconomic status, physical appearance, and the nature of the problem (e.g., academic problem or behavior problem) for which the student has been referred.

Criticisms such as these, while not to be ignored, should not deter us from continuing the use of teams for decision making but rather should stimulate us further to explore and study how to improve the team process. Many other writers (Pfeiffer 1980; Armer and Thomas 1978) share our concern that negativism about the value of teams may inhibit activities to improve team functioning.

It cannot be denied that the indictments made of teams can be equally, in fact possibly more strenuously, applied to decisions made by individuals or groups of two or more professionals (such as a principal and a psychologist, social worker, or teacher), as was the customary practice in the past. We believe that the involvement of specialists from several disciplines, along with the participation of the child's parents, is likely to deter decision making on the basis of a single test or of invalid measurement instruments. The various specialists act as checks and balances upon one another, questioning or asking for evidence rather than blindly accepting one finding. Moreover, the presence of the parents is similarly likely to deter the making of a decision about a child based upon extraneous factors like those cited by Ysseldyke (1982). Rather than constituting shared ignorance, bias, duplication, or wasted effort, we firmly believe that the team *can* work to improve the likelihood that correct and constructive decisions will be made about children.

As we mentioned earlier, however, the positive potential of teams has not nearly been realized, and we do acknowledge that the team approach has been a source of some problems, such as those described by Tolor, Ysseldyke, and others.

Furthermore, the reason for the apparent paradox of the split between the team's positive potential and its negative reality is essentially unrelated to the bad practice found by Tolor and Ysseldyke, which could afflict any decision-making process. The reason for the team's difficulty is that, although the law places a heavy procedural responsibility upon the team, few school officials who conduct team meetings, few school staff members who must attend them regularly, and few parents who are invited to participate feel comfortable or competent with these procedures. This is true regardless of the level of competence or the good intentions of the participants. Team problem solving involving parents and school staff may appear highly desirable and relatively easy for those of good intentions to implement. However, the process is complicated and more difficult than it first appears, requiring new process skills in addition to the specific professional skills of various team members.

This book has two essential purposes. One intention is to help professional team participants to understand what actually happens between parents and school staff when they attempt to work together in a team setting, with the expectation that a clear understanding of the dynamics of the probable interactions will improve team operations and make the team meetings more constructive, thus helping them to achieve their positive potential. The second intention is to assist the professional staff members themselves in their interteam *professional* relationships and functioning.

While each school may have a core of one or more permanent team members, staff participants will change from meeting to meeting, depending on the children involved. It is probable that eventually every teacher in every school will need to be involved in some team meetings. These meetings may become a regular, albeit intermittent, activity of all teachers, yet few if any teachers have had any formal training in how to participate in such procedures, which follow the model of the "case conference." The teachers may feel that their own past performance or professional competence is somehow vulnerable to criticism if one of their students is having difficulties, and that their judgment about the future programs and placements for the child is under critical scrutiny.

Unfortunately, some of these apprehensions may be realistic, as some parents may be eager for the opportunity to find someone to blame for their children's problems and failures. Moreover, teachers, administrators, and other staff members, unaccustomed to dealing with negative parental reactions in situations where they are "exposed" to their colleagues, may add to one another's apprehension. They may sometimes engage in behavior seemingly directed at exonerating themselves from responsibility and hence, directly or indirectly, shifting blame or parents' ire to others. Thus, it is extremely important for staff members to learn what their roles are at these meetings, how to deal with their own anxieties and doubts, and how to maintain productive relationships with parents and colleagues in the team setting. Only when they feel comfortable functioning in case conferences will they be able fully to utilize their own competencies.

In addition to dealing with the special relationships noted above, the book examines the group dynamics of team processes which make for greater or lesser problem-solving efficiency. Some discussions draw on current communications theory and firsthand experience in working in groups with parents, staff, and administrators to explore the practical aspects of how school staff and parents can work best together.

Finally, we do not live in never-never land! And therefore, we realize that even the most professionally constituted, well-trained, thoughtful, competent, and constructive evaluation team may have to make a recommendation for a child based not upon what is ideal for that child, but upon the limitations of the law, financial pressures, the parameters set by the school board, and with an eye to what precedents the team and the board are willing to set or anxious to avoid. Hence, the book deals with the professional and personal conflicts that may be created by the intrusion of the real world into the theoretical ideal. It discusses how to deal with those conflicts so that children are well served, and so that professional integrity is not compromised while practical realities are not ignored.

SUMMARY

In this chapter we have reviewed the concept of the multidisciplinary team in relation to the federal law requiring its employment for decision making about children in need of special education. It is our position that despite some of the problems associated with the imposition of legalistic procedures on educational decision making, and despite objections to the team concept from theorists such as Watras (1981) and Tolor (1978), the basic concept of the multidisciplinary team is sound and useful. The team provides a vehicle for the interaction between schools and parents required by law. Its skillful utilization can motivate parents and school systems to rethink their relationship and can encourage cooperative rather than adversarial relationships.

The multidisciplinary team serves children well because it focuses a variety of different professional skills and perspectives on children as individuals. We predict it will serve education well, in general, as it may come to be used increasingly for decision making about non-special-education children as well. Particularly in light of the urgent focus on education in the nation during this decade, the multidisciplinary team may become a ubiquitous vehicle for forging a stronger partnership between professional educators and parents, to everyone's benefit.

2

Team Meetings: Purposes, Personnel, Preparation, and Problems

PURPOSES

Team meetings fall into two basic categories, depending on the purpose for which they are called:

1. Planning meetings. At these meetings evaluation material is reviewed and, if it is determined that special education is needed, an individualized educational program for a child is developed.
2. Review meetings. These can occur whenever it is felt that there is a need to review progress or to change the program.

For every child who has been determined to need special education services, the law requires at least two meetings the first year—at least one planning meeting, and at least one monitoring meeting at the end of the year to assess the program and plan for the following year. The law requires at least one review each year thereafter (referred to as the annual review), although progress reviews may occur more frequently.

13

The specific tasks to be accomplished at these meetings are the following:

1. To review the referrals of students thought to be in need of special education services. To be considered at a team meeting, there must have been a formal referral and the parents must have given written approval to certain evaluation procedures.
2. To decide whether a child should be classified as "exceptional." (Under some state laws, this term may include children who are gifted as well as those who are considered "handicapped.") The term handicapped, for the purpose of the law, has a far broader definition than the vernacular, and may include children with even minor disabilities (handicaps) if the disability interferes with the child's capacity to profit from a regular educational program.
3. If the child is so classified, to decide what the particular needs are so as to develop a program of services. (At present, the law does not require services for gifted children. Programs for the gifted are purely optional on the part of local school districts. It is certainly possible, however, that the inclusion in several states of gifted children under the term "exceptional" has established some basis for future broadening of the law to require that the special educational needs of all "exceptional" children be addressed.)
4. To assure parental awareness of the entire process and to encourage parent involvement in all facets of it. This includes obtaining formal parental approval for all evaluations, communicating to parents the results of evaluations and their implications for the child's educational program, getting their agreement to provision of special services, encouraging them to participate in program planning, and obtaining formal written parental agreement to the program and to any subsequent changes. To formalize efforts to involve parents, to facilitate obtaining necessary parental approval, and to assure the school district's compliance with federal regulations, it is advised that the school systems develop standard procedures for notification of parents and other procedural matters.
5. If it is determined that a child requires special education, and if the parents agree, to formulate an adequate and appropriate "individualized educational program" for each child and to commit that program to writing in a formal document commonly referred to as the IEP.
6. To recommend an appropriate placement for each child that is the "least restrictive environment" in which that child can prosper educationally.
7. To review and monitor the IEP and modify the child's program, services, or placement whenever necessary.

The first six tasks are accomplished in planning meetings. The last task is accomplished during the review meeting.

PERSONNEL

The responsibility for carrying out the tasks of the team, as enumerated above, is shared with the parents. Even if they do not accept the legally required invitation to participate, they should be kept informed of the team's deliberations and decisions and should continue to be encouraged to take an active role in decision making about their children.

The parents have the legal right to invite someone to accompany them. This may be a friend or neighbor or relative, or (as is more often the case when parents actually accept this invitation) the guest may be an attorney representing the parents or the child or an independent specialist whom the parents have consulted.

The number of people attending the meeting needs to be kept manageable and realistic and should be related to the primary purpose of the meeting. If the meeting is the year-end progress review to determine the child's future program, any staff member who might be involved in prospective program changes should be invited to attend. If the objective of the meeting is simply to reaffirm the continuation of the child's current program, only the minimum number of staff members required by law are needed. This variable approach to staffing team meetings is practiced in many school systems, in contrast to the often time-wasting alternative of requiring routine attendance at all meetings by predetermined special education staff members whether or not they are actively involved in a particular child's program.

The advantage of flexible, as opposed to routine, staffing of team meetings is evident. The flexible approach makes it possible to accomplish team-task objectives more efficiently and is the approach of choice when staff members are overburdened by huge caseloads and have too little time to get their work done. In fact, it is clear that to overburden staff in such circumstances by requiring routine attendance at team meetings would be contrary to the "full service" intent of 94-142, in that it would reduce the time available for the special education staff to work with other children.

Another factor affecting the decision about who shall attend has to do with the question of relevance, i.e., should a specialist who has had minimal or infrequent contact with the child be involved in a team meeting? Obviously, in meetings where new information or fresh input is desirable, attendance by such staff members might be encouraged. Otherwise, the general practice of inviting only the staff directly involved is probably sound. Parents tend to become annoyed by a staff member whose remarks do not reflect sufficient familiarity with their child. Such questions as "How well do *you* know my child?" or "When was it you said you worked with Sally?" are not unusual in such circumstances. In fact, the law, as implemented in many states, requires that the staff members attending a team meeting be directly involved with the child in some way.

There are, however, several other factors affecting the decision about staffing which should not be ignored.

1. In most instances, a team meeting is usually *not* a good time to introduce either a new staff member or a new approach, and it probably is not the best time to initiate a potentially anxiety-producing idea such as the need for counselling or therapy. A defensive reaction on the part of parents would not be surprising under such circumstances, so that what might have seemed like a timely idea could prove disruptive if introduced without some preparation.

2. The team leader may wish to exclude certain staff members because of a history of antagonism or disagreement between them and the child's parents. If negative feelings still exist and the staff member's contribution is not vital to the review of the child's performance, excluding that staff member from the meeting is probably desirable. However, if a staff member is to have a continuing role in the child's program, the decision to exclude him or her should not be made without that individual's agreement. It is very important under such circumstances to obtain the staff member's understanding of the purpose to be served and his or her agreement to remain out of the proceedings. At a later time, the differences with the parents should be addressed. A follow-up conference should be arranged for the purpose of resolving such disagreements as soon as possible to insure a cooperative relationship.

The invitation sent to the parents should indicate which staff members are likely to be in attendance. They may be noted categorically—i.e., "a speech therapist"—rather than by name. In general, it is probably wise to avoid including anyone not specified on the notice. Parents often feel at a slight disadvantage to begin with, meeting on school turf with a host of "experts." That discomfort is likely to be increased if they need to contend with the additional surprise of encountering a specialist whose presence was neither requested by them nor anticipated as a result of the notice.

PREPARATION

Staff Roles and Expectations

Staff members should have a clear idea, before the meeting, of the roles they are expected to play. They should know in advance what data they may be asked to explain and whether they will be asked for specific descriptions of the child's present performance or suggestions for the child's future program or whether they will be asked only to answer questions. They should also have an idea of what kinds of questions are likely to arise.

Staff should also have a clear understanding of the specific objectives of the particular meeting. Classroom teachers who may not have attended team meetings previously should be briefed about the nature of the meetings, informed of the specific objectives, and told which other staff members will be in attendance. Staff members should also know the order in which they will speak.

This advance planning is not meant to predetermine outcomes or to control staff input but to be certain that staff members do not find themselves working at cross-purposes or confusing the parents. Staff members should also understand whether, when an IEP is developed, they may be asked to assume responsibility for implementing the services, attaining certain objectives, monitoring the child's progress, writing future reports, and the like.

Without advance preparation and clear understandings among the staff, communication problems are likely to develop. These problems may be exacerbated if the team leaders are uncertain of their leadership roles and/or if the parents are harboring resentment or antagonism or are fearful of the meeting. Furthermore, unless staff members are aware of the procedural requirements of the meeting and the due-process safeguards that must be formally offered and explained to parents, they may find the meetings overly formal and intimidating. Obviously, this is most likely to occur in the case of teachers who may have attended few meetings. It is expected that special education staff and administrators who regularly attend these meetings will be knowledgeable about the procedural aspects and take them in stride. However, as the procedural matters become "pro forma" to the staff, they should not be treated carelessly, omitted, or neglected. Omissions may be the source of serious legal complications later if parents disagree with team decisions and wish to invoke their legal rights.

Occasionally, serious communication problems can develop when the meeting is run by a dominating leader who fails to insure that everyone has a chance to contribute. No matter how clear or well-prepared the other members are regarding their potential contributions, the tone and pace will be set by the leader. It is the leader's expectations, more than anything else, that will ultimately determine whether everyone will finally leave the meeting satisfied with his or her role. A more complete discussion of leadership factors in terms of their effect upon group communication and problem-solving efficiency will appear in Chapters III and IV.

One other factor related to team members' expectations is often neglected. With increasing frequency, regular classroom or subject-area teachers are being involved in team conferences, but most are prepared poorly, if at all, for the role they will be expected to play. Consequently, the teacher's attitude may vary from feeling completely left out, to defensive reactions to parents' or other staff members' questions about their work with the student, to annoyance that a special education student has been "dumped" in their classroom. Therefore, unless these mainstream teachers are better prepared for their part in the team process and feel comfortable about the extent of their contribution or responsibility for the program or the child, their active involvement in the team meeting may, at best, be meaningless and, at worst, disruptive.

To accomplish the job of better preparing mainstream teachers for such roles, the federal law requires each state to develop inservice training programs to acquaint all teachers with special educational issues and procedures. PL 94-142 funding is available to both the states and the local school districts for such activities. But the ordinary facts of life—i.e., time pressures on teachers, budget demands in other school program areas, lack of inservice trainers—often inhibit the development of effective, continuous inservice training to the extent needed.

Therefore, it usually remains for the special education leadership to do the job of preparing mainstream teachers for their team involvement. The team chairperson can encourage teachers to learn about available special educational and support services. The principal can and should inform all regular staff of their potential responsibility for team involvement, and of the need to have them, as well as special education staff, assist in the planning for special children. Prior to a meeting, the team coordinator can inform specific teachers of what will be expected of them with regard to a particular child. However, unless the general expectation that he or she will be, and needs to be, involved has been established through leadership of the principal or other appropriate administrator, the mainstream teacher is not likely to be the informed colleague that the special education planning process requires.

It is not infrequent to overhear teachers, upon leaving a team meeting for which they had not been prepared, making comments such as:

"What a waste of time—I don't know what they needed me there for at all!"

or

"Is that what these meetings are all about—just sitting around, shooting the breeze?"

or

"Is that what I was pulled away from my class for? Next time would you please see if you can do without me?"

or

"All of this time, and so many people pulled in just for one kid—how do you justify it?"

Such comments, after what has been perceived as a meaningless experience, are clearly indicative of why it is important to prepare mainstream teachers better. Though the law requires their participation, unless regular teachers better understand the importance of what they have to contribute and accept their role vis-à-vis special needs children, their forced participation can undermine the whole team's efforts.

Parents' Expectations

Much of the success or failure of efforts to involve parents and elicit their cooperative participation depends upon the nature of their expectations prior to team meetings and how those expectations are fulfilled.

Parents whose children are experiencing difficulty in school are likely to be apprehensive. Their reactions may range from fear about their child's future to feelings of guilt over their own possible role in the youngster's difficulty, whether it is a physical handicap, an emotional disorder, or a learning disability. Some of these reactions may be irrational. However "guiltless" they may be in reality, parents whose youngster suffers from cerebral palsy, for example, may harbor some secret feeling of responsibility over possible genetic causes, birth trauma, or other causative factors for which they blame themselves.

Similarly, they may feel defensive if their child seems to suffer from less specific difficulties, particularly if there appear to be social or emotional overtones for which the parents may either blame themselves or feel others hold them accountable.

Even in the absence of these personal negative feelings, the idea of coming to school for a conference with the principal and other specialists may be difficult for some parents to handle. Their associations to "being called to the principal's office" may go way back to their own school days. Regardless of the source of their apprehension and the groundlessness of their fears, it is important to understand that these feelings may exist and to be prepared to deal with them.

Some parents, rather than being apprehensive and defensive, may feel extremely angry or resentful toward the school system or toward particular school staff members. They may believe that their child has been "singled out," "mishandled," or "labeled," or that the child has not been given enough attention and that his or her difficulties have been overlooked, ignored, exacerbated, or—in the extreme—even caused by the school. In addition, the formality of the contacts required to assure that all legal procedures regarding parental notification and assent to evaluation have been met may add to, or create, negative parental reaction.

However, it is also often true that a team chairperson may be happily faced with parents glad to see the school staff interested in their child and eager and happy to cooperate. If so, that chairperson is blessed and that team fortunate. But negative feelings are equally as likely to be present.

It is hoped, therefore, that the initial contacts with the parents preceding the team meetings in which parents are first informed of their children's school difficulties and notified of the advisability of evaluation for consideration of special education, can be cordial and productive and thus serve to allay at least some of the parents' initial apprehension. For a fuller discussion of ways in which parents' anxieties, fears, hostility, and the like can be turned into constructive channels, see "Parent Conferences in the Schools" (Losen and Diament 1978).

Parents should be treated with courtesy and introduced to all staff members present. Each staff member's role should be explained. An attempt should be made to answer all questions that may arise, and parents should not be intimidated or rushed into signing an IEP but should be given time to consider the staff suggestions if they seem hesitant or confused. It is better to wait a week or two—even to have another meeting if necessary—than to risk having to deal with uncertain, angry, or resentful parents all year.

Regardless of whether parents' feelings are basically negative or positive, it is also extremely likely that, knowing that there are many special education service alternatives available and possible, parents may naturally feel that their child is entitled to the best possible situation and that the staff will recognize and recommend what would be ideal for the child. Given these expectations, parents may react negatively to suggestion of programs or services that fall short of the ideal. To help avoid such a situation, therefore, the school district should give parents a written description of general program alternatives. This should include details of the law's requirement that a program be appropriate and adequate and also a full explanation of why, within the financial resources of a public school system and under the limits of the law, it may not be possible to provide what might be "ideal" for a child.

The school staff should be very straightforward with the parents in explaining their due-process rights, including the fact that the parents may have a right to obtain an independent evaluation at school expense, to employ the counsel of an attorney, to challenge recommendations, and so forth. It should also be made clear to the parents that they do not have to agree to the classification of their child, to the services suggested by the staff, or to a special education placement. They should understand that they have the right to request additional or different services or a different placement, and that their request will be considered. The more parents feel assured that they have a real voice in the decision-making process and that they are not powerless to affect decisions about their child, the more they are likely to be persuaded of the good intentions of the planning team and to be willing to cooperate with the staff.

The time and place to inform parents about any of their child's difficulties that may have been diagnosed through staff evaluations, should be carefully chosen. If it is suspected that a child has a serious problem, the parents probably should have the opportunity to discuss this, and to deal with their own feelings about it, in a more intimate meeting with the staff member who has the most direct knowledge of their child, rather than at the team meeting. The meeting when general evaluation findings are discussed and an IEP planned is probably too late to break major news about a child.

Similarly, if in the absence of adequate progress, the parents have not been regularly informed of problems, the annual review meeting is probably not the time to bring in new negative information, as the following illustration may demonstrate.

As they were ushered into the small conference room adjacent to the principal's office, Mr. and Mrs. M. became aware that the mood of the group assembled to meet with them had dramatically changed. A few minutes earlier, while they were still seated just outside the office awaiting their annual review of their son's progress, they had heard loud voices and laughter from the conference room. Now all had become hushed and businesslike. There were introductions all around of people they knew, and some they hadn't met before, and Mr. Harlow, the principal, whom they remembered from a number of previous meetings, occupied the opening moment with what seemed to be a repetitive and endless description of their "due process" rights and challenge procedures. He then described the role and function of all the staff members present, in so far as each had had something to do with Johnny's special education program during the course of the school year. Mr. Harlow seemed to be trying to make them feel comfortable but at the same time reminding them of the importance of the annual review process to which they had received a formal written invitation. The M's weren't comfortable. Instead, they felt ill at ease—as if they had been summoned before some high tribunal, intent upon judging their continuing fitness for parenthood.

Some of the staff members—the school psychologist, Johnny's special education resource teacher, and his fifth grade homeroom teacher—described their impressions of what Johnny had learned during the school year. The speech clinician also reported that Johnny no longer needed help with sound discrimination. Finally, Mr. Harlow summed up the various reports, with the comment that Johnny "obviously has done very nicely this year."

Ms. Parks, Johnny's homeroom teacher, had earlier made a comment which suggested that she didn't seem to share Mr. Harlow's enthusiasm, but she did not say anything further after the principal's summation. The psychologist also reacted noticeably to some of Mr. Harlow's superlatives, but she, also, made no further comment. It was, therefore, quickly agreed that Johnny would continue to receive supplementary tutoring as part of his IEP for next year, but that other support services were no longer necessary. Mr. and Mrs. M. were thanked for coming, once again apprised of their challenge rights, and everybody stood up and shook hands as they left—all wishing all a pleasant summer ahead.

It had indeed seemed very routine and matter of fact, but instead of leaving feeling pleased about Johnny's progress, the M.s felt vaguely troubled. Why had Ms. Parks not expressed further her apparent reservations? And what had stimulated the psychologist's reactions to Mr. Harlow's summation? The businesslike tone of the meeting had not made it easy for Mr. and Mrs. M. to pursue such questions. And there was something about Mr. Harlow's management of the meeting which seemed predetermined, overly controlling, and not at all conducive to the more open sharing of information about their son that they had anticipated. Nevertheless, the news about Johnny sounded good, and Mr. and Mrs. M. weren't going to let their vague apprehensions preoccupy them for very long. They soon afterward dismissed their doubts and allowed themselves to accept the team's judgment.

This special education team meeting with Mr. and Mrs. M. is probably not unlike those that take place in public schools around the country. It was, basically, the kind of evaluation meeting that provides the opportunity for the school staff to report about a student's progress. Unfortunately, if limited to that purpose, such meetings often prove to be little more than an exercise, and their effects tend to undermine Public Law 94-142, the "full service" guarantee for all public school handicapped children and their parents.

Many aspects of the meeting might be considered procedurally sound. Mr. Harlow ran the meeting smoothly, with appropriate reference to the parents' challenge or due-process rights. He reviewed the functions of the staff in attendance and tried to make the parents feel comfortable. He also kept the focus of the meeting on the child's progress and directed attention to plans for the coming year. All of his efforts were consistent with the purpose of an annual review as required by law. There were, however, two major flaws in the conduct of the meeting which seriously detracted from the value of the whole process.

A major fault was the fact that Mr. Harlow had permitted little, if any, expression of staff disagreement with his overall progress evaluation. Recognizing the time constraints most teams face at annual review time, it is nevertheless self-defeating, and ultimately more time consuming, to allow parents to leave the meeting with an unrealistically optimistic picture of their child's progress. In this case, therefore, the concerns of the homeroom teacher and the psychologist, having never before been expressed, should at least have been explored. An annual review *ought* to provide the opportunity for as objective an appraisal as possible of a child's progress and future needs. Otherwise, all involved, including the child's parents, engage in a superficial interchange which tends to produce mutual distrust and suspicion at future meetings. Mr. and Mrs. M. may have forgotten their post-conference concerns as they turned their attention to their vacation plans, but their sense that things were left unresolved or incompletely stated is likely to increase their uneasiness about their son's reported progress the next time.

Perhaps of even greater significance was the fact that the M.s were evidently not adequately prepared for the annual review. They had not been made aware of Johnny's difficulties *during* the school year, despite the fact that they had had previous conferences with members of the school staff and Mr. Harlow. Consequently, the most potentially troublesome factor in the staff's annual review meeting with the M.s was that some of the staff's reservations or concerns about Johnny's school performance, which were only indirectly alluded to at the meeting, had never been reported or discussed at any time during the year in individual conferences with the M.s.

In one important sense, it could be argued that Mr. Harlow's summation about how well Johnny had performed during the year, having gone uninterrupted by his staff, was probably best left that way without any further reaction by the homeroom teacher or the psychologist. If they had taken initiative at that time to introduce divergent points of view at the annual review, it might have proved disconcerting for everyone and have raised serious, perhaps justified, questions about the staff members' communications with one another and with the principal. At the very least, it would have come as a shock to Mr. and Mrs. M. to hear negative reports about Johnny for the first time at the annual meeting.

Unfortunately, time constraints do often lead to the unexpected disclosure of new information to the parents at an annual review conference. The point here is that although such new disclosures may have to be acknowledged when they occur, the risk of distressing parents with negative or surprising information at such times can and should be avoided.

Parents' expectations at annual meetings are likely to be attuned toward hearing either what they are hopeful about or what they already fear concerning their child. Therefore, introducing new and unexpected information at an annual review may produce an equally unexpected and dramatic reaction from the parent who exclaims "Why wasn't I told about this before!"

Consequently, one of our major theses is that parents should always be informed well before the end-of-year meeting about any serious questions or concerns a staff member may have regarding their child. In other words, changing a parents' expectations for their child as a result of what has happened during the school year should not be attempted during the limited time available at an annual review. There are usually enough issues concerning plans for the future, which need to be collaboratively addressed, and which require mutual trust. Discussion about what transpires during the year should be initiated prior to the annual review. Thus, parents' expectations for their child, stemming from the child's performance during the year, need not become the major focus of the meeting. Planning for the future is hard enough. Introducing something new about the past may make planning for the future impossible.

Parents' expectations prior to team meetings should be fully explored and discussed before annual reviews or any other major decision-making conferences. Schleifer (1979) underscores a number of reasons why this is important. His article describes parents whose experience with an efficiently run end-of-year conference is negative because they were not helped to understand either the preconference evaluation procedures or how the various "program pieces" were put together. As a result, they later expressed the feeling that they had been "railroaded" into the team's plan without a firm sense of what was going on. In this case history, during the prior year the parents had had their child in a private school special education program. They were regularly apprised of their child's progress by the private school staff. They were impressed with the coordinated efforts of the private school to maintain contact with them as well as communication among various staff members. The parents' subsequent experience with the public school had proved disappointing when, despite earlier verbal assurances about the need for close communication, they were ushered into an annual review of their child's progress with little prior contact with the staff and meager understanding of how their child was being evaluated.

It could be argued that the parents had been spoiled by the private school's approach and that the public schools cannot be expected to duplicate the resources of specialized private schools, but that argument is specious. In such a situation, the parents' expectations for their child and the program devised by the public school must be carefully explored beforehand so that any differences and similarities between current and past programs can be explained and understood, even if not fully accepted. Predictably, parents whose children have been in other programs will have expectations based upon their previous experience. Again, we believe the annual review is not the time to begin exploring expectations or differences arising from parents' prior experiences. That job should be done when the child begins his or her new public school program.

Similarly, we believe that parents' long-range expectations for their child's future should be explored and clarified with them prior to any program change or decision-making sessions called at times other than the annual review. Unless *both* parents already are familiar with the staff's view of a child's strengths, limitations, and potential, and unless differences regarding such views have been essentially resolved in prior individual conferences with parents, no meaningful plan is likely to evolve from the team meeting.

In addition, prior to the planning meeting, it is imperative that parents be apprised of the nature and purpose of all evaluative instruments, grading systems, behavior rating schemes, and the like which were used by staff to arrive at a diagnostic conclusion. Parents should not have to be in the position of needing to exercise the veto guaranteed them by 94-142 regarding the kinds of diagnostic instruments employed by the school staff, and they will be less inclined to use that veto at a planning session if they sense that they can trust the school staff to explain the nature, purpose, and results of the procedures. Specific methods of working with parents toward understanding evaluation devices and procedures are elaborated in other works, such as

"Parent Conferences in the Schools" (Losen and Diament 1978). The point to be emphasized here is that appropriate prior conferences to explain the evaluation process are important to offset parents' fears that important decisions about their child will be based upon procedures about which the school staff prefers to keep them ignorant.

Parents' Prior Notice Rights

The law requires that parents receive notice of team meetings to identify a child's special needs and to plan or modify a special education program appropriate to the child's needs. The law further stipulates that such notice be communicated to parents in language they can understand, within a prescribed period of time prior to the meeting, and that it contain information apprising parents of their due-process rights. In addition, the notice must state that regulations consistent with the intent of PL 94-142 have been developed to urge active parent participation in team meetings, to allow for surrogate parent representation when appropriate, and to encourage parents to bring their own advisors to assist them in their team involvement. These advisors may be professional specialists of their own selection, attorneys, friends, or anyone the parents wish to invite.

These statutory rights are obviously intended to increase parental involvement in school decisions. However, their implementation has resulted in at least three unexpected negative side effects which tend to be antithetical to the best interests of the children the laws are intended to serve.

First, the paperwork and attention that needs to be devoted to procedures (e.g., written notices of meetings, records of having mailed notices and subsequent telephone calls, preparing arrangements for taking accurate minutes or recordings of meetings, the need to sign a variety of release forms, waiver of notice forms, permission for testing forms) have created an aura of red tape around all formal team meetings which is time consuming and frustrating.

The requirement to wait a certain number of days before school personnel and parents can officially meet is a necessary but often time-wasting precaution. Waivers signed by the parents can alleviate some of this red tape, but then the proceedings may be slightly tinged with an aura of illegality because of the omnipresent feeling that everything needs to be done just right, that the "case" may have been jeopardized in some way, or that certain due-process rights will have been violated. This whole matter of following legally prescribed procedures also tends to be alien to the school staff, teachers, and parents who have not been legally trained. Administrators, who may be more generally comfortable with procedural matters, are also frequently uneasy about special education regulations because such procedures are dictated by state or federal statutes rather than by local or district board of education policies with which they are more familiar.

Most team members, therefore, including many parents, frequently perceive the bulk of regulatory procedures as unnecessary and time consuming even if they do protect the parents' rights. Consequently, many view the parents' due-process rights as a boon to lawyers more than as a genuine aid to parents. However justified these or opposing views may be, the fact remains that the imposition of regulatory procedures creates, at the very least, the subtle awareness that over and above the desirable circumstance that all parties might *want* to get together, the team *must* get together and *will be recorded.* This fact of current special education life is also what creates the second and perhaps most important negative side of the law's effect: the reinforcement of adversarial attitudes and the anticipation of conflict between parents and staff.

Sometimes adversarial circumstances are justified in a particular situation. But, apart from the possibility that an adversary relationship might develop anyway, given a set of potentially antagonistic circumstances, formal references to the law and to parents' due-process rights tend to raise awareness, arouse suspicion, and encourage a quickness to challenge and an equal quickness to defend or disguise ulterior motives. This is especially true when the source of a child's school difficulties is hard to pin down or rectify, e.g., when a child's difficulties seem to be primarily emotional in origin, or when the child's symptoms or difficulty suggest an undisclosed home or family problem. Although the law requires that some positive action be taken by a team to meet a child's identified needs, adversary channels created by due-process regulations often tend to be used too quickly by parents or school personnel. What may be lost as a result is the necessary airing of underlying issues and concerns that might aid in developing the most comprehensive and mutually desirable program of remediation. In other words, now parents and staff can avoid uncomfortable confrontations about real causative issues by pursuing due-process procedures and by turning matters over to the lawyers.

Finally, there is the realization that formal notices and formalized procedures, however protective, often arouse mistrust and suspicion as well as unnecessary or premature defensiveness when no such feelings previously existed. Comments from parents like the following are unfortunately becoming increasingly commonplace:

> "Do I really have to sign all these permissions? What are you planning to *do* to my child?"

"Are all these forms and waivers really necessary? I trust you!"

"I received your letter and am planning on coming in with my husband next week, but I almost get the feeling we ought to bring our lawyer too."

"Is there something you're not telling me about Jackie—this notice scared the hell out of me!"

"I thought my child was just going to be tested—what is all this due-process stuff about?"

Obviously, laws and regulations have been enacted primarily as a means of correcting existing injustices. And, with regard to parents' rights, the clear intent of the law is to involve parents meaningfully in those school situations that have in the past either discouraged or circumvented parent participation in the decisions affecting their children. There is little point in arguing now for an alternative, non-statutory way to proceed. PL 94-142 and its effects are likely to be with us in some form for some time to come. Therefore, to enhance effective team functioning, we must acknowledge the fact that potential negative expectations may be aroused by the law and its concommitant regulatory procedures. Such reactions must then be confronted, discussed openly, and resolved as fully as possible if the team is to do its job. Otherwise, a procedural step like prior notice, which is intended to start a helping process for a needful child, may become the *final* notice that very little can or will be done.

POTENTIAL PROBLEM AREAS

Even with the most careful planning and preparation the nature of the process is such that there are potential stumbling blocks which need to be faced. Among the most frequent are negative or defensive reactions by staff to the presence of parents' advisors, common procedural difficulties, conflicting opinions among staff members, and extreme parental attitudes such as excessive passivity on the one hand or an overly dominant stance on the other.

Staff Reactions to Parent Advisors

PL 94-142 encourages parents to invite others to attend team meetings. These may include lawyers, outside professional specialists, or others who parents feel will support or help them to articulate their concerns. The positive intent of this aspect of the law is to provide parents better representation via informed advocacy, thereby increasing their power in the decision-making process. It is most suitable in school situations in which the parents' contribution usually has been ignored, minimized, or circumvented. Unfortunately, in those school situations where parents have characteristically been encouraged to participate actively in the team process, the net effect of the presence of expert guests brought by the parents is, at the very least, distracting. At worst, it is potentially disruptive, if not demoralizing, for the school staff who believed they were trusted and respected, but who may view the parents' utilization of outside advocates as evidence that they are not.

To make matters worse, school personnel are generally not trained in matters of law. While they probably are familiar with the special education regulations and with school policy, they may feel uncomfortable regarding formal legal issues and procedures they do not fully understand. They may feel that involvement in quasilegal processes should not even be part of their job. In the presence of lawyers, most staff members react with feelings ranging from defensiveness and agitation to outright fear and open antagonism. At the very least, they appear to be easily intimidated by lawyers who are obviously more at home in confrontational situations and who seem to have no qualms about openly challenging a staff member's background, training, experience, and other qualifications. Most teachers are not used to being challenged or having their credentials regarded with skepticism when they make evaluative judgments about a child's performance in school—particularly if they have worked closely with the child for some time. Similarly, support services staff, (i.e., school psychologists, social workers, and counselors) are threatened by the implication frequently present in a lawyer's questions that they are not looking at things from the point of view of what might be best for the child, but rather from the point of view of the school system or the staff.

The situation becomes particularly difficult when the parents who have invited a lawyer to attend turn matters entirely over to the lawyer and refrain from any participation in the meeting themselves. Communication under such circumstances can sound more like a series of courtroom-style exchanges than a discussion about a child's needs or problems. It is too easy for such a meeting to deteriorate rapidly into a flurry of charges and countercharges if attention is not redirected to the child's present difficulties and the team's purpose in meeting about them.

For their part, lawyers ordinarily do not feel bound by the team's usual procedures, especially if they have been asked to pursue a complaint for the child's parents or guardian. They will sometimes behave provocatively, or state a position prematurely—e.g., "We've heard enough! Whom do we contact to arrange for a hearing?"—well before the parents would normally have even considered that possibility. On the other hand, if the lawyer and the parents have not predetermined their course of action, there is no reason to anticipate undue unreasonableness simply because a lawyer is present. It may be quite possible that a lawyer, despite his or her potential to be intimidating, will be anxious to assist the team to pursue full consideration of all relevant issues and concerns. The point is that the very presence of an attorney is a significant variable to be taken into account regarding what, and with what ease, matters of importance will be discussed openly. It is often helpful, therefore, for the chairperson to acknowledge at the outset that the very presence of the lawyer may have a negative or inhibiting effect on communication.

> "We ought to recognize that Ms. Pardon, here representing the Clarks as their attorney, may be helpful to all of us in our proceedings, but since most of us are unaccustomed to working with lawyers present we will need to be sure that our own discomfort does not lead us to be overly cautious in what we say or how we say it."

or

> "Mr. Martin is here as the Smiths' lawyer and advisor, but let us try not to be distracted by legal or due-process issues, until we've worked through the main purpose of our meeting today, which is . . . "

or

> "Ms. Dayton is here today representing Barbara as her lawyer. We expect, however, that we have a lot of work to do together as a team to come up with an appropriate program for Barbara before we get involved in legal matters."

Recognizing the probable impact of a lawyer's presence upon the rest of the team, openly acknowledging that fact, and proceeding from there to the main business of the team meeting is about all that a leader can do at first to diminish the negative impact of the lawyer's presence upon communication. The lawyer's behavior will then determine whether or not his or her presence seriously impairs open communication. Specific strategies for coping with lawyers' tactics during team meetings will be discussed in more detail in Chapter VI, but it must be reemphasized that a lawyer's presence invariably has a profound effect upon everyone's level of comfort in communicating.

The presence of other specialists invited by the parents may have a similar, but often not quite as profound, impact as the presence of a lawyer at a team meeting. For one thing, guest psychologists, social workers, and reading or other educational specialists are more often than not perceived by the staff as having expertise similar to their own. They are seen as being, if not totally sympathetic with the staff's interests and problems, at least cognizant of them. Their role is more familiar to the staff (although the reputation of a particular guest specialist may evoke awe, concern, or contempt, depending on the individual). The guest specialist, unlike the lawyer, elicits, in some instances, a more urgent need to communicate more material, in greater depth, and with more substantiation. More effort tends to be directed toward exchange of professional opinion, possibly in an attempt to impress a guest specialist in a staff member's field. Jargon often flows more freely, and consequently communication may suffer not from inhibition but from too much specificity. To maintain perspective, comments from the chairperson may be in order, such as:

> "What we seem to be getting into about the comparative validity of these two tests is fascinating, but we may be losing the point of our discussion . . . ."

or

> "We may disagree over the interpretation of this particular sub-test, but can we get back to what this all means relative to Susan's program?"

or

> "We seem to be talking about the program for Tommy from two entirely different perspectives. What do we need to do to come to some sort of agreement?"

The clear message to be conveyed when a guest specialist is present is that we share similar knowledge and skills, perhaps to varying degrees, but we know a lot about one another's ideas to begin with and therefore can communicate more openly and less defensively. As a result, the communication problems which occur with guest specialists (which will also be discussed further in Chapter VI) may be addressed differently than those which occur with lawyers present. The communication-inhibiting, anxiety-provoking factors surrounding a lawyer's presence must be minimized or neutralized as much as possible to facilitate communication. With guest experts present, rather than being inhibited through anxiety, communication may become bogged down in irrelevant detail or academic disagreements. Therefore, considerable attention should be given to the relevance and flow of discussion and attention to the team's primary objectives.

To ease the strain being felt by everybody at the meeting, and to immediately acknowledge the adversary-reinforcing properties of the guest's presence, the team chairperson should quickly affirm the parents' right to have legal or specialist assistance at the meeting. But the leader should also note that the presence of the outsider, particularly if unexpected, is likely to make the school staff feel somewhat guarded in what they wish to say, especially if the session is to be taperecorded. In addition, the team leader should note that, while guests are welcome, it would be helpful for them to clarify their interest in the case or their relationship to the parents. In that way, any adversary attitudes or preexisting antagonistic views may be made clear at the outset. Thereafter, it is probably a good idea to encourage the guest to participate in the proceedings whenever it seems appropriate to elicit the parents' reaction to something reported or presented. Attempts to limit the guest's participation should be kept at a minimum, because the danger of unnecessarily alienating the parents, who are undoubtedly depending upon their guest's aid, is great. However, the leader may intervene when the guest pursues a line of discussion or inquiry that seems premature or inappropriate to the task at hand or when the guest's point of view appears to be at odds with the parents' previously expressed attitude. The point to be made in such situations is that the meeting was called to fulfill a particular objective and the guest's contribution should not be allowed to deviate too far from or detract from the team's purpose, as occurs in the following incident:

Mrs. Q.'s lawyer had been commenting throughout the early moments of our annual review of Jackie's progress that he would be recommending to the Q.s that they request a central office or administrative review of our local proceedings and program decision. As the team leader, I finally felt constrained to acknowledge the fact that the Q.s could pursue their due-process rights and request such a review at any time, but that the prior assumption that there would be a need for such a review was premature and served to undermine the very purpose for which the meeting had been called—to arrive at a mutually acceptable special education plan and IEP for Jackie. A good-faith attitude would assume that the team decision would be one to which the parents would agree and that there would not be a need for a review. To automatically assume otherwise was self-defeating.

The lawyer agreed that he might be prejudicing our efforts, but he assured us that he was only trying to keep the Q.s aware of their options, so that they wouldn't feel overwhelmed by the school staff's presentation—and feel pressured into concurring when their own inclinations were to disagree. He did, however, agree that his frequent reference to their intent to challenge the team's decision might undermine our immediate purpose and he said he would refrain from further comments along those lines.

Later on, when, fortunately, a mutually desirable plan of action *was* agreed to, I urged the lawyer to spell out the due-process procedures which the parents could pursue if they felt, at any time, that the program we had devised for Jackie was not being implemented to their satisfaction.

More often than in the illustration cited above, the guest expert or lawyer is difficult to manage, contain, or draw into the team process as a mutual ally. Frequently an outside consultant has been engaged because the parents are already doubtful or concerned about what they perceive the school staff to be doing and are considering challenging the program. Consequently, guest experts often arrive with a protective or negatively biased view, especially if they have come to know the child in another setting. Therefore, we need to try to state our objectives and impressions as openly as we can to enlist the aid of the guest expert in our mutual problem-solving effort. If we are less than candid or are defensive ourselves, or if the staff becomes unduly awed, cowed, or mute in the presence of the guest, the parents are likely to feel that their lack of faith in the school staff has been justified.

Administrators must be particularly aware of the need to assist staff to prepare for such potential encounters. In-service training should include simulated role-playing exercises which provide staff with the opportunity to explore their likely reactions to a variety of possible encounters with parents and parental advisors in potential or actual adversarial relationships. The better prepared all staff members are, the more successful they will be in turning potential adversaries into working allies.

Procedural Problems

The team-meeting difficulties which frequently plague even the most efficient of team leaders are those stemming from procedural oversights or misunderstandings. Such problems range from minor frustrating delays, e.g., needing to wait for one teacher while everyone else has gathered to meet to failure to allot the necessary number of days for parents' receipt of notice of the meeting, to neglecting to include one or more staff members who have something significant to contribute. Such procedural difficulties are troublesome, but not difficult to overcome if it is understood that such difficulties are bound to occur. Notice-of-meeting issues can be resolved by having a parent "waiver of notice" form available to reduce the legal implications of an oversight or error. And, if an absent teacher is needed to round out the staff's review or presentation of a child's performance, it may be possible to arrange for that teacher to meet with the parents at another time or to join the meeting immediately if a standby aide or substitute can be found. In fact, in large school systems when several meetings have been scheduled and the likelihood is great of needing someone to attend a meeting who has not made prior arrangements to do so, having a standby substitute may be desirable.

Procedural problems, though always frustrating, can be resolved if it is anticipated that some such problems will occur despite careful planning and if the team, including the parents, are willing to solve such problems as best they can and not let them destroy the meeting. In other words, such problems become big problems only when they are incorporated into an already formulated adversarial attitude.

Conflict among Staff Members

A more difficult problem occurs when, during the presentation of evaluation data for program planning purposes, one or more staff members disagree with the general consensus. The pre-meeting resolution of such staff-member differences, and related role-contribution conflicts will be discussed in greater detail in Chapter VI, but it is imperative that:

1. Such differences or dissenting opinions should be annotated to the team's decisions.
2. Such differing opinions must ultimately be resolved through further examination of a child's performance—possibly via further, independent evaluation.
3. Such differences should not diminish the team's effort to reach a *tentative* decision regarding a child's program, pending further evaluation.

Parental Passivity

In Chapter VII, the specific methods of encouraging parents' active participation in team meetings will be developed within the frame of reference of the "dynamics" of parents' passivity. For the time, however, it should be noted that continuing passivity generally thwarts efforts to involve parents more meaningfully in helping their children, reinforces defensive or resistive behavior, and often portends future difficulty. Gilmore (1974), the present authors, and others have therefore cited the importance of encouraging in parents an active participatory role. Passive, reticent parents are usually, for one or more reasons, deferring too readily to the team's authority. While such deference may reflect a complex and significant history of deferential behavior on the part of the parents, it is the immediate task of the team to encourage a change via whatever concrete ways the team can devise, beginning with some acknowledgment that the parents have thus far felt comfortable in their passive role.

This may be more difficult than it seems, because the staff may too readily perceive and dismiss these parents as nonchallenging, undemanding, or uncaring. The team must guard against a tendency to do nothing about such parents' passivity and to take advantage too quickly of the opportunity to move on to more pressing issues with other children and other parents.

Parental Domination

In sharp contrast to the need to draw out the passive parent into an active team role, the vocal, demanding, usually hypercritical parent needs to be eased into a more receptive stance. Such parents are already too active and tend to dominate team meetings to the extent that *mutual* problem solving is impossible. Again, the dynamics of the aggressive, dominant parent as team member must be addressed immediately rather than, as is often the case, briefly tolerated and then ignored or avoided as much as possible. True, such parents are not easily ignored or avoided; they keep letting you know that they must be dealt with somehow. But the frequent error, in such cases, is to remain on the defensive—a stance continually reinforced by the parents' aggressive actions—and not come to grips with the potentially undermining character of the parents' behavior.

It is more difficult to respond immediately to a parent's aggressive stance during a team meeting than to the passive parent's behavior. Because such parent behavior is often a function of defensive reactions against feelings of helplessness and vulnerability, but certainly not an immediate reflection of such vulnerability, it is best for the staff member who has worked most closely with the parents to meet with them separately, and to point out the disadvantages of their attitude and behavior. If this is attempted during the team meeting, it is likely that the aggressive parent will misconstrue the message and react with statements like:

"Why are you trying to shut me up?"

"Are you telling me that you know my child better than I do?"

"I had to make special arrangements to be here today, so I have no time to waste with all your talk, I simply want to know what's wrong with Eric and what you are going to do to help him."

In other words, the parents' aggressive behavior ought to be more carefully investigated in terms of the purpose it serves them before efforts are made to get them to listen or reflect on what the team really has to say.

Problems in Initial Meetings

The first coming together of team members to share information about a child is like any other encounter between people meeting for the first time for some purpose. The overriding objective needs to be clearly stated and agreed upon. Surprisingly, it often is not. Everyone "knows" or at least "says" the team has gathered to help a child "do better in school," "enjoy school more," or "realize more" of his or her potential. These generalizations are easy to make. But the most meaningful and tangible objectives often remain ambiguous in everyone's mind. Therefore, more than merely stating generalizations it is important to identify one or two specific goals for reference, such as "helping Brian overcome his low self-esteem" or "helping Joanne compensate for her writing difficulty," or "reducing Johnny's distractability." When some specificity has *not* been achieved during the team's first meeting, it is not uncommon to hear parents remark in later meetings:

"What is my child's problem anyway?"

or

"Why is it necessary to have so much testing?"

or

"Wouldn't it be easier to keep him back a year?"

The single most important emphasis in a problem-solving approach to team meetings is the importance of clearly stating, restating, and adhering to a few specific, mutually agreed upon work objectives. In the absence of consistent group interest in delineated objectives, hidden agendas, unresolved personal concerns, within-group alliances, intra-team squabbling, and a variety of other non-child-help-related issues can all seriously undermine the important purpose of the team.

SUMMARY

In this chapter we have discussed the different purposes of team meetings (essentially, initial planning and placement and later review and change) and the different tasks to be accomplished at the different meetings. We have stressed the importance of meaningful parental involvement, not only because the law requires that parents participate but also because parents' attitudes of cooperation or resistance (or anything between the two extremes) can have a significant effect on the success or failure of a child's program. We will return frequently to the primacy of the parents' role in later chapters of this book.

In considering who among the professional staff ought to attend team meetings, we have supported the principle of flexible size and membership. This approach assures that everyone who *ought* to be present will be there, while avoiding placing an undue time burden on staff members. We also pointed out some possible pitfalls in staffing, stressing the inadvisability of including staff members toward whom parents of the child in question have historically been antagonistic (and vice versa).

We emphasize the following principles of effective preparation:

1. Staff members should be aware of due-process requirements, be cognizant of how extensive a part they will be expected to play, and be briefed on the questions they are likely to be asked and the type of data they will be expected to supply.
2. Parents should be notified of and afforded all their legal rights and treated with courtesy and respect at meetings.
3. Parents should have been kept informed all along of their child's progress so that they will be unlikely to hear at the meeting for program planning unexpected, upsetting news about their child's progress.
4. Staff members should be educated to the fact that for parents these meetings may be occasions that provoke anxiety, guilt, defensiveness, and/or resentment.

We have reviewed potential problems that may occur and made suggestions for avoiding or dealing with the following difficulties, among others:

1. Staff anxiety caused by the presence of parents' legal counsel. The leader should always keep the focus on the primary objective of the meeting and permit relevant discussion only.
2. Staff concern about the presence of guest professional experts. The leader should make use of the guest's expertise and try to develop an alliance.
3. Procedural oversights. These are bound to occur; the leader should stay calm and not escalate antagonism.
4. Professional disagreements among staff. Staff conflict should not be

ignored but neither should it be permitted to destroy efforts to reach tentative conclusions.

5. Extreme parental attitudes (e.g., passivity, aggression, domination of meeting). The leader should try to involve passive parents as, while they may seem tractable, they may later undermine the progress of the program; the leader should not permit bullying parents to impede decision making. Sources of the parents' behavior may need to be explored.

Chapters V, VI, and VII deal with these issues relative to parents in greater depth. Chapter III will deal with the concepts of communicating and problem solving as a team.

3

Communicating and Problem Solving in Team Meetings

INTRODUCTION

The decision-making process is affected by many variables, including the size and composition of the team and the interaction among team members. There may be considerable variation in the size and make-up of special education teams within a school district. That variability is limited, to some extent, by local and federal regulations governing who may (and who must!) attend team meetings, and by the availability of staff and the extent to which parents participate actively. In addition, such factors as the clarity of purpose for which a meeting has been called, whether or not the child under consideration is in attendance, and how much staff preparation has gone into a meeting, all have a significant effect on what is communicated and how easily communication occurs as the dynamics of the team process unfold. Furthermore, the issues of who says what, how and when information is shared, and what sort of findings have occurred are all important variables which can affect team decision making.

Another important point is the extent to which the "apparent" decision making and problem solving taking place during a team meeting are "genuine." For, though federal regulations forbid decisions about a child's program or placement to be made outside a team

39

setting, it is an unfortunate fact that many meetings are called simply to "rubber stamp" decisions that actually have been predetermined.

This chapter, therefore, is devoted to exploring the communications and problem-solving processes which vary with or are affected by several of the factors noted above. Factors relative to questions about leadership and the effects of different leadership roles upon the problem-solving process in team meetings will be touched upon in this chapter, but leadership styles per se and the specific roles of team members will be more fully explored in Chapter IV. For the moment, the focus is upon what may or may not happen during special education team meetings as a function of size, structure, mode of communication, parent or student involvement, purpose, and attitudes about problem sharing. There will also be references to the professional literature on communications theory and practice in small-group decision making because, in effect, a special education team constitutes a small group problem-solving unit. However, the main focus will be upon the application or relevance of theory and published findings to the authors' own actual experience and the experience of others in the public schools.

This chapter also includes potential strategies to improve the efficiency of special education team meetings, with specific references to procedures and methods to facilitate administration and coordination, improve communication within the team, and raise team morale with respect to its usefulness as a decision-making body.

FACTORS AFFECTING COMMUNICATION

The Effect of Size and Structure on Information Sharing

The dynamics of information sharing during a team meeting are probably less affected by the team's size than by the prevailing atmosphere which generally regulates how such meetings shall proceed. It is of greater significance, for example, that the meetings are run in a certain manner, i.e., in an autocratic, a democratic, or a laissez-faire manner, than that they are generally attended by few or by many members. Despite its lesser importance, however, the size of a group clearly has some impact upon ease of communication and, therefore, deserves attention.

Many authors (Hare, Borgatta, and Bales 1962) have described the optimal size of a variety of problem-solving or decision-making groups, with general agreement that the most effective or constructive work is accomplished in groups of no fewer than three or four members and no more than eight. Apart from mini-team meetings called for routine purposes, that same principle also applies to special education team meetings. Team meetings that include more than eight members have been known to intimidate parents and are, therefore, usually counter-productive.

The membership of the special education team will vary with the child being considered, but the law requires the categorical representation of the administration, the pupil-services staff, and the regular instructional staff. This means that, at the very least, a team meeting must include an administrator (usually the building principal in an elementary school, a lower echelon member in secondary schools), a member of the pupil personnel staff, and one of the child's teachers. Often, if an outside placement is being contemplated, the team meeting will include a representative of the outside school district or agency or institution where the child may be placed. Various specialists from the pupil personnel staff are included when and if their presence is relevant.

When determining team size, it is important to strike a balance between the number of staff members who have the most pertinent information to share and can best communicate with parents about their child, on the one hand, and the number of participants who will assure the most effective input for evaluation and program planning, on the other. Since the law requires that a chairperson, a coordinator, and a teacher be present and that strenuous efforts be made to include one or both parents, theoretically the number options lie within the four-to-eight range recommended for optimal functioning. Practically, however, the closer the size is held to the bare minimum, the more effectively the team is likely to function. For one thing, the larger the group, the more time is needed for presentation of findings and discussion of data (much of which may better have been reviewed and discussed in prior meetings with the parents). Furthermore, the more members attending, the more divergent points of view or options are likely to be considered—with more time required for thoughtful consideration.

In many cases the team coordinator will have received and discussed the findings of one or more special education specialists and integrated those findings into an overview of the child's functioning. Unless the findings are of primary importance or the data is so technical, specialized, or difficult to understand that it requires the actual staff member who has conducted the evaluation to explain it to the parents, it may be wise not to invite everyone who has *ever* seen the child to the team meeting. One might establish as a working principle, therefore, that larger group meetings should be arranged when more varied input is needed for problem solving and when time limitations are of little or no concern, and that more routine evaluation and program reviews should be scheduled with fewer staff members attending.

The actual determination of which specific staff members should attend should be made by the special education team coordinator, often in conjunction with the team chairperson.

Obviously, the above considerations are irrelevant in those unfortunate situations in which the team is dominated by one member—the leader. Such a circumstance obviates the factor of the relationship between group size and problem-solving efficiency because the dominating team leader may manipulate group size to serve predetermined objectives.

An additional factor about group size is important: the extent to which group pressure influences decisions may vary as the size of the team varies. Asch's classic research (1952) into the influence of the majority opinion upon individuals who are in the minority (or alone) in group problem-solving situations described an interesting phenomenon which is sometimes also observed in special education team meetings. Asch discussed the pressures upon individuals who felt pitted against the majority's "expert" viewpoint to "yield" to the majority opinion. He described situations in which a minority of one had yielded to the majority rather than appear foolish, uninformed, mistaken in judgment, or somehow incapable of making an appropriate judgment.

Parents in a team meeting may frequently be in this minority position and often may yield to the judgment of those they consider to be experts, particularly when the school staff appears unanimous in an evaluation or decision about their child. There are also instances when staff members may reluctantly "fall into line" despite their differing professional judgments and against what they consider their better instincts, when it appears that there is unanimous opposition to their deviant point of view. This yielding tendency, whether it occurs in parents or staff members, must therefore be recognized when a team, which is genuinely interested in pooling *all* their thinking, is intent upon arriving at the best decision affecting a child's program or placement. The larger and more expert the team or group working together, the greater the danger that a deviant point of view will be suppressed, possibly to the detriment of the child.

In another phase of his studies, Asch found that, particularly in large groups, even a single supporter for a group member's differing viewpoint often overcame the tendency of the lone dissenter to yield. Therefore, in the absence of a dissenting opinion during the team's deliberations, expecially when the group is large, it is incumbent upon the chairperson at least to check out what appears to be the group's unanimous decision to make sure that there really is complete agreement, and that anyone with reservations about the decision has had a chance to air them.

The yielding phenomenon, of course, also varies with the general tone set by those in the group who exert influence and leadership. Chapter IV will deal more fully with the differential impact upon group decision making of different approaches to leadership. It should here be noted that yielding to the powerfully influential judgment of the majority is more likely to occur in large meetings than in small ones and in autocratically run meetings than in those where all members feel they have an equal share in determining the outcome.

The Effect of Mode of Communication
upon Sharing

An important factor affecting problem-solving efficiency and team morale is the manner in which information is shared by the team members. In the early fifties some interesting communication network studies were conducted (Shaw 1954) to explore the comparative problem-solving efficiency on both simple and complex tasks, of groups sharing information in different ways. The most relevant findings disclosed that, for simple tasks, the greater the extent to which access to information was initially limited to one member of the group—who then served in a central information-distribution capacity—the greater the group's performing efficiency. However, as tasks became more complex (resembling the tasks frequently confronting planning teams), it was more important to group morale for all group members to have a sense of equal sharing of information. And as group morale improved, the increase in problem-solving effectiveness was notable.

Members of groups that continue to use, for more complex tasks, the mode they had previously employed for simpler tasks—that of depending on one central authority to collect and disperse information—became increasingly discouraged by their minimal, somewhat isolated roles when tasks became more demanding and time consuming. It appeared that when group members felt that their roles were not particularly important to the team's problem-solving effort, they tended to lose interest, withdraw effort, and, in some cases, complain about the unfairness or the inefficiency of the whole operation. As a result, their problem-solving efficiency dropped below the performance level of the group where all members felt they had an equal share in the group's effort.

In special education teams, when the flow of information is too deliberately directed or is overly managed by the chairperson or any other individual, the remaining team members, including the parents, begin to feel like excess baggage, as if what they have to say is not especially important. They may begin to develop the feeling of being manipulated, as part of an already determined scenario; they may or may not express their resentment, depending upon their feelings of personal security in the work situation or other similar factors. The team leader often is not aware of this reaction because, as the team meeting was called to accomplish a relatively simple task within a short period of time, it seems to make the most sense to proceed as directly as possible to a decision, with as few "side trips" as possible. Granted, there are many occasions when time restrictions require wasting as little time as possible on discussion that may not seem directly to the point. When such occasions arise, team members who may not be expected to play an active role, or who do not have significant information to share with the team, should probably either not be invited or at least be given the option not to attend.

It may be contradictory to the intent of the law if the team procedures employed result not in increasing but in diminishing the opportunity for equal sharing in decision making for any members—including the parents. As the Shaw studies show, having a more significant share in the decision making process increases the positive feelings of members about their contributions and improves their ability to work effectively together.

A speech clinician from Palm Beach County, Florida, described this kind of positive experience most succinctly. She said that the chairperson of her team was the school principal, who generally set the direction and tone of most of their meetings but made it clear that all members had an equal say in the team's decisions. As a result, she reported, there was a lot of opportunity for "interdisciplinary sharing which I feel good about." She then noted that "in addition, it helps me learn about others' techniques and terminology. You also become more familiar with certain aspects of children's problems with learning disabilities which your own training never touched upon." This particular speech clinician went on to describe some of her team experiences as somewhat lengthy or drawn out, in that a lot of information (some of which perhaps could have been discussed with parents beforehand) was openly shared at the team meetings, but it was evident that she had been reinforced in the view that she had a significant role to play, vital information to contribute, and an important part in the decision-making process. As Shaw's studies would suggest, the procedures she describes were more than usually time consuming. However, their positive impact upon team-member morale (and professional skill development) is equally evident in her view of her experience.

Interestingly, from the speech clinician's descriptions, one of the ways in which the principal conveyed to the team that each regularly attending member was an important contributor was to express the idea that the judgments she expressed were only hers, and that her point of view might be overruled by the group's collective thinking. This did occur occasionally, reinforcing the genuineness of the principal's position and enhancing the members' views of their own roles in the decision-making process.

The Effect upon Communication When Children Attend Team Meetings

Public Law 94-142 urges that "when appropriate" students be invited to meetings called for the evaluation of their special needs and the development of their educational program. The rationale for this recommendation is that the students should have some direct say in what is being planned for them. Experience supports the validity of this approach when the student is of junior high school age or older, and it certainly holds for students over eighteen years old, who are legal adults. But for elementary-school-aged children, and for many junior-high-school-aged children as well, the question of whether or not the student is aware, mature, or responsible enough to contribute meaningfully to the team's deliberations constitutes the major consideration and should determine whether it is appropriate to include the student. Another, perhaps even more important, consideration, which is sometimes overlooked, is the extent to which the student's presence is likely to inhibit communication between parents and staff and actually diminish the group's problem-solving efficiency.

> Tommy, age fourteen, an eighth-grader in our junior high school, had been invited to attend a program-planning team meeting. Despite his long-standing learning difficulties, which he and his parents were freely able to discuss, Tommy had always impressed the staff as a boy who was surprisingly self-assured, and who was acknowledged as a leader among his peers. He was quiet throughout most of the early phase of the meeting while the team specialists described their recent diagnostic impressions and reports of his progress, but shortly after his parents expressed their agreement to the recommendation—a resource room program of supplementary services to help him with his "word-attack" skills and his expressive writing difficulties—Tommy surprised everyone with his comments and suggestions about a few changes he thought should be made. Though obviously a bit self-conscious, he pointed out that the classes to which he was to be assigned included two former friends of his whom he described

as "trouble makers" who "had it in for him," and who he felt would make it hard for him to "get much from the class." Discussion ensued about the ability of the teacher to help ease the difficulties he was experiencing with those and a few other prospective classmates he was concerned about, but it turned out that those staff members who knew the other students in question agreed that his concern was a realistic one that had been overlooked. Tommy seemed a bit reluctant to pursue the issue himself lest he put himself in the position of being disloyal to his peers, but he made further comments which underscored a fact of junior-high life—that one's peer relationships have a powerful influence upon one's receptivity to learning and school performance in general. Tommy artfully managed to avoid incriminating any of his fellow students when pressed for details about some of the negative peer pressures he was under. He dismissed further inquiries by his parents and by some of the staff by saying that there were some things he preferred to handle by himself, but he stuck to his point that some schedule changes might be important for him if he was to get the most he could out of the program.

Tommy isn't really an exception to what might be expected when a student is asked to take part in a team meeting. There are many students in his age group who can contribute to the team's planning in a responsible way. But the younger the student, the more likely it is that he or she will feel overwhelmed by the team procedures, the perceived reasons for having to be there, the sense of being in a fishbowl, and by a whole host of other factors related to how the student feels about certain teachers, about parents, and about the other staff discussing his or her problems and needs. When this occurs, the communication between team members, including the student's parents, is dramatically affected, and this generally limits what can be openly discussed.

Martha, a sixth-grader, had expressed willingness to participate in the annual team meeting called to assess her progress during the current school year and to plan for the next school year. Her parents, who had requested that she be allowed to attend, were therefore somewhat disappointed and a bit nonplused when, at the meeting, Martha seemed not to want to say anything when asked for her opinions. She simply nodded or said nothing when her parents urged her to comment and did not respond to gently worded questions from her teachers. Before long, parents and staff stopped prompting Martha to participate, but all the others present were uneasy and became increasingly guarded in their comments. As one teacher noted afterward, "I thought she was on the verge of tears." Martha was asked, in fact, if she would prefer to leave the meeting, but she demurred, saying that she preferred to be there to hear what was said about her. Interestingly, after they were over their mutual disappointment about Martha's reticence, her parents began to talk freely about what they thought Martha felt about the progress she had made during the year— which she had, indeed, discussed with them. Occasionally they looked over in her direction, again to try to get her to comment, but Martha ignored their glances. The team chairperson tried to carry on, but it was soon evident that the rest of the staff, sensitive to Martha's discomfort, really did not want to go into any but the most superficial aspects of her performance. Planning for the following year was conducted in a similarly cursory fashion and the meeting soon ended. Later on, Martha's teacher said she'd had some important issues to discuss regarding certain inconsistencies in Martha's work habits, but she became apprehensive about introducing anything new because she felt the youngster might respond defensively and she wasn't sure that her parents would be supportive enough in view of their obvious disappointment with her behavior at the meeting. In other words, in this case, the child's presence at the meeting served to inhibit what might have been a freer exchange of ideas had she not been there. Later, it was determined that Martha had misunderstood the reason for the meeting, and when she saw both of her parents and a lot of school staff present she simply "got scared" and thought some "big decision was going to be made."

Obviously, Martha should have been better prepared and given a clearer understanding of the meeting's purpose, but the fact remains that students brought into team meetings are often not well prepared. Consequently, the usual effect of their presence ranges from distracting and inhibiting to disruptive. The younger the student, the greater the chance that the parents and staff will feel constrained to watch what they say or will try to respond to how they see the child reacting. The older the student, the more likely he or she may be able to contribute to the purpose of the meeting—provided the student has been counseled about the meeting's purpose and procedures and about what to expect from the other members who may attend.

Having a student attend a team meeting can be a valuable opportunity for the staff to develop a "contract" with the student to foster the feeling that he or she is importantly involved in decisions affecting his or her future schooling. However, this may be better accomplished in a one-to-one situation. This is true because, as was the case to some extent with Martha, a student, regardless of age, is likely to be somewhat overwhelmed by a team meeting and may react with fear or bewilderment that can last beyond the meeting.

Students experiencing the kind of problems in school that require referral to a special education team are likely to be undergoing some degree of emotional stress regardless of the source of their difficulties. They may be struggling to retain feelings of "normalcy" and to avoid feeling "different," "singled-out," "peculiar," or "stupid." For some students, having their problems be the focus of attention at a large meeting of professionals may serve only to confirm their worst fears about themselves. They may be so distracted by the feeling of being "under the microscope" that they may fail to apprehend meaningfully what is going on. Except where it is known in advance that the evaluation findings are certain to provide them with reassurance, it is probably better for students with moderate to severe learning disabilities not to attend the meetings where their programs are discussed. However, one sympathetic staff member who knows him or her well may meet with the student following the meeting to discuss the decisions and explain the objectives the group hopes will be accomplished.

Equally as important as preparing students for team meetings is preparing staff for how to deal with students. Children may feel that they are being grilled when staff and parents throw questions at them. They may not be ready or able to respond to questions. It may work better for the team leader to say, "We would be interested in your view of the problem" (or of a proposal), rather than to ask directly "How do you feel about ―― ?" The less directive approach gives the student two important options: the choice of saying "I'm not ready to react; I need to hear more," or the like, and the choice of giving the group information, opinions, and reactions about aspects of the situation other than what was directly asked.

A staff member who knows the child well should discuss with the leader whether the child's input should be sought first, or later in the meeting. There should also be some agreement—and the child should understand this—as to whether the child is there as a team member with equal input or whether the child will actually be able to exercise "veto power" over a proposed course of action. On the one hand, the program can't work without the child's cooperation. But on the other hand, putting the child in a veto position may be giving the child power that is inappropriate, frightening to the child, and not in the child's best interests.

Sticking to the Purpose and the Attitude of Sharing

If students who attend team meetings tend to inhibit the adults who are there to make decisions about them, one would certainly expect increased uneasiness in the presence of other guests and lawyers, as discussed in Chapter II. The main thing to be kept in mind is that the meeting has been called for a specific purpose and all invited need to try to remain committed to that purpose for as long as possible. If the leader refers to the primary purpose—which is to evaluate a child's special education needs and provide a suitable program—when redirection of the team's deliberations seems needed, an attitude of sharing can be reinforced, despite differing staff and parent attitudes, and despite some of the inhibiting or disruptive factors noted above. The desire to share information, observations, or impressions about a child; views about different available programs; and other relevant information is likely to prevail in all members of the team, including the child's parents, at least at the outset of the team meeting.

The parents may already have reservations about what they expect from the school staff, and members of the staff may have similar concerns about a child's parents. Similarly, the team meeting may be viewed in advance by the administrators as routine, or as potentially troublesome. But, given that the meeting has been called to solve a problem of mutual concern, that primary objective can and should be readdressed whenever the meeting seems to be drawn off course—for whatever reason.

The one constant, binding issue that characterizes these team meetings (which few other problem-solving groups have going for them) is the fact that the team efforts are directed toward helping a particular child in whom each team member has a professional and/or a personal interest. The existence of this common, binding purpose or super-ordinate goal increases the probability that there will be stronger mutual interest in resolving matters of disagreement than might be expected in other problem-solving groups who need to pool their knowledge and skills. The Sherifs (1956), in their classic studies of groups working to overcome intergroup antagonism and prejudicial attitudes, found that the most powerful agent available to diminish effectively and finally dispel adversarial and antagonistic feelings was the acceptance of an overriding goal or primary objective which could be cited as transcending the needs or views of individuals.

Similarly, a team meeting can be salvaged from adversarial, or disruptive, or antagonistic quagmires—when it is apparent that the desired attitudes of sharing views and receptivity to joint planning are deteriorating—if the primary reason for everyone being there is *reaffirmed.* Indeed, it will not be enough for the leader simply to say:

"Let's not forget, we are all here to help Jimmy."

or

"Aren't we forgetting our main purpose—to agree upon a program for Ellen."

but to redirect the team to the specifics of the main purpose while at the same time acknowledging what seems to be blocking more constructive efforts.

"We seem hung up on some important issues which are getting in the way of our reaching agreement on which of these program options will best meet Margaret's need for improving her visual-motor skills. It seems that we *do* agree on her need for tracking exercises—the question is, in which of the programs we've described will she get the most help with her perceptual difficulty with the least danger of feeling singled-out or different? For Margaret's sake, we need to come up with something—one of these program alternatives we've discussed, or perhaps some modification of one of them—to start with. What do you think we can or ought to do?"

Obviously, anyone—the parents' lawyer, an antagonized or defensive teacher, the guest expert, even the student, herself—may still thwart pursuit of the team's primary objective and block further constructive sharing. Nevertheless the "strong suit" of the team's purpose, the acknowledgment of the child's needs, should be reaffirmed to be the primary concern. These efforts should be continued until it is unquestionably clear that the goal cannot be further pursued without the imposition of due-process or third-party intervention.

METHODS OF FACILITATING COMMUNICATION

There are many instances when communication is blocked for other reasons and the problem needs to be addressed in order to make the meeting productive. The following is an illustration of an instance in which the parents' mistrustful attitude was the source of blocked communications and needed to be dealt with before any other constructive team work could occur.

The team meeting seemed to have begun on a constructive note when, at the outset, the staff and Ms. Gardner, the school psychologist, informed Ms. Gonzalez, the principal, and Carol G.'s parents that the recently completed evaluations clearly pointed to a perceptual handicap which had not heretofore been suspected. Carol, who was repeating first grade, had started the school year successfully, but by late fall she had become increasingly frustrated when, because of her painfully slow progress, the other first graders, all much younger than she, were beginning to surpass her in school work. The staff evaluation disclosed a partial hearing loss which certainly was contributing to the youngster's difficulties and might even have been the primary cause. The staff was somewhat "excited" by this finding, which was so "clearcut" in a situation where frequently a child's problems are hard to pin down. They quickly began to discuss ways to help the little girl compensate for her hearing problem and build her confidence in her approach to school work.

Carol's parents, on the other hand, were astonished at being told that their child had a hearing difficulty. They listened intently to the explanation of how it affected her auditory discrimination and slowed down her ability to develop word-attack, sound blending, and other reading skills. They continued to listen to what was described as the generalized effect of Carol's hearing loss upon other aspects of her learning. But when the team arrived at the point of specifying and developing an appropriate IEP to help Carol, the parents seemed reticent—almost as if they were unwilling to participate in any further discussion. Ms. Gardner, taken somewhat aback by the parents' passivity, asked if they weren't "feeling good" about the fact that something could now be done to help Carol. Carol's mother seemed agitated by the question. She said that of course she was gratified that the evaluation had pinpointed Carol's problem, but she said she was also feeling upset about the fact that Carol's kindergarten and first-grade teachers had not spotted the problem earlier. Carol's father then angrily elaborated his similar feelings of disappointment about "so-called professional educators who can't spot a child who can't hear." It was obvious that the need mutually to develop an appropriate program for Carol had become sidetracked.

Perhaps the staff had been naive not to anticipate that, while parents may be relieved to find that their child's learning problems have a specific cause (and, by extension, possibly a specific remedy), they would still naturally be upset upon being told that their daughter had a very real physical handicap that no one had suspected before. Natural reactions to such a disclosure might range anywhere from alarm and confusion to fear and anxiety. Many parents would find it hard to accept such news and might wish to deny it or certainly to seek corroboration before making any decisions based on this new, unpleasant information.

Moreover, hostility and anger toward the bearers of bad news being common, parents might react with hostility toward the professionals who broke the news. Some parents' feelings might be compounded by reactions of guilt over not having suspected the problem themselves, or —even more guilt-producing—over having suspected it at some time but repressed it out of fear, anxiety, or similar causes.

It is not surprising then that rather than feeling "delighted" that the cause of the child's school difficulties had been isolated these parents were angered by what they considered the incompetence of her previous teachers, and that they further expressed doubts that anything very effective would or could be done about Carol's problem in the future—despite the team's enthusiasm.

Very wisely, the principal responded quickly to the parents' expressed annoyance. She acknowledged their sense of mistrust, and asked the psychologist and the speech therapist to take a few moments to talk about whether or not the parents' concerns were valid. Much discussion ensued about the fact that it wasn't easy to spot the effects of Carol's hearing loss, because it was the kind of problem that was confounded by developmental considerations and other medical factors such as upper-respiratory infections and seasonal allergic reactions.

However, after some time, although the parents' doubts and annoyance were somewhat allayed by the discussion, it was still apparent that they weren't entirely convinced that her previous teachers had handled matters competently. Sensing that the meeting was likely to remain unproductive and that the timing was not right to push on to "mutual problem solving," Ms. Gonzalez urged that the meeting be postponed until the parents had the opportunity to review the staff's opinions with their pediatrician. The parents were receptive to the principal's suggestion and were gratified that everyone was willing to postpone the development of the IEP until they had had time to absorb the news and seek corroboration. Within a week, having been reassured by their pediatrician that Carol's problem, although it was real, was a marginal one and not easily discernible, "even by well qualified teachers," the parents were now willing to cooperate and asked Ms. Gardner to reconvene the meeting.

In this incident, the principal's response, though time consuming, was necessary to reestablish the parents' trust in the school staff so that productive problem solving and idea sharing could proceed. The IEP could have been pushed through during the first meeting, but the parents' mistrust would have lingered and might have impeded full implementation of the program. Instead, the principal's actions actually facilitated eventual consensus.

The cause of these parents' negativism was fairly clearcut and the method of dealing with it was not complex—merely requiring a minimal postponement of decision making. Some advance discussion among the chairperson and the staff might even have avoided the initial parental negativism. When evaluation data show this kind of clear, dramatic, previously unidentified handicap which can be corroborated by referral to a physician, this probably ought to be disclosed to parents before team meetings to give them the opportunity to absorb the news and follow up with any private consultations they may want before utilizing the information in decision making.

Other sources of parental negativism may be far more difficult to identify or attribute to a specific cause. Some parents may be generally mistrustful of school personnel because of previous negative experiences, in connection with their child's program or even as a result of negative experiences with their own schooling far in the past. Others—particularly those whose children's problems are of long duration—may have become accustomed to an adversarial relationship with school personnel. Finally, in instances where a child's difficulties are thought to be related to home situations or parental relationships, the parents' defensiveness may be difficult to deal with. Regardless of the source of the parental attitude, however, the critical issue is that their aroused negativism should be acknowledged, addressed with consideration for their concerns, and resolved, if possible, before the actual task of joint planning is undertaken.

There are still other instances when efforts to share ideas and plans may be momentarily blocked when a particular staff member feels that his or her role has not been sufficiently recognized or that a contribution he or she wishes to make has been overlooked, or otherwise overshadowed or diminished. We already know, from the Shaw studies regarding communication in small groups (1954), that morale suffers when team members feel bypassed or do not have a sense of equality in the problem-solving process. In the next section of this chapter we will discuss how individuals should prepare for meetings to minimize the chance of being bypassed or having their contributions overlooked. When this does occur, it tends to result in a particular kind of communication difficulty which deserves special attention.

The kinds of comment at meetings that signal that someone feels bypassed include:

> "I didn't know Mrs. Walsh was going to talk about Phillip's reading comprehension skills—that was included in the battery of tests I gave him a few weeks ago."

or

> "Of course, if Barbara is going to be placed in that resource room program, she won't need to keep coming to me."

or

> "Will I have time to go over the results of my tests of Billy's listening skills?"

When such comments occur during a team meeting, the call for attention they signal should not be ignored or treated lightly. Someone is feeling "stepped on," or at the very least overlooked, and that fact should be faced immediately to avoid increasing tension.

It may be that a deeper problem exists for the team, in that one or more of the members may have been feeling overlooked for some time. It is possible that the more complex problem of role differentiation needs to be addressed, but the immediate and pressing matter is that the bypassed staff member needs to be heard. If there has been merely a momentary oversight, then the problem may be easily resolved by acknowledging that this has happened and by taking up immediately what has been bypassed, or by deferring it for logical consideration at a specific point later on during the meeting. Unless a deeper problem exists, the following comment should suffice:

> "You're right, Mr. Byron. After we hear what Ms. Walsh has to report about Phillip's reading comprehension, we need to see how that compares to your findings—we didn't mean to overlook your report."

However, when more complex problems, including underlying inter-staff antagonism, do exist, a more direct confrontation may be necessary. It should, however, be an acknowledgment that nevertheless directs resolution of the personal matter to a more private arena, or implies that there are more pressing issues for the moment.

> "Mr. Byron, let's hear Ms. Walsh out about Phillip's reading skills, then if there is any disagreement between your report and hers we'll see how it affects what we need to plan for him. Will that be OK for now?"

If it is not "OK for now," it may be necessary to specify a time when Ms. Walsh and Mr. Byron can get together, after the meeting, to iron out what is evidently a misunderstanding or other disagreement which is not appropriate to try to resolve at the moment.

When staff members openly express concern that they have been bypassed, that impression needs to be corrected immediately if, indeed, an oversight has occurred. If spontaneous acknowledgment of the oversight isn't sufficient, the more complex interstaff relationship problem underlying the issue will need to be deferred to a later, more private, discussion. Maintaining the delicate balance between acknowledging staff problems and deferring their resolutions to more appropriate times is difficult but necessary if the team is to be able to go on with its primary business. Fortunately, this kind of problem will occur only rarely, if staff members are prepared for and familiar with their roles and functions at team meetings.

Staff members will not always be given as much time as they may feel they need to make their contributions. The leader may be able to resolve any resentment by pointing out the time limitations and the fact that there may not be enough time to explore peripheral issues. If someone feels bypassed frequently, then that issue also needs to be resolved more appropriately afterwards, as a staff relationship issue.

Facilitating sharing to maintain ease and openness in communication is a complex process. It requires awareness and diplomacy in judging what sources of resistence need, in addition to being acknowledged, to be dealt with immediately or deferred for resolution following the meeting. The more complex or deep-seated the issue, the greater the likelihood that any attempt at immediate resolution will fail; it may then be necessary to review roles and relationships within the broader context of staff expectations and feelings of discontent.

TEAM MEMBERS' ROLES: PREPARATION FOR TEAM MEETINGS

The communication impasse that arises when staff members feel bypassed or ignored can and should be avoided. Nothing discourages parents more about the effectiveness of the school than witnessing intrateam squabbling or apparent discontent among team members. By contrast, a Philadelphia-area high school principal described the primary strength of the special education team in his school as its ability to work effectively with parents "because our special education staff comes to team meetings well organized and directed—pretty much knowing what they have to do and comfortable in their relationships with one another." The principal attributed much of this harmonious "comraderie" to the caring, sensitive leadership of his special education chairman who, in turn, stimulated a caring, concerned attitude among the special education staff, which the parents seemed to sense. But the key ingredient in the success of the team's efforts was the leader's emphasis upon preparedness. "They are all well prepared for the presentation they have to make, and the chairman can sit back and let them do their thing."

It was apparent in this principal's account of the team process in his school that letting "people do their own thing" was not simply a manifestation of leadership style, but required careful, deliberate planning so that each staff member's role and expectations were clarified in pre-team meetings before anything was presented during the meetings where the student's parents were present. Such preparation is extremely necessary and does *not* mean predetermination of decisions about a student. However, there are three decisions that should be made in advance to insure the smooth running of the meeting where the decision about the student will be made.

First, a decision needs to be made about who is and who is not to attend or make presentations at the team meeting about a particular student. When the special education staff in a school is small, the members generally get to know fairly well each other's strengths and shortcomings, and the varied areas of overlap among them—e.g., school psychologist, social worker, special education teacher (and/or diagnostician), counselor, speech and language development therapist—are often clarified gradually through successive experiences with one another. Consequently, the decision about who should attend a particular team meeting is frequently based simply upon who has had the greatest amount of contact with the student. This decision is generally made easily by the staff members themselves, particularly when they like and respect one another. When they do not, the team coordinator needs to make this decision based upon who has done the most evaluating of or has had the most continuing contact with the student. Similarly, when the staff in a particular school is large or more diverse, and possibly less familiar with one another, the decision about who shall attend (beyond the minimum required by federal or state statutes) should be made by the coordinator.

The second necessary advance decision is the order in which data will be presented. The classroom teacher needs to be cued into this procedure also, so that the timing of the teacher's description of first-hand experiences with and impressions of the child may be scheduled for most effective juxtaposition to other specialists' findings. In addition, the timing and relevance of the sequence of presentation of each specialist's findings should be reviewed in situations where the team has not yet evolved its own sequential, preferred order on the basis of experience with one another's strengths in making one's own or supporting others' presentations. For example, if the team coordinator is also a specialist (e.g., a social worker or psychologist) who has evaluation data to present, then he or she may coordinate the presentation of other specialists' findings around his or her own summary impressions, which may be set forth very early in the meeting.

However a particular team may develop its own usual sequence for presentations, it is important that there be some organization of the various staff members' reports, tied together by the main report—the impressions and recommendations of the particular specialist whose evaluation is most directly related to the future program objectives for the student. The decision about sequence of presentation needs to be made beforehand by the coordinator so that anticipated reactions of the parents and their consultants, or of the mainstream teachers and visiting administrators, can be addressed most effectively, at the most appropriate time, and in conjunction with the overview or plan for the total presentation.

Third, a decision must be made as to who will coordinate follow-up interpretive discussion or act as the staff spokesperson in fielding questions from parents or their consultants and handling their reactions to the data, suggestions, and recommendations presented by the staff. The spokesperson is most often the coordinator or chairperson, but need not always be. For example, if the primary recommendation under consideration is a supportive speech-and-language-development program for a child with a hearing or communication disorder, then the coordinator may organize the team presentation around the findings of the speech and language specialist. The parents would be encouraged both to raise questions and to react directly to the program objectives recommended by that specialist and to follow up the team meeting with an individual conference with the specialist. That specialist will thus serve as the key follow-up contact and staff spokesperson. Similarly, if special-class placement is being considered, the coordinator may channel the parents' reactions and questions into further discussion and elaboration by the special-class teacher, who will then serve in the key capacity. If a support service primarily involving psychological or social work consultation is likely to be the program of choice, then the psychologist or social worker may be "assigned" to be the team's major spokesperson.

It is also often wise to elect the team member most involved with the student's program (as per the IEP) to be the future team contact person to be most available to the parents to discuss their child's progress. (In some systems, however, the coordinator or team chairperson always assumes this role.) When a contact person other than the chairperson or coordinator is likely to be assigned, that specialist probably should assume the spokesperson's role during the IEP development meeting as well.

Individual Staff Member Roles and Expectations

We can assume that special education staff members and teachers are trained and certified in the professional and technical essentials of their job. However, they may not have received any training about how they ought to function as members of special education teams. It probably also is true that in many, if not most, school systems there may be considerable overlap among specialists' roles and functions so that there may be more than one specialist qualified and available to work with or provide similar data about a child. Any confusion regarding the role or status of each of the various specialists, whether or not their functions overlap, can create communications problems unless overlapping as well as delineated functions are commonly understood and respected.

Special education staff members may learn a lot about other specialists' contributions through the team meeting process and may come to have a high regard for one another's work. If left to chance, however, encounters that have the positive potential of producing mutual respect can instead lead to role confusion, jealousy, antagonism, and enmity. Therefore, clarification of roles, understanding of different specialists' skills, awareness of status attributes, and regard for one another's strengths and limitations are all necessary for effective team communication, and they must be facilitated by the team leadership through whatever means are most readily available. Provision of inservice training sessions or workshops on different specialists' functions constitutes one approach for facilitating better understanding and appreciation of one another's roles. Perhaps the best way, however, is for team leaders to encourage staff members to use others' special talents, skills, or expertise whenever possible to complement their own—especially (as is often the case) when caseloads are heavy and time is short. The highest possible mutual appreciation among team members can best be realized when individuals are encouraged to know how and where the complementary efforts of others may be more a real help than a possible hindrance.

Rather than engaging in "territorial" disputes, staff members should be able to use each other to support and supplement efforts. The need for assistance from others should not be viewed as an indication of inadequacy. Rather, all staff should be encouraged to consider cooperation as their prime responsibility, the better to serve the children.

Problems arising from the fact that the staff members on a team enjoy differing status levels in the school may be more complex, but not insurmountable. Status differences spring from a number of sources —most frequently from background factors such as seniority, salary, level of experience, where people were trained, or the number of degrees they possess. Higher or lower status may also be a function of a staff member's on-the-job effectiveness. Certain staff may also be seen as having a close relationship with the principal, the team leader, a board member, a teacher-union official, a parent group, or some other source of power.

Status differences may surface destructively in the form of competition, or status can be acknowledged and used in the "aid of the cause." The effective team leader can employ a member's status advantageously for the team, to the satisfaction of other team members, if status differences are acknowledged but then set aside as having no personal advantage-producing value *within the confines of the team.* The subordination of individual goals and status to the team's purpose should be reinforced as a working principle. Inservice training to help staff understand role differences will be limited in usefulness until the entire staff can comprehend the value and power of using those differences to complement and supplement each others' efforts and to communicate with parents as a team.

The Parents' Role in Team Communication

Thus far, we have emphasized the staff role in communicating in team meetings. In Chapter V we will consider specific strategies for involving parents effectively as *active* team participants in the team problem-solving process. There are, however, a few important basic principles pertaining to parent involvement that need to be addressed here.

It is imperative for the school staff to view parents not as enemies but as important, helpful allies with an active, major role to play in the schooling of their children. It is equally important for the school staff to help parents to see their own role in this light. The need to treat parents as equals—experts *in their own right* about the growth and development of their children—has been amply developed in "Parent

Conferences in the Schools" (Losen and Diament 1978). Unfortunately, however, parents are still too frequently not accorded equal status in special education identification and planning matters affecting their children; they are too often viewed apprehensively as potential antagonists, whether or not adversary circumstances have arisen.

Obviously, what one says to someone and how one communicates with a group are affected by one's expectations of the listeners' receptivity to one's own point of view. If a staff member views parents as never-satisfied potential antagonists, or if a parent views the special education staff as school officials whose primary function is to fend off costly parental demands and services, then communication will fail. A child's parents must feel a *part* of the team in order to work *with* the team, and to communicate with ease within that team for effective problem solving. The team staff members, individually and as a group, must convey the message that the parents are welcome—really welcome—that they will be respected for what they have to contribute, and that they are considered capable of joining in a process where everyone's views will be heard. This is a necessary condition for effective communication and problem solving. More than lip service to this attitude is required, and it will be up to those who prepare parents for team meetings, as well as those who run the meetings, to develop the mutual sense among parents and staff of pursuing a "superordinate goal" which transcends individual concerns—the goal of best meeting the needs of the child.

Unfortunately, the preparation of parents for team meetings is rarely given high priority, nor do many school staff feel they have the time to devote to such exercise. Nevertheless, there are certain opportunities to begin the preparation of parents for the team process. For example, PL 94-142 requires that "appropriate notice" be given parents prior to evaluation and prior to the planning for or placement of special education children. Since notice must be given to parents literally before anything can begin to happen, it is possible to use these notices—whether they are mailed forms or face-to-face conferences—as opportunities to encourage parental awareness and active involvement.

To begin with, the referral process requires parent approval as well as awareness. The presentation of approval forms offers the first chance to talk with parents about what procedures, meetings, staff contacts, options, and joint decision-making opportunities lie ahead. Then, following initial screening and diagnostic evaluations, many chances arise for discussing subsequent steps and for helping parents actively share in the ensuing procedures which will culminate in the IEP. Losen and Diament (1978) described procedures for sharing test data that actively involved parents in the process of assessing their children's needs. The following illustration best exemplifies that process:

Mrs. V. grimaced when I commented that there were several indications in her son's Sentence-Completion test responses that he was feeling sad or depressed. I had previously explained that no single response was of as much significance as the recurrence of persistent themes which seemed to characterize a number of George's responses. But when Mrs. V. frowned, I saw that she didn't really accept my interpretation and I asked if she would like to review some of George's test responses with me. "Yes," she said. "I would like to see what possibly could have made you arrive at that conclusion. He certainly hasn't said anything to *me* that would make me feel he is depressed."

I again described the test instructions which George had been asked to follow: I noted the variety of ways he might have responded to some of the sentence stems, and some of the ways other nine-year-old children often responded. Then, as I read each of his responses, I asked Mrs. V. what *her* interpretation of his sentence completion might be. After attributing a few of his initial responses to chance or to the sort of flip comments George might ordinarily make, Mrs. V. grew increasingly quiet until, after one particular response, she groaned, "Oh my God, I didn't know he felt that way . . . . He must have heard us quarreling about him . . . . My husband and I had a fight one night a few weeks ago about disciplining George and some other things I was angry about . . . and he must have overheard us."

We then discussed a few of his other responses which implied that the youngster's self-doubts, stemming from earlier years when he'd been in a number of foster homes, were evidently not yet resolved despite his apparent good adjustment to his adoption at age four by Mr. and Mrs. V. He had learned to cover his feelings and rarely revealed to anyone that he still felt sad—often with no apparent reason. Mrs. V. expressed concern over what the testing had disclosed and we were able to begin planning for referral for outside professional counseling to help George and the V.s better understand what was still depressing him. But just as we were about to conclude our meeting, Mrs. V. admitted that she had been skeptical about my initial interpretive comments and she said she was glad that I had taken the time to go over the test materials so that she could see what I was talking about, and could relate her son's responses to things that had happened at home. I chose that moment to point out that the rest of our work together, including how we might work out the IEP to meet George's educational needs, would involve similar sharing of what we knew about George. I told her that to be sure we had the whole picture we would be seeking active sharing on the part of her and her husband regarding what was happening at home, and what she and her husband might be doing with George via family counseling. Mrs. V. agreed that reviewing the test results as we had indeed had been helpful and she now looked forward to a more active part in planning for George than she had realized was possible.

"You know, I had pretty much intended to do whatever you recommended for George, because of our concern over his terrible school work, but I appreciate the feeling that I've got something to say about what happens . . . and that Mr. V. and I will be part of the process."

While Mrs. V. was readily drawn into active participation, the process doesn't always work that easily or effectively, but the opportunity to involve parents actively should never be overlooked. We may make ourselves more vulnerable to criticism when we are more open with parents, and we indeed make ourselves extra work and lengthier discourse when we show an openness to consideration of parents' alternative solutions to problem situations. But whatever the price paid for this active, constructive parent involvement, it is likely to be less than what follows when parents and school personnel stare at each other over the "double barrels of due process."

The involvement of parents in a sharing process can be accomplished effectively only if the school setting is supportive and if the school staff and officials responsible for the development of team procedures exert the kind of leadership necessary to facilitate active parent involvement. The following chapter will be a more comprehensive consideration of what constitutes effective leadership, and of which leadership models make the most sense for special education team work.

SUMMARY

In this chapter we have discussed the factors that affect group communication and problem solving either positively or negatively, and reviewed some ways to facilitate communication.

The size and structure of the group are important variables in the group's functioning. The minimum size is delineated by law to some extent. We recommend generally that the size of the group be kept as small as possible so as not to overwhelm parents (or students who may be present) and to insure that all members of the team who are present are given the opportunity to play an active role that they themselves see as significant.

To optimize group interaction, the leader should avoid having all information presented or processed by a single individual. However, the leader may summarize and present data and opinions of staff members who, though they have worked with the child, may not be present at the meeting.

Older children may be invited to attend group meetings if staff members who know them well are sufficiently confident that they will not be intimidated or made anxious by the attention focused on them. Of course the parents must consent to the child's presence if the child is a minor. Often a child's participation elicits the cooperation to make a program succeed (through, for example, the contract process), but the child should be thoroughly prepared for what will be discussed. A student at the meeting should be treated with courtesy and respect, and his or her opinions should receive thoughtful consideration. When a youngster attends a meeting to decide his or her program, the youngster should be in on the jury's deliberations, not just there to hear the judge pass sentence. On the other hand, a child should not be given virtual veto power over a program decision. Though the youngster may appear to want to exercise absolute power, it is not appropriate for a school-aged youngster in need of special education to be the sole decision maker about his or her educational process.

The leader should be aware that the child's presence may inhibit the staff and parents and thus prevent the necessary free and open discussion. Similarly, discussion may be inhibited or the meeting undermined by the presence of parental advisors whom the staff may see as threatening. The leader must constantly reaffirm the purpose of the meeting and stick to relevant points. If the parents' mistrustful attitudes, hostility, resentment, or anxiety threaten to undermine the conference, the leader should openly acknowledge the parents' concerns and attempt to resolve them before proceeding. Parents should be regarded as allies—as experts about their own children—and treated without condescension.

The leader should prepare for the mechanics of the meeting so that the staff knows who will be expected to present what data and in what order. Staff members should be helped to understand and appreciate one another's skills and areas of expertise to minimize competition and conflict among staff and to maximize cooperation. Staff should be trained to subordinate their own individual goals and status needs to the team's purpose and the child's well-being.

Having discussed the effect of other variables on the team's functioning, we now, in Chapter IV, will discuss team leadership, emphasizing the impact of different leadership styles on the decision-making process.

4

Leadership in Team Meetings

INTRODUCTION

It is not by chance that the law refers to the special education decision-making body as a team rather than a group, committee, cabinet, or any one of many other possible terms. The choice of the term implies that the group shares many characteristics attributable to a team. A team is a group working toward a common goal. To achieve that goal, a team's members are usually willing, when necessary, to subordinate individual interests to the common end. Team members pool their collective expertise to create opportunities for success, often playing roles that complement or supplement one another's efforts.

There may be many paths to the development of an effective team and many different types of effective teams. But the key element in the evolution of a group of disparate experts into a decision-making body that is, in the truest sense of the word, a team, is the leader—and the way in which the leader exerts authority and nurtures the development of shared responsibility and a shared sense of achievement.

This view of the centrality of the leader's role and the critical effect of leadership style is shared by other professionals in the field. Pfeiffer (1980) cites a number of studies concerning the effects of different kinds of leadership on the special education team. He reports, for example, that if chairpersons exert too directive a role in resolving problems confronting the team, their attempts at intervention tend to be perceived as unacceptable, and in fact, may "generate hostility."

63

In one study, team members apparently did not mind that certain other members' roles might be more influential than their own, as long as they felt they had some voice in decision making and in the process of sharing ideas and suggestions.

Pfeiffer further emphasizes the importance of "shared responsibility" as the "key principle of collaboration, and the fact that team members need to feel that the problem will not be handed over to any one individual or professional discipline." He asserts that at least two team participants should share responsibility for *all* aspects of the problem-defining-and-solving process, rather than leaving any one member with sole responsibility for any aspect. Pfeiffer contends that the cooperation thus engendered increases other team members' involvement, insures greater validity in decision making, and increases the probability for successful implementation of recommendations.

Pfeiffer's excellent advice is consistent with the research findings noted in Chapter III which emphasize the greater problem-solving value of genuinely shared communication over controlled, or autocratically manipulated, information sharing. But the process of sharing communications and sharing responsibility for decision making doesn't simply happen—it evolves. There is no doubt that effective sharing of responsibility must be nurtured and then reinforced by the purposeful, sensitive direction of the leader.

A Philadelphia-area high school principal underscored as one of the chairperson's main strengths "the ability to encourage shared participation in all aspects of the team process." Similarly, a speech and language clinician interviewed emphasized the value of interdisciplinary sharing which was facilitated by her building principal, who, as chairperson of the special education team, "clearly set the direction and tone" but nevertheless fostered shared participation and decision making.

It could be argued that any team or group left to its own devices would evolve a leadership structure appropriate to the group's collective needs and purpose. Whyte's classic study of the Norton Street Corner Boys' Society (Whyte 1955) and the Sherifs' studies of competitive boys' groups (Sherif and Sherif 1956) certainly posit that leadership structure emerges and stabilizes as the group's needs are clarified and supported.

But a district or building special education team does not have the latitude or time to evolve a leadership structure peculiar to its needs. For one thing, the team's composition, its designated leaders, and the purpose and occasions for which it is called into action are all prescribed by statute. Therefore, the kind of leadership necessary to bring about the team sharing advocated by Pfeiffer and others, as well as ourselves, must be actively sought and developed and appropriately reinforced to obtain desired results.

THE EFFECT OF DIFFERENT LEADERSHIP STYLES ON GROUP PROBLEM SOLVING

Some of the classic studies of the effects of different leadership styles on the members of small groups were conducted by Lewin, Lippitt, and White and first reported in 1938. A summary of their findings (White and Lippitt 1960) compares the reaction of groups of boys to three kinds of leadership: autocratic, democratic, and laissez-faire. According to these studies, autocratic leaders, who, characteristically, gave orders and clearly directed all the activities of the group, tended to elicit hostile-critical reactions; aggressive scapegoating behavior; subdued, submissive, and other dependent attitudes and an attitude of shared frustration; but little individuality and little "group-mindedness."

The democratic leaders were characterized by lack of concern for their own status; confiding and jovial attitudes; well-timed, guiding suggestions; willingness to provide information; and efforts to praise or stimulate self-direction. They tended to elicit genuine, spontaneous work-interest; greater persistence at tasks without redirection; greater originality, creativity, and efficiency in task performance; much higher morale; friendly attitudes; and positive "group-mindedness."

The laissez-faire leaders, who were less inclined to give guiding suggestions and primarily confined themselves to giving technical information, elicited poorer, much less organized, less efficient, apathetic, uninterested, and less satisfying performance overall, despite a high degree of friendliness. Surprisingly, however, despite low cooperation, group-mindedness seemed to result from laissez-faire leadership. But close analysis of the data suggested a qualitative difference between those under democratic leadership and those in the laissez-faire groups. The latter had expressed more of a desire to have group unity than a feeling that they had actually experienced it.

In summary, therefore, White and Lippitt concluded that while the laissez-faire condition was most conducive to relaxed attitudes, the democratic condition was the most efficient, productive, and creative for mutual problem solving. The autocratic condition tended to elicit more morale problems, discontent, and feelings of frustration among individuals.

The application of these findings—which have been affirmed by a host of more recent studies using the Lewin, Lippitt, and White study model—to special education team functioning would automatically suggest that team chairpersons and coordinators should clearly shy away from characteristics of autocratic leaders such as:

1. Giving direct orders
2. Interrupting proceedings with personally proposed solutions
3. Ignoring individuals' suggestions
4. Withholding praise or encouragement
5. Making generally critical, nonobjective comments
6. Demanding respect or allegiance

The White and Lippitt summary would suggest that the following forms of behavior, characteristic of democratic team leaders, should prevail:

1. Offering guiding suggestions
2. Providing information which is timed to be of greatest value
3. Stimulating self-direction
4. Appreciating others' values, points of view
5. Respecting differences in opinion
6. Appropriately acknowledging the humor in certain situations

Since the Lewin, Lippitt, and White studies, at least two or three other distinct lines of research have highlighted further exploration into the question of what constitutes effective leadership. One intriguing point of view which attracted many proponents up until midcentury, and which still lingers whenever we speak of leaders who have "charisma," was known as the "great person" theory of leadership. As described by, among others, Gibb (1954) and Lindzey and Aronson (1969), the theory posited that great men and women, who were identifiable by certain physical and personality traits, would gain leadership ascendency among others in a wide range of situations regardless of differences in the nature of the group's aims or objectives. Stimulated by studies of small military units during World War II, the proponents of this theory would seek team leaders from among those who were:

1. Intelligent but not difficult to comprehend
2. Physically strong and attractive
3. Self-confident
4. Socially aware and considerate
5. Articulate, forceful in expression, and open to communication equally with superiors and subordinates

6. Self-starting, assertive, persuasive, and goal-directed
7. Loyal and essentially conforming to group norms and values

So much for great persons! It seems apparent that even if such godlike persons exist in any appreciable number, one would be unlikely to find enough of them in the employ of the public schools. Nevertheless, practically speaking, it is to be hoped that at least some special education team leaders have arrived at their present positions through having demonstrated some or many of the above characteristics, in addition to having completed a number of years of successful experience in teaching, supervision, or specialized professional experience. And, as the next line of research into leadership suggests, while the "great person" traits may be viewed as desirable standards for anyone to strive for, they are not necessarily enough, in and of themselves, to guarantee leadership success in all situations.

As Borgatta, Couch, and Bales (1962) point out, great people "tend to make great groups," in the sense that two major factors—group performance-productivity and satisfaction of the members—are simultaneously enhanced. However, it is necessary to look beyond these truisms to see what both the great and the less-than-great still need to accomplish in order to bring about effective team functioning.

By the late 1960s, Lindzey and Aronson (1969) reflected a gradual trend toward the view of effective leadership as "an interactional phenomenon." Leadership was described as a function of the interaction between personality traits and specific factors in the task, problem, or social situation. Leader behavior was found to be subject to group determination, based upon the expectations of the followers, the nature of the task, and the traditional norms of the group which the leader was chosen *to represent.* Dynamically, therefore, the leader-follower relationship was viewed as successful when *both* felt satisfied. As group goals changed, leadership needed to change, and different forms of leader behavior might be demanded.

Current thinking is moving increasingly toward the view that the possession of task-oriented skills is paramount for effective leadership. The recent literature says less about the more global personality traits or characteristics of effective leaders. Evidently, as problems in society require more technologically complex and precise knowledge to aid in problem solution, the best providers of those specific skills and necessary information are the most likely to provide ad hoc, if not continuous, leadership.

The best special education team leaders are, therefore, those who, on the one hand, clearly possess the knowledge, skills, and personal qualities which best facilitate group performance, and, on the other, are abreast of rapidly changing technological demands and understand the need to develop new skills. A good example of this phenomenon is the evolving need for team leaders to be quasilegal authorities as well as effective group facilitators who are knowledgeable about special education. Therefore, the determination of various effective leadership models appropriate for modern-day special education teams will have to include the following complex and imposing list of job requirements essential to effective leadership of special education teams:

1. Sensitivity to, and awareness of, the child's educational needs, parents' concerns, and the needs of individual staff members.
2. Awareness of available special education programs and alternatives within the system, the immediate region, and the larger area.
3. Familiarity with regular curriculum, scheduling, transportation, and related community support service options.
4. Familiarity with the intricacies of budget allocations and financial constraints.
5. Familiarity with local and federal special education regulations, including parents' due-process rights and pupil-records policies.
6. Possession of parent conferencing skills to encourage active parent participation.
7. Ability to articulate and communicate information about team members' specific roles and functions.
8. Familiarity with psycho-educational and language development diagnostic procedures as well as standard achievement measures.
9. Awareness of within-system lines of responsibility, school schedules, and tables or organization.
10. Ability to assist others in making program decisions for children.
11. Ability to follow up team decisions with regular staff contacts and parent "progress" conferences to meet timelines for program implementation.
12. Ability to encourage parents' use of due process and independent evaluation procedures when appropriate.

LEADERSHIP MODELS FOR SPECIAL EDUCATION TEAMS

The freedom to choose among a variety of leadership styles or models is somewhat limited by certain of the functions prescribed by PL 94-142. For example, it would be inappropriate for a leader to assume a completely informal attitude because of the requirement to follow certain prescribed procedures, such as notification of parents of their due-process rights, and the necessity to develop an IEP for a new special education program or placement which meets with the expressed approval of the parents. Because the team leader must assume responsibility for enacting such statutory procedures, at least a touch of formality cannot be avoided. Beyond that kind of responsibility, however (which also includes assuring that parents are aware of their other rights—such as those concerning timelines for program implementation and the right to inspect their child's records), there is certainly room for varied approaches to running team meetings and managing the efforts of the special education team. Three particular approaches are worth consideration. All of these leadership models have basic strengths as well as limitations. The three models may be labeled process-oriented, task-oriented, and child-oriented.

The chart below shows graphically the likelihood of wedding the personal leadership styles discussed, (democratic, autocratic, laissez-faire) with the methodological approach to running a special education team meeting.

As the term process-oriented is characteristically used in the literature, it usually refers to the position that the *process* of arriving at a decision is as important, or nearly as important, as the decision itself. Its proponents are concerned about the immediate feelings, responses, and reactions of the group participants. However, one should not dismiss this methodology as appropriate only to self-help, values-clarification, and personal growth groups, though they may certainly have given rise to the approach. Proponents of this approach to problem solving would contend that employment of this method *not only* makes the participants feel better, *but also* results in better decisions. This approach is most certainly the one most useful for a leader who is comfortable with a laissez-faire style. It probably is not possible for the leader whose style tends toward the autocratic to employ this approach. It probably could be used effectively by the leader whose personal style leans toward the democratic model.

The task-oriented approach would be quite comfortable for autocratic leaders who, in the interest of "getting a job done," might rationalize giving orders, imposing a unilateral structure on the meeting,

Model for Conduct of Special Education Teams	PERSONAL LEADERSHIP STYLE		
	Laissez-Faire	Democratic	Autocratic
Process-Oriented	Very Likely	Possible	Very Unlikely
Task-Oriented	Unlikely	Possible	Very Likely
Child-Oriented	Possible	Possible	Possible

even manipulating the team toward a predetermined decision. In the hands of a democratic leader, however, the task-oriented method could be exceedingly effective and efficient in terms of both time and money. A laissez-faire leader could probably not function in this model.

Regardless of personal style, a group leader could be basically child-oriented. Such a leader might be less cognizant of the needs of the school system as a whole and certainly less concerned with the system-wide financial ramifications of a particular decision.

The term child-oriented may elicit the most positive reaction, as does, probably, the term democratic style. But this is deceptive; these terms don't necessarily go together. In fact, the most ardent child advocates may unwittingly abandon democratic approaches and resort to extremely autocratic behavior in their zeal to provide the best for their children.

Process-Oriented Leadership

As noted, this orientation is perhaps most closely likened to a number of human-relations group problem-solving approaches popular for the last twenty years. The leaders who employ this style with greatest ease are often experienced in one or more of the "effectiveness training," "values-clarification," or other group problem-solving techniques which emphasize the development of awareness or sensitivity to others, risk taking, and assertiveness in small group situations. The following illustrates the process approach:

> Mr. Renzulli, the team chairman and building principal, began the planning and placement team meeting by introducing everyone. He then asked all staff members to talk briefly about their roles and functions in the school and particularly about that aspect of Paul's special education evaluation for which they were responsible. He then turned to Mr. and Mrs. S. and asked, "Do you have any questions you would like answered about any of our staff before we begin discussing our findings on Paul?"
>
> Mr. S. asked why so many staff members were at the meeting. The chairperson explained that Paul had been evaluated by a number of specialists on the staff and he thought that, therefore, each should take part in the presentation and be available for questions from the parents.
>
> He then added, "If you feel heavily outnumbered by the five of us, I can appreciate that feeling."
>
> The parents smiled and nodded a bit self-consciously but denied they were feeling uncomfortable.
>
> Mr. Renzulli then commented offhandedly about the fact that Mr. and Mrs. S. probably were already familiar with their rights as parents, including the due-process procedures they might pursue if they left the meeting in disagreement with the findings or recommendations. Mr. S.

seemed on the verge of a question but did not ask it. He and his wife were anxious to hear the reports.

Mr. Renzulli then asked who would like to report first. Paul's classroom teacher began, followed by each of the specialists. The speech and language clinician discussed her evaluation of some aspects of Paul's school performance. The reading specialist described her assessment of the youngster's reading and spelling skills, as compared to other third graders. The school social worker gave an overview of Paul's school work and specific difficulties in light of personal, peer, and family factors. After each report, Mr. Renzulli made a comment or two himself and invited the parents to react.

Mrs. S. expressed surprise and asked for clarification only when the term "dyslexia" was alluded to in the reading specialist's report. Mr. S. was silent throughout the various reports.

"Are you sure you have no questions?" asked Mr. Renzulli.

"No, I guess I'd like to hear what you plan to do for Paul before I say anything further—I didn't realize his reading was so far behind the others."

"No questions about the tests we used?"

"No, what's the next step? What do you recommend for him?"

"You would like to get to his IEP—is that what you are saying?" (He was sensing their readiness.)

"Yes, if that's what you call it." Mr. S. was obviously a bit edgy and impatient. Mr. Renzulli explained how the IEP forms had been developed and that the task was to specify long- and short-term objectives, along with the timelines detailing who would provide special instruction and when such assistance would be provided. Then, as staff members proposed the objectives they would recommend, Mr. Renzulli asked the parents if they understood how each objective was related to the evaluation.

Finally, when all were finished with their suggestions, he asked the parents for any suggestions they might have about Paul's program. Mrs. S. asked about the advisability of some outside tutoring.

Mr. Renzulli asked if any of the specialists had "any feeling one way or another about Mrs. S.'s suggestion." Everyone had and expressed opinions—generally in the negative, regarding the danger of too many different people working with Paul. Mr. and Mrs. S. therefore agreed not to pursue that idea and signed their approval for the IEP objectives which the team had recommended. Before concluding the meeting, which had run an hour and fifteen minutes, Mr. Renzulli announced when Paul's program would be reviewed and asked if Mr. and Mrs. S. agreed. He then thanked the members for their "input" and asked for comments about how the meeting had gone. Mr. and Mrs. S. however, had already stood up and were putting on their coats to leave, so there were only a few mumbled positive-sounding comments as the parents shook hands and walked out of the room.

There might not be too many objections raised to Mr. Renzulli's considerate approach in running this special education team meeting. The meeting ran well over an hour in length, but it would appear that everything that needed to be done was actually accomplished. Also on the positive side, this model is, indeed, probably most appropriate for school districts where the staff's heavy caseloads prohibit time for individual conferences with parents prior to such team meetings. However, one practical problem is that the meeting took too much time. Mr. Renzulli made frequent efforts to draw Mr. and Mrs. S. into active participation, and to assure that all staff members had a chance to "do their thing." While this may have been an effective process exercise, the parents and the staff were probably ready earlier for conclusions and decisions. As a typical process-oriented person, even when he sensed this readiness, he did not push it but asked if that's what the parents wanted. In a sense, he made them push him. Therefore, while this approach may seem admirable in that it covered adequately the legal steps required by law and insured attempts to include the parents actively, most of the chairperson's well-intended efforts were probably wasted. His efforts at parent involvement were poorly timed and therefore resulted in mildly irritating the parents rather than in genuinely involving them. The problem in Mr. Renzulli's timing was not so much the question of what was done when in the meeting but the fact that so much was attempted during the team meeting that might better have been accomplished beforehand in individual conferences between the parents and some of the specialists, or in a preparatory conference with the social worker.

As a general rule of thumb, meetings for the development of an IEP should not run more than forty minutes. The job here being attempted should have, at least in part, already been reviewed in a preliminary meeting or series of meetings with those staff members who had done most of the evaluating. Had that been done with the parents prior to the meeting, Mr. Renzulli's approach might have been more effective in encouraging them to raise and explore alternative objectives and procedures which the preliminary meeting or meetings might have led them to consider.

Finally, a major drawback inherent in Mr. Renzulli's style was his tendency to let things happen without any plan. For example, there was no order of presentation established for the various staff members' evaluations. He allowed any of the staff who wished to report or comment to do so whenever they chose. He engaged in no plan of data presentation, nor did he make any effort to redirect efforts to what might or might not be relevant to the task of developing an IEP appropriate to Paul's needs. His staff may have felt gratified, in that each member probably appreciated the time afforded their report or comments, but one wonders whether or not there might have been a more efficient way to use some of that time. The obvious suggestion would be for prior communication among staff members.

Task-Oriented Leadership

At some risk of overorganizing or predetermining the outcome of special education team meetings, the task-oriented leadership style focuses upon getting the job done. Team leaders are not as much concerned about group process and seeing to it that everyone who attends makes some contribution. The task-oriented leader wants primarily to keep everyone on target and arranges matters so that all elements of the task are accomplished in as little time as possible—considering the collective time of all staff members involved in team meetings. This leader is business like and encourages assertiveness for problem-solving purposes, but detests wasting anyone's time. The task-oriented leadership style can be very effective, as all team members are encouraged to behave purposefully and professionally. Provided the leader is not overly autocratic and does not push a unilateral, predetermined outcome, helping the team members to structure their contributions can result in cooperative teamwork and positive outcomes.

The following is an illustration of a task-oriented approach.

Ms. Rosen began the meeting promptly on time, introduced staff, and briefly referred to each member's role in Delia's evaluation, noting that the school social worker would be summing up each staff member's findings as part of her overall presentation of the results of the evaluation.

She then specified the due-process procedure to be followed by Mr. and Mrs. J. if they "wished to challenge or disagree with the team's decision at the end of the meeting." Ms. Rosen further specified the parents' right to know about and receive copies of the various records accumulated concerning their child's referral and evaluation, and gave the parents a booklet describing the school district's special education services and programs and parents' due-process rights and procedures.

Ms. Rosen then asked if the parents "understood their rights" and, when they nodded, turned to Mrs. Brown, the social worker, to "sum up what the staff agreed were Delia's problems as related to the need for special education."

Note the difference between her approach and Mr. Renzulli's. His inquiry about the parents' understanding of their rights, while probably meeting the letter of the law, was cursory. If they later found themselves in an adversary position, the S.s might—almost legitimately—claim that they were not given full and adequate information about their rights. Ms. Rosen, on the other hand, was methodical in her attention to this important legal requirement. This is advisable regardless of which general leadership style one espouses.

The social worker spent some time reviewing the collated account of various assessments which the staff had made. She asked Delia's teacher to amplify on some classroom observations about the child's awkward handwriting. She also asked the reading specialist to explain the term "dyslexia" which appeared in her report—anticipating that Mr. and Mrs. J. might want to know what the term meant. She ended up with a preliminary listing of the long-range and short-term goals and objectives which had been recommended by the staff for the parents' approval.

Mr. J. asked about outside-of-school help with Delia's writing problem, but Ms. Rosen informed him that if the team felt it was necessary, the school staff would be responsible to provide such assistance.

"However," Ms. Rosen added, "that decision is up to you, if you feel private tutoring might also be desirable—as long as you arrange for it to be coordinated with what we are providing in school." She then asked the J.s if they had any alternative suggestions for the IEP.

The J.s had no suggestions, questions, or comments. They signed their approval of the IEP as recommended, with the understanding that they could have a copy of the IEP form including the objectives and timelines for service delivery, as soon as it was typed up in final form. Ms. Rosen thanked them for coming to the meeting, and they left. The meeting had been concluded in twenty-five minutes.

The meeting with Mr. and Mrs. J. had run smoothly, and the task of developing an appropriate IEP to meet Delia's needs was successfully concluded. The J.s were informed of their rights, had had a chance to ask questions and provide input, and had signed their approval of the IEP as recommended—all in less than half the time needed for Mr. Renzulli's meeting with the S.s. This approach is perhaps particularly suitable in school districts where time is of the essence because of heavy staff caseloads. Similarly, during the end-of-the-year rush to conclude large numbers of annual reviews, the administration and staff might find this style of getting things done most desirable. But while Mr. Renzulli's process-oriented approach included much that could have, and perhaps should, have been done at a prior meeting, Ms. Rosen's task-oriented approach would be far more successful if there actually had been prior meetings with parents. Whichever of the various "great-person" traits Ms. Rosen might call upon to charm, persuade, or reassure her staff and the parents that they are meeting to make a "joint" decision about Delia's special education needs and program, unless the parents had had a prior meeting with one or more of the staff about their child, most parents would have been ill-prepared or unwilling to arrive at a decision in twenty-five minutes, and might have felt "railroaded." In other words, where preparation would have been *desirable* for Mr. Renzulli's meeting, it is an absolute *necessity* for a really successful conclusion of the type of meeting conducted by Ms. Rosen. Otherwise, the parents might later justifiably complain that they were really being asked to rubberstamp the team's proposed IEP, without adequate opportunity for input or sufficient knowledge of what had been done in assessing their youngster's needs.

Child-Oriented Leadership

The following anecdote may illustrate what occurs in a meeting where the leader is basically child-oriented.

Ms. Collins, the school psychologist, had met with Peter's parents during the early months of the school year about several teachers' complaints that the fourth-grader's behavior had been disruptive. As team coordinator, Ms. Collins had completed a psychological evaluation herself, and had arranged for an assessment of Peter's attentional difficulty by the speech and hearing clinician, who suspected an auditory perceptual problem. Prior to the team meeting, Ms. Collins met with Peter's parents to discuss the psychological test results, and she and the speech clinician had reviewed the fact that Peter was reacting badly because of several factors. He did have a moderate hearing impairment which contributed to his apparent inattention and restless behavior. But most of Peter's disruptive antics were found to be due to his hypersensitivity to being picked on by his classmates because he was one of the smallest boys in class. To make matters worse, he was often "put down" by his older sister and brother at home. Furthermore, Peter had fallen considerably behind his classmates in reading comprehension because of the auditory disability. Both Ms. Collins and the speech clinician were, therefore, considering the advisability of recommending placement in a small self-contained special class for learning-disabled children. The team meeting was called by Ms. Collins to help make that determination.

Ms. Collins introduced everyone. Peter's parents, the G.s, already knew most of the assembled staff, so a review of each staff member's role was unnecessary. Mr. Cartwright, the building principal, also said he expected that Ms. Collins had already amply familiarized the parents with their due-process and other rights—which, indeed, she had. Ms. Collins then summarized the results of the various tests, reporting as much to inform Mr. Cartwright and the homeroom teacher as Peter's parents. She called upon the homeroom teacher to comment about any recent changes in Peter's behavior, but there had been little change since the evaluations had begun. She then asked Mr. and Mrs. G. for their reaction to the testing impressions.

"We've had a good chance to think over what we learned about Peter's difficulties since our meeting with Ms. Collins," Mr. G. remarked, "and we feel you've all done a good job pinpointing his problem. But what do we do next? What can you do to help Peter here in school?"

Ms. Collins, with the agreement of the speech clinician, described what she felt would be in Peter's best interests, a placement in a small, self-contained special class for children with difficulties like Peter's in a neighboring school system. In that class, Ms. Collins argued, Peter could benefit from the special individualized attention he might receive, he would obtain and learn to use a corrective hearing aid which had been further recommended by the child's pediatrician and an EENT specialist, and he would not have to contend with bullying classmates while he was learning to compensate for his other problems.

Mr. Cartwright and one of the special education resource teachers worried about the possibility of moving him out of the mainstream entirely too quickly. One suggested that it might be better to try him a while with supplementary resource help while keeping him in his regular program. The principal also appeared anxious to avoid yet another costly out-placement for which the school system would have to pay the tuition and transportation.

Ms. Collins persisted in her view of what was best for Peter. She feared that if he stayed with his present class, the children would continue to make him feel bad about his size and his inability to do the same work they were doing. She also was afraid he would be teased about his hearing aid.

Mr. Cartwright did not persist with his objections to the placement, because Mr. and Mrs. G. quickly responded to Ms. Collins' suggestion. "I think that's the way we've got to go," said Mr. G. "We'd hate to see Peter put down some more. We're having a hard enough time at home keeping his sister and brother off his back." "He's become so sensitive to everything," added Mrs. G. "It's painful to see him getting hurt all the time—and the kids here in school, even some of his friends, can be vicious at times, without realizing it."

With the parents' support of the recommendation, and with Ms. Collins herself at her persuasive best, only Mr. Cartwright seemed interested in pursuing other alternatives, but each idea he proposed for consideration was set aside. The meeting, therefore, was soon concluded with the detailing of the special class placement in IEP terms and a timeline established for further arrangements to be made to implement the team's decision.

After the G.s had left, Mr. Cartwright objected that Ms. Collins had pushed too quickly for an outside placement, but she insisted that the school district would have to find the money for Peter, because there was no suitable alternative for him, or children like him, in their elementary schools.

The team followed Ms. Collins's lead, over the understated objections of the principal, who knew he couldn't argue against Peter's tuition placement on primarily financial grounds. The team had clearly been influenced by Ms. Collins's child-oriented stance and the persuasiveness of her arguments.

It is not unusual for pupil-personnel-oriented staff in leadership roles to pursue "client-centered" objectives. But was Ms. Collins's argument on Peter's behalf entirely justifiable? Could not a supportable case be made for at least considering the options suggested by the principal?

For one thing, the schools are required by law to provide adequate and appropriate special education programs for "special needs" children. But they are not required to provide, or financially support, what might be "ideal" or in the "best" interests of the child if other, less costly but educationally viable alternatives are available and have not yet been exhausted. In Peter's case, such other options might even conform better to the "least restrictive environment" principle of PL 94-142.

The intrinsic problem in the child-centered leadership approach is that, while the child might be served in ideal fashion, the approach does not always take into account the justifiably limited obligation of the schools to provide what might be suitable or appropriate without being necessarily ideal. The child-centered model sometimes fails to recognize appropriate administrative as well as legal constraints. Mr. Cartwright's position, if adopted for *purely* financial motives, might not have been entirely justifiable, but the important issue of the extent of responsibility of the schools was essentially bypassed. It frequently receives minimal consideration in the face of the primary concerns of child-oriented staff. But, while seemingly acting only in the interests of children, the staff that consistently ignores the real issues of financial demands on the district and the limitations of a school system's obligations may unintentionally be working against those interests. The backlash against provision of special services is already being felt in school systems which, hard-pressed to meet the needs of all school children, are forced to allocate what many regard as disproportionate sums for handicapped children. Respected observers and critics of the American educational systems such as former *New York Times* education editor Gene Maeroff (1982) are including "over" emphasis on special education among the things that are "wrong" with American education, and are beginning to take the position that the public schools have been called upon to solve social problems better solved by, and meet needs better served by, other agencies.

Apart from concluding that Ms. Collins was clearly "child-oriented" —perhaps to a fault—one might also note that she tended to be autocratic in her style. She seemed determined to pursue her own objective, she may have predetermined the appropriate placement for Peter, she overruled the principal's objections, and she gave rather short shrift to staff members arguing for a placement more in the mainstream. A more democratic leader operating in the child-centered mode would have been more open to alternative suggestions. While the outcome might have been the same, the more democratic leader might have avoided the principal's obvious discomfort with the placement.

To avoid this situation, it probably would have been advisable for Ms. Collins to have consulted with Mr. Cartwright prior to the meeting to discuss the financial consequences of what she intended to propose.

She might have been able to settle the issue of the cost of the placement with him and other concerned administrators beforehand, or they may have been able to persuade her to consider *their* point of view: that the least restrictive environment (which might have been more advantageous for reasons above and beyond the financial) option should have been more seriously considered. It might have been advisable first to try supplementary help for Peter before going to the more restrictive, self-contained special class, which probably included youngsters with far more serious handicaps.

Child-oriented leaders who genuinely advocate providing what is the best available are more effective when they give serious consideration to the limitations of a school system's obligations. When they fail to do so, and continue to press for costly "ideal" services, they tend to arouse unnecessary antagonism and create adversarial relationships between parents and the school. This sort of dogmatism should be avoided except in a situation when a practitioner is convinced that the school's position is truly neglectful of the interests of the child.

The three alternative leadership models described have been purposely delineated in rather stereotypic fashion, to highlight some of the strengths and weaknesses characteristic of each orientation. None of the three types of behavior was entirely acceptable or entirely deplorable. Not surprisingly, the most effective leaders borrow the better features of each. There can be no doubt about the appropriateness of a leadership role that is primarily child-oriented, because the needs of a child are paramount to the very existence of the team; but the leader should not lose sight of the limits of the jurisdiction and capability of a publicly funded institution.

Similarly, the task-orientation model is valuable to keep the team's deliberations on target, but not at the expense of overwhelming the parents and thereby diminishing their participation. Finally, a leadership stance that reinforces active participation by all team members (the process orientation) is also admirable, but not when it leads to unnecessary waste of time.

It is the contention of the present authors that a dual leadership role for special education teams—a model reinforced by federal and state statutes—can effectively capitalize on the strengths of the three types of orientation and minimize their limitations.

A DUAL LEADERSHIP MODEL
FOR THE SPECIAL EDUCATION TEAM

The development of the team process has seen the evolution of two fairly constant and permanent team members. This has resulted in their being affirmed as the two basic leadership roles, thus constituting a dual leadership responsibility for team tasks. The two "constant leaders" are the team chairperson and the team coordinator.

The chairperson usually represents the administration point of view. Either the building principal or the principal's designee, the chairperson is generally a professional educator and tends to be most aware of the interests of the school system. However, as an astute building administrator, he or she often recognizes that if parents' interests are well served, in the long run the district's interests will be served as well.

The coordinator is more likely to be a special education or social or human services professional, and may be more likely to assume the role of child or parent advocate and be less concerned about budget and other constraints. The coordinator will generally be most knowledgeable about the child's needs and press to assure that the best available services and programs the system has to offer will be provided.

Therefore, while there may be some inherent conflict between these two individuals because of basic orientation, both have an investment in assuring that the team arrives at a mutually acceptable decision. Both wish to help children, and neither wishes to make parents unhappy (even though, at times, parents may perceive the joint leadership of the team as aligned against them and interested only in what might best serve the immediate interests of the school system's "management"). Also, perhaps for different reasons, both the chairperson and the coordinator have a stake in seeing to it that matters run smoothly. Neither usually has the time or inclination to engage in due-process challenge procedures, and both will probably experience gratification when the rest of the team reflects their successful leadership efforts. Whatever intrateam competitive pressures or other issues might separate them, the chairperson and coordinator usually strive to have the team work well. In addition, because the coordinator is often subordinate to the chairperson in line-responsibility, the dependency of the chairperson upon the coordinator for technical expertise is offset by the coordinator's dependency upon the chairperson for administrative authority. This interdependence provides the basis for mutual support and diminishes the danger of prolonged conflict.

Sometimes, if both team leaders have similar backgrounds or professional training in special education areas, those similarities may fuel competitiveness. Leadership style differences can also create conflict, just as those same style differences can be managed to complement one another. But the administrative status of the chairperson as building administrator is likely to result in deference to his or her overriding authority when competition tends to become too disruptive. The success of dual leadership is dependent upon mutual recognition and acceptance of the fact that one of the two leaders, usually the chairperson, has *final* authority or responsibility for the team's decisions. The acknowledgement of that distinction will then permit effective sharing of leadership functions as the process requires different skills or competencies.

The Primary Role of the Chairperson

The most important aspect of the chairperson's role is that of *director of operations* toward meeting the team's task objectives. It should be up to the chairperson to:

1. Provide clear information about team members' specific roles and functions as part of the introduction of parents to the team.
2. Apprise parents of team procedures and remain sensitive throughout the meeting to the parents' need to ask questions or express concerns, thereby encouraging their active participation.
3. Determine that parents are aware of all their legal rights, know their responsibility, sign all necessary approval forms, and receive program descriptions and other literature.
4. Provide information to parents about personnel with responsibility and about organizational structure.
5. Provide information and resource assistance regarding the regular curriculum and current budget, program, or service allocations and constraints.
6. Be informed about school scheduling and transportation and community resources or support services available to assist in programming for handicapped children.
7. Be aware of the various within-district and regional special education program options or service delivery systems.
8. Be attentive to and aware of the "flow" of meetings; be articulate and decisive; be compassionate and, with a sense of humor, able to provide focus for the group's perspective when redirection seems appropriate.

The chairperson is the main expeditor of team procedures and is most responsible for the development of inservice training for the staff as that becomes necessary to keep up with changes in regulations or procedures.

Finally, the chairperson is responsible for the provision of interpreters when needed (as when parents do not understand English), the assignment of substitutes to free teachers for meetings, the completion of the IEP, and the provisions for other necessary record-keeping and followup functions such as taking the team's minutes and assigning an appropriate contact person for the parents.

The Primary Role of the Coordinator

Similarly, to meet the task objectives of the special education team, the coordinator should be assigned primary responsibility for the following:

1. To be aware of the accumulated evaluation data about student's educational and support service needs.
2. To communicate with each of the team's specialists who have evaluated any aspect of the student's school performance, and to discuss their reports and anticipated roles in team meetings.
3. To recommend to the chairperson which specialists or consultants may be most needed for various meetings, and whether or not interpreters may be needed.
4. To be "custodian" of special education records for the team, and the primary source of information to the team about local, state, and federal statutes or regulations on special education.
5. To be able to describe clearly and explain the purpose of the various evaluation procedures used by the team's specialists, and to be able to translate technical terminology included in reports into language parents can comprehend.
6. To assist other staff members in making evaluation procedure decisions appropriate to referral questions and to ultimate program or service options.
7. To schedule parent conferences for the presentation of certain evaluation data and for discussion of identification or programming procedures prior to team meetings, and to coordinate the presentation of data for meetings.
8. To facilitate parents' active participation in team meetings.
9. To be knowledgeable about community resources, and to be able to explain in detail for staff as well as parents any and all details pertinent to special education program options or service delivery systems which might be considered for a student within the district, in the region, and in or out of the state.
10. To oversee the development and the writing of the IEP objectives and the timelines for the delivery of services, clarifying the interrelationships of components of the IEP and determining appropriate future review dates to evaluate progress.
11. To coordinate or provide inservice training about special education regulations, statute changes, information to aid in "mainstreaming" special education students, and the like.
12. To follow up team decisions to assure that the timelines for the delivery of services are followed and necessary programs or services implemented.

There is obviously considerable overlap between the functions of the chairperson and the coordinator. Allowing for negotiation between the two to find the "best fit" of role and function delineation, the essential differences in the two roles should be clearly understood and maintained. The chairperson should always be seen primarily as the expeditor, the final authority, or the director of operations. The co-ordinator must be seen as the most knowledgeable about special education programs and services, and the most aware of the inner workings of the team process. The chairperson sets the interpersonal tone, provides for the communication bridge between parents and school staff, and oversees the administrative aspects of the team's functioning within the regular school setting. The coordinator provides the informational glue, the staff's preparation, the technical knowhow, and the employment of group-process or decision-making skills so that the child's needs, and programs to meet those needs, remain the primary focus of the team's efforts. It is not impossible for either one to serve in both capacities. In fact, in many school districts that is exactly what happens because of time and economic constraints. But the dual-leadership model outlined above is, in our experience, probably the most effective by far to accomplish most fully the team's nine task objectives.

The Case Manager's Role

The role of the case manager is assigned by the team to one staff member. Usually that will be the person who will actively implement the IEP as one, if not the major, support person, or the teacher who will have the most ongoing contact with the child. The case manager is also designated as the primary person for parents to contact when they want immediate information, or for school staff to consult when they need some information about things happening at home (e.g., the reasons for excessive absenteeism from school or behavioral upset seemingly caused by something outside of school).

The case manager must keep both the coordinator and the chairperson aware of major incidents affecting the child's progress. In effect, the case manager, is the program director for the child and is responsible for carrying out the team's decisions.

THE PARENTS' LEADERSHIP ROLE

When parents have initiated special education procedures and are pressing for a suitable program or services to meet their child's needs, those parents have gone beyond "active participation" in the team process and are likely to continue to play an important, determining role in the team's deliberations. Such parents' functional leadership is particularly evident when they bring in their own psychological or psychiatric consultants, legal representatives, or other educational specialists to aid their efforts.

In other instances, parents who are themselves professional educators or educational specialists may take the lead (beyond active participation) and clearly chart the team's direction by virtue of their knowledge or dynamic presence. In these circumstances, unless the team simply "submits" to the expert-parent's will and reaches the decision pushed by the parent, the expertise of the professional parent can readily be utilized by the team's leaders if that expertise is acknowledged and respected. Most of the time, the team's leaders can and should encourage such parents to assist actively in the team's deliberations and planning so that the staff as well as the parents may enjoy valuable exchange of ideas which such interaction engenders. This is possible only if no one on the staff becomes hypersensitive or defensive about "letting the parents in." The team leaders should try to assure that such defensive reactions are minimized.

However, the parents who, with or without personal expertise or private consultants, try to *impose* direction on the team's planning for their child constitute a slightly more difficult problem for the team. Taking the initiative, and bringing in consultants is fully acceptable. But, when parents either impose their own direction or bring in consultants to *force* the team's judgment, decisions, or plans in accordance with their own views and against the team's findings, such attempts need to be channeled appropriately into constructive, mutual action.

In other words, short of raising the specter of due process, educators should try to highlight the fact that the parents' efforts to force their own position may not be necessary, or, indeed, may be detrimental to efforts to develop a mutually acceptable plan. Statements like the following may be helpful in such circumstances:

> "Mr. and Mrs. O., let's look at what's happening. It's quite clear that your view of Jonathan's problems and what might be necessary to remedy them has led you to take the position you have—as strongly as you've stated it. We may not really disagree, but we don't think you're giving us a chance to state our case, present our findings, or consider, with you, some of the alternatives suggested by our findings. If we wind up in disagreement we can always go to an independent evaluation, but let's see first if we really disagree."
>
> "Mr. and Mrs. O., you have expressed your view quite forcefully. But unless we can have a real chance to describe what *we've* found, and what *we* think needs to be done for Jonathan, we're going to get nowhere. We have to come out of this meeting with a team decision that covers our

view as well as yours—so please hear us out. If we can't agree, there are things we can do to arrive eventually at an agreement. Are you willing to listen to what we have to say?"

The point is that the views expressed by the parents must be acknowledged, and to the extent that the parents have been adamant, or have underscored their strongly stated position with credentialled expertise, that effort or stance also needs to be acknowledged—particularly if the parents' manner or expressed views have suggested no willingness to consider any other alternatives. A strong position, a demanding position, taken by the parents needs to be noted as such. The team's leaders can then bring matters back into perspective by reminding all that the team's overriding purpose is to arrive at a mutually joined decision.

Furthermore, the law provides for alternative strategies to be employed when parents and team leaders have reached a deadlock. The one obvious strategy, due-process challenge by either party, really only delays the battle and postpones matters to be judged at another battlefield—generally further away from the child. The resort to independent evaluation and judgment, however, is entirely in keeping with the spirit of joint decision making because it puts matters off (and allows time for things to cool down) until there is the opportunity to re-evaluate the child's needs in the light of an additional, professional opinion—preferably an opinion which is mutually arranged and therefore likely to be mutually accepted or respected.

It is probably also evident that effective leadership can translate into finding strategies for coping with parents who may be acting aggressively or defensively out of concern for their children or because of some hidden agenda which may be the result of an unpleasant previous experience with the schools. The next chapter examines how best to overcome such unhelpful attitudes and how to involve parents actively and more helpfully in decision making without undermining the respect or capability for active participation which we wish to accord them.

SUMMARY

This chapter has dealt with the importance of the team leader to the effective functioning of the special education team. The leader is key in organizing disparate individuals with different skills into a smoothly functioning team. The operation of the team can be affected by different personal styles of leadership (e.g., autocratic, laissez-faire, and democratic) and also by different methodological approaches to leadership—which we have labeled process-oriented, task-oriented, and child-oriented. Certain personal leadership styles are more or less likely to be compatible with particular methodological approaches. The so-called democratic style can be compatible with all three, while the laissez-faire style is most compatible with the process orientation, and the autocratic style most compatible with the task-oriented approach. The following are significant advantages and disadvantages of the various personal styles:

1. Autocratic personal leadership style:
   Key advantage—efficiency, time saving
   Key disadvantage—apt to generate hostility and resentment among other team members
2. Laissez-faire personal leadership style:
   Key advantage—creates relaxed attitude which promotes cooperative decision making
   Key disadvantage—may be wasteful of time, directionless
3. Democratic personal style:
   Key advantage—builds team morale and promotes shared responsibility
   Key disadvantage—may delay decision making

Regardless of personal style, the most effective leaders display at least some of the qualities recognized as characteristic of "great persons." Whether or not they are highly charismatic, however, effective leaders of special education teams need to possess skills specific to their field so that they may make a concrete contribution to the team's work. They also must be knowledgeable about special education laws, local options, and board of education policies.

In the discussion of the various methodological approaches we pointed out the following key advantages and disadvantages to each approach:

1. Process-oriented:
   Key advantage—promotes cooperation and tends to create high morale. (Some theorists believe it results in better decision making.)
   Key disadvantage—it is most time consuming and could appear directionless.
2. Task-oriented:
   Key advantage—encourages professionalism among participants; most efficient and least time consuming.
   Key disadvantage—could encourage unilateral decision making and

manipulation of participants by a dominant leader.

3. Child-oriented:

Key advantage—suited to all types of personal leadership styles; most attuned to spirit of the law.

Key disadvantage—could encourage unrealistic expectations, promote staff tendency to ignore real legal, logistic, or financial limitations to the school district's obligations.

The best leaders borrow the better characteristics of each approach and some are even able to alter their personal styles to fit different circumstances.

We support a dual leadership model that divides responsibilities between the two individuals most likely to be permanent team members: the building administrator (or designee) who acts as chairperson, and a special education professional who acts as team coordinator. The chairperson directs the operation, expedites procedures, sees to legal notifications, and the like. The coordinator consults with other professional staff, collects and reviews data, synthesizes where appropriate, facilitates parent participation, and makes sure follow up occurs.

Sometimes parents who are active and knowledgeable share functional leadership. While their active participation should be sought, parents should not be permitted to intimidate or manipulate team members, nor should they be allowed to usurp leadership functions more appropriately exercised by professional staff members. Chapter V deals with strategies for involving parents effectively.

5

Effectively Involving Parents in Decision Making

INTRODUCTION

Prior to the passage of PL 94-142 in 1975, few state statutes required any sort of special education identification procedures, special education team meetings, or consistent efforts to involve parents in decision-making processes. Furthermore, most school support personnel ranked parental involvement in decision making as desirable—but of low priority, according to a study done by Gilmore (1974). Given these facts and attitudes, it would be appropriate to question whether most school personnel really wish to involve parents more effectively, or, in fact, to any greater degree than they absolutely have to, to meet legal requirements. And, regardless of whether school personnel wish to involve parents at this time, it is necessary to address the issue of whether active involvement of parents in team decision making is a *genuinely desirable* objective.

Most school people would probably agree that parent cooperation is highly desirable. But effectively bringing parents into the power structure calls for commitment to the belief that such a process *really helps children.* Otherwise, the law will be obeyed in the letter, but not in the spirit. There are some reasonable arguments against the position that parent involvement necessarily helps children. First, the amount of time which may be necessary for an already over-taxed staff to encourage active parent involvement may be excessive. Second, scheduling conflicts often requires special efforts to get everyone together, while valuable time is "lost." The arrangements to meet after school, for example, to accommodate working parents, often mean inconveniencing one or more staff members who may have after-school commitments. Third, some parents do not desire to be involved. Fourth, some who do wish to participate may have a hidden agenda or an axe to grind. A not uncommon staff reaction, therefore, is "Who needs it? We have work to do—let us do our job!"

Time and scheduling difficulties for the staff may not be the only obstacles to effective parental participation. The attempt to involve parents in decision making, surprisingly, may sometimes be met with anxiety, unexpected resistance, or defensiveness on the part of the parents themselves. Yet, if they are genuinely interested in helping children with special needs, the staff should not evade their responsibility to involve the children's parents actively. The reasons for this are obvious:

1. Parents normally spend much more time with their children than any member of the school staff and therefore have more time available which can be directed toward supporting special educational efforts.
2. To the extent that parents' difficulties or family problems have influenced a child's school difficulties, the child's progress in school is likely to be slow unless the parents are aware of and take an active part in remediating any familial source of the problems.
3. The parents' relationship with their child preceded, and will follow, the staff's involvement. The potential for long-range impact on a child's development inherent in the parent-child relationship would therefore be wasted if parents are not actively involved.
4. Given the undeniable importance of preventive early intervention, active parent involvement in decision making is absolutely necessary. It would clearly be a waste of a valuable resource to give in too easily to parents' resistance or defensiveness or to staff resistance, whether based on concerns about time or on other factors.

There are other reasons for more actively involving parents in the school-team process. A recent description of the rationale for improving parent consultation procedures (Brown, Wyne, Blackburn, and Powell 1979) emphasizes the value of parent involvement for obtaining greater support for developing special school programs and communicating more information about their suitability for exceptional children. In other words, the authors promote parent consultation to bridge the chasm which "has developed between our schools and the home . . ." (p. 192). The consultation session, they argue, is in itself "an expression of the school's concern" for the child's unique problems and conveys information about the effectiveness of various pupil-service programs. The primary value of parent involvement is underscored by what these authors have to say about the need for active parent consultation to overcome the barriers in communication and about staff frustration in attempts to make effective interventions to help a child when they are "blocked at every turn by the family."

SOURCES OF PARENTS' ANXIETY

A report on the implementation of PL 94-142 from the Council for Exceptional Children in "Insight" (Ballard 1981) revealed that parents attend only one half of scheduled IEP meetings and that their role, when they do attend, is generally passive.

Parents' passivity can stem from a variety of causes, including subtle encouragement of their passive behavior by the staff through direct or indirect reinforcement. But parents' unwillingness to participate at all, or their discomfort in taking an active role, just as frequently may arise from their own anxiety, from their uncertainty about what is expected of them, or from their expectation that little will come of their attempts to influence the decisions being made about their children.

What makes parents anxious? Perhaps the primary source of parents' anxiety is their concern over what is happening to their child. They feel dependent upon the team to identify their child's difficulties accurately and provide the necessary remedial services or programs. As a result, they may feel somewhat at the mercy of the school staff's expertise about what should be done, particularly if they are not themselves knowledgeable or have done little independent investigating about their child's problems. Under such circumstances, parents are especially anxious not to appear stupid, confused, or indecisive. Their response to this anxiety may be resistance to the team's suggestions, but it is also, often, a tendency to remain passive.

Another source of anxiety which reinforces passivity may be their feeling of having somehow failed their child. Such anxiety or guilt over a feeling of inadequacy is not at all uncommon. Having done everything for their child during the preschool years, parents may feel that their own competency is on the line when a problem requiring remediation is brought to their attention. Even though indirectly or directly assured by the staff that they are not to blame, parents will still often feel that their parenting skills are being negatively judged and that they have made mistakes somewhere along the way or their child wouldn't be in his or her present predicament. Such doubts reinforce passivity. They may feel, "If our judgment and actions have caused this child's problems, maybe we'd better leave the decisions about solutions to others who know better."

Another source of concern for some parents is their mistrust of the school staff. They may feel the staff has misdiagnosed the problem or, if they believe the problem to be correctly identified, they may doubt the staff's competency to remediate it. Parents' reactions to such a sense of mistrust vary considerably, but one response is to accept with resignation whatever the staff decides, providing it will make little difference to the outcome. Parents experience a feeling of helplessness under such circumstances and tend to resist any effort to reassure them. Apart from any negative prior experiences they may have had which may have reinforced doubts about the staff's competence, such feelings may arise from their own self-doubts which, in turn, stem from other earlier experiences with authorities, e.g., their own parents, physicians, preschool or nursery school educators. Whatever the specific source of a belief that they can expect less than adequate service from those upon whom they depend, the parents experiencing such doubts tend to be cynical. Their attitude produces little active participation in a process in which they have little faith.

One particular concern sometimes expressed by parents, and one which tends to discourage active participation in team deliberations, is the fear that further involvement in special education will exaggerate the perception of their child as "different," not only in their eyes, but in the eyes of teachers and other children as well. Typical comments which may tip the staff off to such feelings are these:

"Does Sally really need to go out for special help so frequently?"

or

"Isn't she missing enough regular class time already?"

or

"Won't Joey feel singled out even more if we increase his special reading sessions—he already feels funny going for help three times per week."

When parents make comments like these, the team leader should try to bring their underlying fears into the open and offer some reassurance. A response might be,

"Mr. K., I sense that you are concerned that Susie might miss out on experiences with her class—or that the other children may wonder why she needs to leave class so often. You probably even fear that the children may react negatively, or tease her. We understand your concern. Susie's remedial program *may* result in her missing something, and it is possible that she will be subject to some teasing. But we have to ask whether her learning problems may not become an even greater source of difficulty if we don't do something to alleviate them."

This response is only an "opener" for an exploration with the parents of their concerns.

Beyond those considerations, the parents who express concerns such as these may not be fully aware of, or willing to accept, *the extent* of their child's problem, and they may simply remain doubtful about their child's real difference from his or her classmates. They may defer to the "experts," but, unfortunately, they may not offer the fullest reinforcement at home.

Finally, parental passivity may sometimes occur when parents' guilt feelings extend beyond concern about their inadequacy as parents to fear that they may also be failing others, e.g., grandparents. They may also fear that friends, relatives, and others will learn about their poor parenting unless they do what they are told by the school authorities. This is a particular concern experienced by parents when their child is one who tends to behave unacceptably or "act out." Warnings that such acting-out behavior may result in increasingly restrictive programming or placement for their child tend to be frightening, even overwhelming. Most parents will not challenge the team's recommendations if there is mounting evidence that the child is endangering others or "disrupting" normal classroom procedures. (This is not true, of course, of all parents; some may be fierce in their denial of their child's misbehavior and/or may seek to place blame on the school, its staff, its program, etc.) But, simple as it may be for the team to deal with parents who accept decisions submissively, the team—and the child—may be missing out on a potentially important contribution to decision making and program development.

SOURCES OF PARENTS' NEGATIVE EXPECTATIONS

It was noted earlier that parents' cynicism or doubts about the staff's competence to provide adequately for their child may stem from prior experience with their own parents or authorities in which the parents felt powerless or unable to exercise any control in stress situations. However, negative expectations may come from more direct and more recent experience with the school.

A recent experience with the child's teachers, for example, may have been particularly disappointing (not uncommon, if the child has just been or is in the process of being identified as needing special assistance). The following anecdote may illustrate this point:

> At the conclusion of the meeting to develop an IEP for Ruth, Mr. and Mrs. G. stayed behind to talk to Ms. Curtain, the principal. Ms. Curtain inquired if they were really satisfied with the program developed by the team, since they had said little during the meeting.
>
> "Did we really have much choice?" snapped Mrs. G. "Ruthie's teacher has had her mind made up that Ruthie has a problem from the first day she was in her class—you heard her say Ruthie was a disruptive influence on the other girls!"
>
> "Why didn't you say something about that during the meeting?" asked Ms. Curtain.
>
> "It would have been futile. Ms. Banks told me only last week that all the other teachers were beginning to complain about Ruthie too. What would have been the point?"
>
> "You might have been able to get my viewpoint on that, as well as the reading teacher's—she sees Ruthie twice a week in developmental reading class."
>
> "What's the point—antagonizing Ms. Banks will only make things worse for Ruthie. We might as well see just how things work out—the special help won't hurt her. We just don't think Ms. Banks understands Ruthie, that's all, even if she does have a little problem."

Whether or not Mr. and Mrs. G. were justified in their view of Ms. Banks, their expectation that the team deliberations would be overly influenced by that particular teacher obviously affected their perception of the role they might play. Mrs. G.'s view that Ms. Banks was not sympathetic toward her daughter had not been sensed and explored by any other staff member. Consequently, the G.s sat through the meeting in apprehensive silence and left with many concerns unresolved.

Parents' negative experience with their child's previous teachers can have a similar effect. Their sense of being powerless to do anything about a teacher whom they perceived as incompetent, insensitive, or antagonistic can color expectations for many years. Again, the validity of those perceptions is not the relevant issue. The issue is the parents' persisting cynicism or sense of having no real say in anything affecting their child's education.

Passivity can also occur when parents' prior negative experiences have occurred not with teachers but with the principal, the psychologist, the social worker, or the counselor. This is particularly true if they feel their child has either been mistreated or not treated fairly and might be subjected to retaliation if they should complain. The irrationality of these negative expectations make them difficult to deal with, or to get out in the open. Sometimes the parents may not even have had a negative encounter. They may have "heard" that the principal is "hard-nosed" about children who are disciplinary problems, or that the school psychologist is less agreeable than he sounds, or that the staff makes promises that the superintendent is not likely to approve for budgetary reasons, and that, as a result, parents might as well keep their mouths shut and "hope for the best."

OVERCOMING PARENTS' ANXIETY AND NEGATIVE EXPECTATIONS PRIOR TO TEAM MEETINGS

It is ardently to be hoped that parents' negative reactions are irrational and not, indeed, based on accurate perceptions of the staff. If so, most of the concerns parents are anxious about, and many of their negative expectations, can and should be ameliorated via pre-team conferences. The basic intent, in fact, of such meetings is to diminish usual or anticipated parent concerns about evaluation and team procedures so that the team meeting can be more directly focused on the need to make certain decisions.

It might be argued that pre-team meetings are expensive luxuries and that staff time can better be used for any number of other activities, but careful analysis will show that this is not true. Effective decision making requires all the team members, including the parents, to be ready to pool their thinking and suggestions to decide upon the most helpful course of action for a child. Persisting parent concerns, unresolved doubts or questions about what has gone before, confusion or cynicism about the team's objectives, resistant attitudes which stem from earlier experiences—all of the factors that can get in the way of mutual planning and decision making—are obstructive time-wasters. Considering the fact that at least three or four staff members are giving up time from other duties to attend a team meeting, it would seem a far more efficient use of staff time to have one staff member regularly assigned the responsibility for pre-team parent-preparation conferences to assure that everyone else's time, as well as the parents' time, is not likely to be wasted or abused.

The pre-team meeting requires special conference skills. First, a counselor, psychologist, social worker, or school administrator, trained in conference techniques, needs to review what has already transpired as a result of the staff's evaluation or identification efforts and to consider to what extent the parents are familiar with and comfortable about what has already happened. It is probably not necessary for both parents to be present for this conference, but if arrangements can be made for both to attend, it is certainly preferable. The staff member's initial comments should be designed to elicit questions, doubts, or uncertainties, and to convey the sense that the meeting has been arranged expressly to assure that the parents are aware of what has been done so far and of what lies ahead. Unhelpful statements like the following should be avoided:

> "I won't bore you about all the testing we've done—the staff uses a lot of different kinds of tests to help us get to know your son better."

or

> "The testing procedure we use is rather complicated and drawn out. Do you have any questions about any of it?"

or

> "I guess you already know as much as you care to about the evaluation procedures we use. Let's talk about what comes next."

Such comments do not foster a "co-equal" attitude. They squelch questions the parents might have and may make them feel either foolish about any they may have contemplated asking or angry that their questions won't be answered. Instead, the following kinds of comments are designed to elicit questions the parents may have and to make them feel able to participate actively in the process:

> "Our evaluation procedures help answer questions about your son's performance in different areas. Would you like to see what I mean?"

or

> "You probably are curious about the kinds of testing we do, and why we use certain procedures to answer some of our questions."

or

> "Before we talk about the team meeting and what procedures will be involved, I'm sure you have some questions about the testing and observation methods we use."

The intent here is not to encourage detailed discussion of the *results* of testing prior to the team meeting (unless the staff member who has called the conference has also done much of the evaluating), but to encourage parents to raise issues and questions about the process itself, so that when summaries of results are presented at the team meeting, parents are familiar with the procedures and in agreement with their relevance. In addition, the opening comments will convey expectations about the degree of involvement expected of the parents. Encouraging them to ask questions at this stage helps make parents feel that their active participation is not only desirable, but expected by the staff.

The remainder of the conference should be conducted similarly. The parents' questions or doubts should be reflected:

"You seem doubtful about why we felt the need to check his hearing."

"You had some questions, I thought, about why we did IQ testing."

"It sounds like you still wonder why we are doing any of this at all."

The parents' acceptance of popular myths or misperceptions about specific evaluation procedures also need to be explored. Some opening statements might be:

"Parents often are confused about what is involved in IQ testing, and what it all means."

"The idea of eye or hand preferences, like being left-handed, having something to do with reading problems is often puzzling to many people."

"A lot of people believe that a child's IQ never changes."

Finally, the meeting should not be concluded until the parents have expressed the feeling that they are comfortable with what has thus far transpired and know the purpose of the team meeting and the evaluation procedures yet to be concluded. They may wish to suggest alternative procedures themselves, such as the desirability of observing their child in a variety of settings, if that has not already been done. Other evaluation procedures, such as an eye-ear-nose-and-throat or neurological examination, might be recommended prior to the team meeting based upon pre-team discussion with the parents.

Again, the purpose of the pre-team meeting is to assure that the preliminary procedures during the identification stages are understood and to clear the way for joint planning, unencumbered by persisting doubts, confusion about procedures, parental passivity, or defensive resistive attitudes. This pre-team meeting is also the appropriate time to try to resolve any nagging doubts, guilt feelings, or feelings of inadequacy on the part of the parents related to their perceptions of their own role in their child's problem. These issues can be dealt with more easily at an intimate conference than during the full team meeting. Similarly, parents' negative expectations derived from previous unsatisfactory staff or school contacts can be explored in greater depth, and either put to rest entirely or scheduled for further exploration with the appropriate staff. A lot of later, potentially unproductive use of staff time can be avoided by instituting the simple procedure of a regular pre-team conference during the identification stage.

OVERCOMING PARENTS' ANXIETY AND NEGATIVE EXPECTATIONS DURING TEAM MEETINGS

Desirable as the pre-team conferences may be, they may not be feasible in all school districts. Parental anxiety or resistance to active participation are then likely to have a negative effect on team proceedings unless some effort is made to elicit the parents' doubts or concerns as soon as they seem apparent at the team meeting itself, before those issues sidetrack or undermine the team's primary objectives.

At the start of the meeting, for example, the chairperson might make a few comments to familiarize parents with the main purpose of the meeting as well as with their rights as parents. Then, preferably in connection with the introduction of staff, it is possible to set the tone for mutually sharing by one or two comments like the following:

> "Mr. and Ms. J., you've met (some, most, all) of the staff before, and I know you have talked about Chris with some of them. Today, we will be summing up our findings, and we will need to know how *you* see Chris's difficulties so that we can agree on a suitable plan to meet his needs. We expect, therefore, that if you've had or have any different ideas about Chris than those you hear discussed by any of the staff, you will feel free to speak up and let us know where you stand. We want, in fact we need, your cooperation if our plans for Chris are to work."

or

> "Ms. T., I know you have had some reservations about getting involved with our special education procedures for Michael, but we have completed all our evaluations which we will summarize for you today, and we now must work out a plan for Michael which we can all agree upon if we are going to be of any help to him. That means if you have any doubts or questions about our conclusions, or if you have a view of his behavior different from what you hear described, please let us know. Remember, the plan we come up with for Michael has to be one we can *all* agree to and work with—or it may not be as helpful as we'd like."

As well-intended as such opening comments may be, experience dictates that they often may remain unheard. If parents are uncertain, anxious, or reluctant to participate, they may nod agreement without having really heard a word. Therefore, the ideas expressed at the outset that parent participation is both needed and important will have to be reiterated at various points in the meeting—especially if the parents seem inclined to remain silent. But the reiteration of those ideas should be rephrased or reformulated more as reflections specific to the point being discussed than as a rehash of the opening comments. The following are some examples:

> "Did you agree, Ms. T., with Ms. Bond's description of Michael when she said he drifts off into his own world unless she keeps after him to do his work?"

or

> (To Mr. and Ms. J.) "Dr. Leyton's findings seem to suggest that Chris has more potential than he shows. Does that make sense to you in terms of what you know about Chris at home?"

or

> (To Mr. and Ms. J.) "Those are our findings on Chris. Is there anything in what we've described that suggests we're off the mark, or perhaps should have explored differently, or have had him tested by someone else? Before we talk about our plans for Chris, we'd like to know what you think—especially if you disagree with what we've found."

The intention here must be clear by now. If parents are to be accorded any sense of co-equal status as members of the team, if a genuine attempt is to be made to involve parents in the team's deliberations, it also is important to accord them a measure of respect for their ability to respond in a professional manner—as "parent professionals" who often know their child at least as well as the school's staff think they do. Consequently, remarks and comments during team meetings must do more than convey the staff's willingness to listen. All questions and comments directed to the parents must also convey a sense of respect for their ability to understand what's going on and participate meaningfully. Maintaining that attitude in the face of underlying doubts about the parents' understanding of their child is obviously more demanding than when the staff already *do* respect the parents' point of view. But a respectful attitude is particularly imperative when parents seem less able, or willing, to communicate their concerns—or, in fact, appear defensive or resistive. It is a simple matter to discourage challenge in team meetings. The staff usually outnumbers the parents, and unless parents are aggressively vocal, the staff may easily interpret their silence or passivity as tacit agreement. To do so, however, may in the long run undermine the team's objectives.

The meeting must culminate in mutual agreement on the specific program for the child. Regulations currently call for a high degree of specificity regarding who will provide what services, which program will be attempted, and how much time will be devoted to each special education program or service component of the child's total program. In planning the program, since it is the special education components which render the child "different," special care must be taken that the parents understand and approve the specific objective of each component and understand how much time away from the mainstream may be involved. New forms of resistance to special education identification and programming may appear when the specific program components are developed and need to be resolved. The reality of their child "going out to a specialist," regardless of how frequently or occasionally, often reawakens parents' concern about their child's "differentness." That anxiety should be anticipated, possibly with questions such as:

> "How do you feel about Michael's going to Ms. Brewer for training in listening skills twice a week while the class has art or music?"

or

> "You realize, Chris will be out of class a half hour each day for help from Dr. Leyton. He needs the tracking exercises to improve his eye-hand coordination and his writing ability, but how do you think Chris will react to missing what's happening in class? How do you feel about it?"

Such questions may rearouse old anxieties about "differentness" which might not otherwise have surfaced at that point. But after the program has begun, the child's experiences and comments about going out to the speech teacher or the reading teacher or the "special" teacher are likely to arouse them anyway. It's better, therefore, to raise the issue again and prepare the parents for that eventuality even if they have concurred in the special education plan following resolution of original doubts.

An important factor in gradually resolving parental doubts is careful presentation of the test data about their child which has helped lead to the specific program recommendations.

REVIEWING EVALUATION DATA

There is great value in direct, objective presentations to the parents of child study data from individual testing and classroom observations. Concurring with Trachtman (1972), we have found that parents can generally comprehend and work effectively with test results, including test protocols, IQ scores, actual test responses, and so forth. PL 94-142 required the release to parents (upon their request) of any test data and reports which the school staff have communicated to one another. But the actual use of test data to make certain points about a child's performance, including open discussion about "controlled" information such as IQ scores, has still not gained popularity among practicing school specialists. Perhaps it is because "specialists" still tend to feel that testing and test results constitute a sort of sacred domain where only the initiated may operate comfortably, and where parents are likely to become confused or misinformed. If this assumption is true, then that, precisely, also constitutes a challenge for presenting data meaningfully and helpfully to parents.

This is not to advocate the extensive or highly detailed presentation of any sort of test or observational data at team meetings. Each staff specialist who has done more than a routine evaluation of a child's performance should also have taken the time to review the findings directly with the parents prior to meeting for the determination of an IEP. In fact, part of each specialist's data report to the team meeting should include reference to the parents' reaction to the data.

A staff member may say something like this:

> "Mr. M. may recall how surprised he was when I suggested that Barbara was probably experiencing even greater frustration in her school work than we had at first realized. But when we reviewed the test results, I was able to show him the huge disparity between her eye-hand coordination and her verbal facility. As a result, I think both he and Mrs. M. were then able to see why Barbara needs special assistance right now, to help her with her writing skills. This is particularly important so that she can regain her confidence and begin to succeed with what is expected of her. Do you remember that part of our discussion, Mr. M.?"

Except under extreme circumstances, the team meeting should not be the situation where parents learn for the first time about significant evaluation findings that are likely to have an impact upon their child's program. The team meeting is not the appropriate time or place for such presentations, and even though the practice of making them there is common because of staff and time considerations, it defies every ideal of effective parent involvement. Parents cannot be expected to respond meaningfully, when, at a team meeting, they learn for the first time that their child has "borderline retarded functioning," or "moderate hearing loss in one ear," or "dyslexia," or a "pattern of slow development in visual-motor coordination." And yet such experiences, unfortunately, are commonplace.

The presentation of data at team meetings should usually not go beyond summaries of the evaluations completed by the various team specialists. Those summaries, however, should emphasize the findings most relevant to an IEP being developed. In addition, the summaries should specify the parents' reaction to the findings and should note which aspects of the findings are likely to be most controversial. The following illustration may clarify this point:

At the meeting to develop an IEP for Jay, a second-grader whose troubles with visual-motor coordination had affected his handwriting, the chairman noted that Jay's parents had agreed to a neurological evaluation following a conference with the school psychologist. They had been concerned about the reported possibility that the child might have a central nervous disorder (or "minimal brain dysfunction," often referred to as "MBD") and had pursued the recommendation for further examination. The results of the neurological examination, however, were ambiguous. "Soft signs" of neurological dysfunction were evident, but not clearly distinguishable from developmental factors. Mr. and Ms. P., the parents, had been confused by the neurological findings—as were some of the staff—and the summary of findings was presented by Ms. Conboy, the school psychologist, who was the team coordinator. "It looks like we're no more positive now than we were before about what is affecting Jay's writing," Ms. Conboy began, when asked about her findings. "Mr. and Ms. P. and I are in agreement that Jay has a problem, but we can't pin it down." Mr. and Ms. P. nodded. "If we could say it is clearly a function of minimal brain dysfunction we might want to consider Jay right now for our special class for neurologically handicapped children and save him from the frustration of trying to keep up with the children in third grade next year. We've discussed the fact that he's obviously too bright (his IQ is over 120) and too verbally expressive to warrant serious consideration for retention in second grade. His parents, are, therefore, uncertain and, frankly, I am too."

Ms. Conboy suggested that Ms. Pulaski, the speech clinician, might give her report. Ms. Pulaski recalled her conference with Mr. and Ms. P., at which time she had cited Jay's occasionally slurred speech as another possible MBD symptom to support the need for neurological examination. "But I haven't picked up any slurring at all since then," she added. "He seems fine—especially since this past spring—he's one of the most articulate second-grade kids I've seen this year!"

Mr. Marx, the reading and developmental writing specialist, then interjected that there had been "noticeable improvement in Jay's handwriting and fewer b-d reversals in recent weeks" and perhaps that meant more of a developmental than a neurological problem. "I haven't had a chance yet to discuss Jay's recent progress with Mr. and Ms. P. or the rest of you, but it may throw some light on the situation to know that he's beginning to show definite improvement. If possible, I would suggest we hold off on the special class idea for awhile longer. All the kids shift from printing to cursive writing next year in third grade. Learning cursive writing could actually help Jay because it reinforces a left to right directional orientation. I'd like to see him get a crack at it. I'm for third grade for Jay with continued special help with his writing! Maybe even a bit more than he's getting now to make sure he masters cursive writing successfully."

"How do you feel about that?" the chairman asked. "Do you all agree?"

"It sounds too good to believe" was the father's reaction. "The fact that Jay is reversing less is certainly encouraging, but I'm still not sure he's likely to do all that well in third grade."

"What do you think?" asked Ms. Conboy. "Should we give him a try in third grade? If the progress Mr. Marx has seen continues, there's a good chance he could learn to compensate for any marginal neurological difficulties, and he may not need the special class."

"Obviously, we want what's going to be best for Jay," the parents responded.

"But we're not exactly sure what that is," Ms. Conboy reminded.

"From what I hear you all saying," Ms. P. responded, "I think Jay might have a rough time in third grade, but it would break his heart to stay back—all his friends are going to third grade—and I guess I'm not quite ready to see him go to the special class, even though I hear that it's a good program."

"That's good enough for me," Mr. P. added. "I realize we're taking a chance and that Jay may be miserable in third grade, but we can always move him to the special class quickly if we have to next year, can't we?"

Mr. and Ms. P. were assured that Jay's progress would be carefully monitored to enable the team to make a quick decision during the fall about the possible advisability of a special-class placement. With the expectation that if his progress is poor in third grade, an opening for Jay might then still be available, the team concluded on an optimistic note. Ms. Conboy felt positive about the outcome, despite some reservations about the decision. There was still the possibility that Jay's progress might be shortlived, given the ambiguity of the neurological findings. At least Mr. and Ms. P. were aware of the risks entailed in the team's decision, and were not left feeling unrealistically hopeful.

The earlier conferences with the parents and the prior discussion of the need for neurological consultation set the stage for a successful team meeting. Working relationships had been established which made possible the later, constructive sharing of data and the frank discussion of doubts. Because the ground work had been laid carefully, the team meeting to plan an IEP could be successfully concluded on a constructive, if cautious, optimistic note. The parents had played an active role, and their awareness of the ambiguities and uncertainties presaged well for future cooperation if a program change were to be required.

There are several other important points and suggestions to be made about data presentation. First, to aid the presentation of certain kinds of summary evaluation information, a variety of charts, outlines, or descriptions of some of the tests employed may be helpful and time saving for the parents to follow while the summaries are presented. For example, a chart showing a brief description of what is measured by each of the sub-tests that are part of the Wechsler Intelligence Scales might be helpful as a reference for parents' use. Such descriptions may note, for example, that the Information sub-test is a measure of "recall of previously learned facts," or that the Block Design sub-test measures "grasp of spatial relationships and nonverbal categorical reasoning ability," and so on down the line of the various sub-tests which collectively help the psychologist arrive at an estimate of a child's IQ. The speech and language development clinician may have similarly prepared charts describing the sub-tests included in commonly employed measures of language development like the ITPA (Illinois Test of Psycholinguistic Abilities) or the Goldman-Fristoe, and the teams' reading specialist might come similarly prepared with sub-test descriptions regarding the Durrell, Gates-McGinitie, Woodcock-Johnson, Wide Range Achievement Test, or other achievement tests.

These charts can then be referred to if, during the course of a summary presentation, a question arises about terms used or specific areas of functioning mentioned. The use of such forms also tends to diminish the mystique surrounding certain tests, particularly the standard intelligence or IQ tests. It is most important, however, that the charts be written in clear, layman's language, avoiding esoteric jargon.

Finally, parents need always to be reminded of the variability of specific tests employed and their reliability or validity. They should understand the range of scores their child is likely to obtain at any given time, rather than being allowed to accept test results as absolute. Parents should not be encouraged in any perception that "experts'" knowledge or evaluation instruments are any more precise or exact than they actually are. If genuine participation in decision making is to be encouraged, it is important to convey the impression, as Ms. Conboy did with Mr. and Ms. P., that there are always questions, that measuring devices are neither perfect nor absolute, and that the staff does, often, need the parents to help make some hard decisions about their child.

REVIEWING PROGRAM
OR SERVICE OPTIONS WITH PARENTS

Regulations require a special education team to consider actively a variety of program or service options for a child before settling on any single alternative. This is particularly necessary if the alternative likely to be most seriously considered appreciably diminishes the child's participation in mainstream activities. The principle of "least restrictive environment" is implemented by showing that there has been at least some consideration of programming that is less restrictive than that finally agreed upon by the team. Often, in fact, the alternative, less restrictive programs considered but rejected are recorded either on the child's IEP form or in the minutes of the meeting. The law's intent is to assure that, in fact, less restrictive options *are* brought to the parents' attention for due consideration before the parents are asked to approve a placement in any program that diminishes their child's mainstream participation.

This requirement sometimes works to safeguard parents against undue pressure to accede to a program placement that they feel is not yet necessary or appropriate for their child. It also sometimes deters the team from too quickly promoting a program (such as a self-contained special class) that may unduly isolate a child from former peers or classmates. Unfortunately, the procedures needed to establish and document the fact that alternative options have been considered are cumbersome and time consuming. The law, nevertheless, is intended to safeguard and protect parents and their children. And while the law tends to complicate and bureaucratize what otherwise could be accomplished more smoothly and efficiently when school staff and parents work together and trust each other, it does at least assure consideration of all available program options. Furthermore, in cases where parents' resistance to a recommended program may be more emotional than rational, a strategic review of the advantages and disadvantages of the available alternative options may serve the purpose of convincing the parents that the team is on the right track. Hence, a cumbersome requirement can be turned to good advantage.

The way this is done varies, depending upon the degree of the child's isolation from the mainstream anticipated in the suggested placement and the vigor of the parents' resistance to it. If a self-contained special class or out-of-district placement is being most seriously considered, then it is wise to outline carefully and deliberately why each less drastic possible program placement was not sufficient to meet all the child's needs. Few parents want to feel their children have been "dumped in some class to get the kid out of the way." Most want to feel sure that everything which could have been taken into account was considered sufficiently. This seems particularly important to parents who are already struggling with self-doubts about their parenting effectiveness. It is a good idea, therefore, for the team leaders to see to it that the parents have been informed how and why each of the less restrictive program options was considered insufficient for the child, before seeking final agreement upon more restrictive placement.

When the question is of more or fewer mainstream activities, a routine presentation of program options is not necessary. Instead, the staff should try to show how every hour *out* of the regular school program may benefit the child more than continued efforts at mainstream involvement. Whenever possible, the child should be receiving the needed special help or support during "free time" or study-period time; the next optimum time for special help would be during non-academic time such as art, music, or physical education (unless that activity is an important motivator for the child). A child should be taken out of basic, academic subject time for special education help *only* when it is certain that the special education program offering is more beneficial than the time in regular class would be.

The staff needs to maintain a receptive, responsive attitude while viewing program or service options with parents in either of the two types of situations discussed above, but particularly in the latter, where issues arise over the amount of time the child *needs* to be away from regular class. It is helpful to parents, in fact, for the staff to cite the specifics of the program or describe instructional similarities and differences between the special and regular instructional programs, and to encourage parents' questions about what their child might miss while out of the regular classroom. When important work is to be missed, the regular classroom teacher should be encouraged to provide some activities, exercises, or work the child may be able to do at home with the help of the parents to avoid falling too far behind in the regular program.

LIMITATIONS TO THE SCHOOL'S OBLIGATIONS

Most parents will obviously want the most ideal or best possible programs for their child. In fact, lawyers and other parent advocates who attend team meetings will often consider it their obligation to pressure the schools to provide the best possible programs and services for their clients. But what are the school's obligations? And what are the justifiable limits to what a public school system may be required to provide to meet a child's identified needs?

Regarding the question of the quality of programming, the issue primarily revolves around interpretations of the terms "suitable" and "appropriate" when used in reference to the nature of the programming which must be provided. The schools are only responsible to provide programs or services that are "suitable" or "appropriate" to meet the child's identified needs. They are not required to provide the "best possible" or "ideal" programs which parents and their advocates desire, but they must prove that what is being provided is, at least, adequate. Obviously, the range between appropriate and best can vary greatly from school system to school system. Most actions brought against school systems probably concern the difference in interpretation of those distinctions.

The difference between what the school may deem appropriate and the ideal is likely to be much greater in large urban centers and in poorer socioeconomic areas where prohibitive budget pressures tend to restrict school resources more than in affluent school communities. Parents in those less affluent areas can easily be shortchanged unless they seek appropriate guidance and support from area parent advocacy groups or national organizations like the Council for Exceptional Children.

Each school district, on the other hand, needs to develop internal consistency regarding the provision of appropriate and suitable programs, preferably before the criteria are established for them by the legal system through due-process challenges and hearing-officer decisions. State consultants, for example, if not actively involved in monitoring local districts, are often at least available for helping local administrators judge whether or not the district's programs and services meet minimum standards.

Another check on a system's program suitability and appropriateness for different categories of identified handicapped children can be obtained through assessment by independent professionals called in to judge the adequacy of programs either for specific children or for groups of children. Having thus established some standards of what constitutes suitability and appropriateness for categories of identified children (e.g., learning disabled, educable mentally retarded, socially and emotionally maladjusted), local school officials can refer to those standards when faced with claims that "you are not doing enough for my child." The IEPs for each child should not only include specific language to indicate those alternatives that the team has rejected as unsuitable or inappropriate, but should also reflect the team's and the system's position that what was finally agreed upon *is* appropriate and will suit the child's needs.

END-OF-MEETING DECISION MAKING, GOAL SETTING, AND TIME LINES

We have emphasized the importance of encouraging active parental involvement in discussing and reviewing the variety of alternative program options available before attempting to arrive at a team decison. The actual process of deciding, should then be simple if the parents have actually participated in the consideration of the various options suggested. It may be even simpler if the parents, as well as the team members who may be in the best position to suggest particular program options, have explored or researched those options prior to the team meeting and have presented their suggestions or recommendations with sufficient background information so that a decision about their appropriateness can readily be made. Attempts at decision making when needed information is lacking or when the parents are totally unfamiliar with the program suggested are often a waste of time.

If the team is clearly unready to agree to a program, it is preferable to delay decision making rather than to raise vague, unexplored possibilities. Comments such as the following should be avoided:

> "Has anyone thought about that new regional program for Johnny? I'm not sure if they're interested in taking borderline retarded children, but maybe we ought to think about it."

or

> "I've heard that Ms. Carter's class over in the Brighton school district is a good one for children like Barbara. Anyone know anything about it?"

or

> "Don't you think our child should be in a program for underachieving gifted children? Didn't you once have a special class or a course for children like that?"

Such comments reveal either that the meeting has gone poorly and that no program options seem satisfactory or that parents or staff haven't prepared themselves adequately for the meeting. Such comments tend to raise additional questions which need to be answered rather than to bring the team closer to the point of decision making.

They also suggest by their substance that certain points still need to be clarified, such as whether or not the child in question is actually a handicapped child or an "underachieving gifted child." Consequently, when such questions or comments arise toward meeting's end, the team's deliberations may need to be begun all over again.

When the review of alternatives has been successfully concluded, however, the decision probably merely needs to be reiterated and confirmed, either by vote or consensus. Formal voting should normally be unnecessary; but if the decision does not seem unanimous, a formal vote may be needed as part of the record for a possible due-process action. In general, a lack of unanimity should be addressed and resolved before the meeting is concluded, or, if that is not possible, a plan should be developed to resolve anyone's doubts. Split decisions do not create confidence in the suitability, appropriateness, or efficacy of any program. Therefore, unless a formal record of a split decision must be made in anticipation of a due-process action, it is wise not to try to come to a conclusion based upon a majority vote. The decision should not be final, in other words, unless all attending are in complete accord.

Once consensus has been reached on a program placement or on primary services, the decision is written into the child's IEP. The time allocations for support services are finally determined, the personnel to provide those services is specified, the amount of time in the mainstream for physical education or vocational or prevocational training is similarly specified, and the IEP's long- and short-term educational objectives are reviewed in more final detail as they pertain to the program options which the team has decided upon. The specification of objectives, how they are written, and their framework—e.g., in behavioral, frequency, or categorical terms—would themselves require booklength consideration. For the present purposes it need only be emphasized that educational objectives should be written in clear, simple, and objective language. The parents should be able easily to grasp their intent and question the criteria which determine whether they are realized. In addition, the proposed objectives should be presented to the parents as subject to their comments, questions, and approval and not as recommendations that the parents are automatically expected to accept.

The parents should also be apprised of the fact that the IEP is a working agreement, not a contract, and that changes, particularly in the short-term objectives, can be anticipated depending upon the child's progress.

Finally, timelines must be established for the delivery of programs or services and for periodic ongoing review, as well as for annual review. Local guidelines vary regarding the degree of specificity required, but the general concept of specificity with parents concerning when the accomplishment of educational objectives should be assessed is a good one. The discussion with parents should focus not on whether timelines are necessary but on what constitutes a reasonable amount of time for the accomplishment of an objective. In this regard, the staff needs to be prepared to help develop a realistic frame of reference for what kind of progress can be expected, in which areas, and by what specified date. In development of timelines, the team should not be overly optimistic, because that tends to breed later disappointment, but neither should it be unduly discouraging. With appropriate allowance for both positive and negative exigencies, it should not be difficult to reach agreement about when the program may reasonably be expected to produce progress.

All the issues which need to be covered in team meetings, both to involve parents meaningfully and to arrive at a workable conclusion, can be charted or checklisted for easy reference.

SUMMARY

In this chapter we have discussed what we see as the essential elements in effective work with parents, the key element being the attitude that parental involvement really helps children. This commitment to involving parents in their children's educational programs will help dispel any lingering reluctance on the part of school personnel to admitting parents to the decision-making process. Cooperative parent participation is critical for the following reasons, among others:

1. Parents have more time to spend helping children, and are more motivated to do so, than anyone else.
2. Parental cooperation is mandatory to ease any familial problems that may be contributing to children's educational difficulties.
3. Parents have a long-term relationship with, and impact on, their children.

Parental involvement in team decision making tends to be less than optimal as a result of the following factors, among others: parents' passivity, anxiety, feelings of dependency, guilt feelings, mistrust of school staff, fear that their child will be labeled, lack of full awareness of the child's difficulty, and negative expectations about the school staff or the school's competence.

Since any or all of these feelings on the part of parents can sabotage the work of the team, it is important to overcome anxiety and negativism prior to team meetings, if possible, through preconference consultation designed to identify and overcome parental resistance. Special conference skills are needed to elicit parents' questions and uncertainties. Once identified, parents' concerns should be dealt with respectfully, sensitively, and honestly.

If preconference consultation is not possible, parents' anxieties and concerns should be elicited and addressed early in a team meeting to avoid undermining the team's primary objective.

During the meeting, skillful use should be made of actual data and results to make specific points about children's performance. However, parents should not be overwhelmed with statistics or unfamiliar technical terms or intimidated by professional jargon or unexpected negative "diagnoses" of their children's difficulties.

Parents should be fully informed about available services and program options. The team coordinator should make sure they understand the possible choices and should not permit them to be pressured into accepting a program they feel is not necessary or appropriate for their child.

Parents—and their advocates—need to be informed about the realistic legal and financial limitations to a school system's obligations.

Chapter VII deals with parents' rights as they now exist under the law and as they are likely to develop.

6

Coping with Unusual Team Problems

INTRODUCTION

A large number of team meetings, particularly those called for annual review, are considered relatively routine by many pupil personnel administrators, but other meetings present special problems. "We usually set those up as mini-team reviews at the end of the year, and they're handled fairly easily by the staff member who knows the child best—plus the principal and the homeroom teacher," said one Connecticut administrator. Although he found that sometimes the earlier meetings to identify a child's special education needs and develop a program may go smoothly, most of them present difficulties.

The concerns expressed by administrators can be classified into two general categories: parent-related and staff-related. In the first category were problems involving parents' unduly defensive or belligerent behavior. This often stemmed from their own personal problems, e.g., alcoholism, divorce or separation, psychiatric difficulties, all of which could cause serious difficulty in communicating. Parents who made constant or unreasonable demands or pressured the team with legalistic threats were also included in this category. In the second category were included those problems resulting from staff disagreements, role conflicts, conflicting evaluations or impressions, and staff

111

pressures for placing-out troublesome or more seriously handicapped students—a problem of particular concern at secondary levels.

With respect to most of the parent-related problem situations, administrators often report that they feel constrained from dealing with the sources of the problem in any direct, "up front" way, especially if parents become defensive, assume a pressuring attitude, or display belligerent behavior. In these circumstances, the school staff anticipated that pursuing the underlying problem would only lead to a drawn-out, time-consuming due-process action. It was reported that frequently, instead of examining their own behavior (once they had been confronted), many parents threatened a legal challenge. Many administrators made comments such as "The law is for parents and their lawyers, not for kids!" Others said things like "We can't deal with the real issues, because as soon as we tell parents something they don't want to hear, they tend to want to duck responsibility for their kids' struggling and blame us. They won't listen—especially not in a team meeting. They will say they've heard of parents who pressed their own point of view successfully, with legal assistance. So they're ready to walk out and take us to court instead of really examining their own contribution to their child's difficulties."

Difficult as the parent-related problems may be, the staff-related issues pose no less of a headache for administrators. Although simple disagreements and temporary misunderstandings about role functions can be readily resolved, personality clashes and chronic disputes over role functions tend to persist over a long period of time and have an effect on many meetings. Thus, one administrator might report having to reshuffle the building assignments of certain staff because role conflicts were otherwise unresolvable, or because two particular specialists whose functions somewhat overlapped "rubbed each other the wrong way constantly." In other reported instances, the staff "just had to learn to live with" a particularly irksome, argumentative, or bossy team member.

There are, however, some relatively effective strategies which may be employed in a variety of troublesome situations. Although, admittedly, some problem situations appear to defy permanent solution, there are some recommendations that may be helpful at least to partially ease these situations. Sometimes, as when "unreassignable" staff members' personalities are clashing, or when it is obvious that parents' belligerence will only be increased by efforts to confront their behavior, it is necessary to accept limitations and ride out a difficult situation as well as possible, once reasonable efforts to reduce tensions have failed. This chapter will, however, elaborate on some strategies worth trying, even in such seemingly hopeless situations.

RESOLVING PARENT-RELATED PROBLEMS DURING TEAM MEETINGS

Unlike what may occur in a community mental health or family-child guidance clinic, to which parents have come voluntarily with a problem they openly acknowledge, there may be little willingness on the part of parents to consider what might be *their* contribution to their child's school difficulties when such issues are confronted during team meetings. No matter how expert the team members are perceived to be about family dynamics or the relationship between school and family problems, parents may not be willing to accept even the hint of a suggestion during a team meeting that they are in any way responsible for their child's problems. Consequently, such confrontations should not be attempted during team meetings. If the need to confront has not been acted upon previously, or if prior confrontations have been unsuccessful, then decision making should be deferred until strategies have been developed to insure parental cooperation. The following are some situations demanding this approach.

Legalistic, Demanding Parents

Most of the time, legally knowledgeable parents, including those who bring legal representation to meetings, are interested enough in the purpose of the meeting to accede to requests that the team's efforts remain directed toward serving the best interests of the child, even when the discussion has momentarily become legalistically sidetracked. Indeed, in all problem situations, the first and best recourse is to appeal to reasonableness for the child's sake. And, as noted previously, lawyers will frequently respect such redirected efforts, which, in the long run, are in their clients' best interests, unless they have already determined to pursue due-process action and are using the team meeting for other purposes.

Unfortunately, it is sometimes necessary to contend with parents whose legalistic and demanding stance during the meeting may be primarily a function of their own generally suspicious and defensive attitude rather than a function of justifiable concern over the handling of the case. It is this kind of parent who, paradoxically, tends to react overly apprehensively to routine, protective procedures, such as the procedure involved in obtaining written permission for testing. They also often react impatiently to hearing information presented to them procedurely about their due-process rights. Their vigilance tends to be aggravated rather than diminished by formal procedures designed to protect their own rights. Such parents mistrust the team and mistrust the system, and therefore mistrust efforts to allay their concerns via formal procedures or official statements—which they consider to be designed only to placate them, not truly to protect them.

Such mistrust must be met head-on, as the following example may illustrate:

Mr. D. had been divorced for approximately two years and had retained custody of his eight-year-old child, Tony, although his ex-wife was suing for custody on the grounds that he was not a responsible or otherwise fit parent. Tony had been retained in first grade. He was a bright child, but obviously caught in the middle of his parents' struggles. He frequently seemed moody, depressed, and preoccupied in school. Now in second grade, Tony was doing passing work, but clearly less than he was capable of, and his generally sad manner was interfering with his ability to make friends. The meeting was called to encourage Mr. D. to accept some help in arithmetic and some in-school supportive counselling for Tony and also to raise the possibility of referral to a child guidance clinic for more intensive family therapy. It was obvious that the team was in for difficulties with Mr. D. when he called to complain about the releases he had been asked to sign to approve psychological testing. He said they were too legalistic and formal, but that he would give his approval providing that testing were limited to achievement and intellectual functioning. Mr. D.'s first remark at the team meeting was a criticism of the invitation notice he had been sent.

"Why do you need all these forms? Even my lawyer was surprised at how legal they sounded. I think those forms must put off a lot of people—they certainly turned me off!"

The team chairperson explained why they were required and how they were intended to protect parents' rights; he agreed that the language in the forms should probably be softened somewhat and rendered less legal sounding.

Mr. D. impatiently brushed off these overtures and pressed to get to the point immediately. He asked, "Well, what do you have to tell me about Tony? What does he need and what can *you* do for him?"

The team moved quickly through the various presentations by the staff. Mr. D. nodded, asked a question or two about diagnostic and test terminology, but said little else. He jotted some notes on a little pad he had taken from his jacket pocket, but he resisted most efforts to elicit his opinion until the team began discussing Tony's sad appearance and his apparent need to talk to someone about what might be troubling him. Then the father jumped into the discussion with angry questions.

"Where did you get that from? What makes you think he's depressed? I've seen none of that—he just needs some help with his math. You're going too far!"

The chairperson reflected Mr. D.'s obvious annoyance, but reiterated what had been observed and what had been noted during testing to suggest Tony's depression. He said that the suggestion about counselling was, at this point, seen more as a preventive measure than as "treatment."

Mr. D. was not to be reassured. He burst out angrily, "You folks do your job on his math! I want a statement of what he needs to accomplish, and of when he will be caught up to grade level—and I will hold you to it! Leave his psyche alone! Between you and my ex-wife you'd think I was an incompetent parent, but I've had enough of that nonsense and the rest of what you're proposing is just that—a lot of nonsense!''

"Mr. D.,'' the chairperson said, "we will go ahead with the arithmetic help for Tony, but we really don't think he's going to be able to use it well until and unless he feels better about himself, is less moody and less preoccupied—perhaps with all that's going on between you and your ex-wife—which he may fear could affect him.''

"That, sir,'' Mr. D. told the team in no uncertain terms, "is none of your damn business! You school people are all alike. You talk about this whole-child crap so much, you think everything is related to everything else—well, I don't buy it. If he's unhappy in school it's simply because he doesn't understand the work—that's your job, help him with his math! I don't want you folks tampering with his mind, or his personality. I'm raising him, and that's my job!''

The team meeting concluded with agreement for math help for Tony. The team also agreed to defer on the counselling component of the IEP and the suggestion for outside counselling, *provided* Mr. D. would agree to pursue independently a private psychological evaluation from a qualified psychologist, whom he might choose, at the school's expense.

"Check us out at least,'' the chairperson suggested. "Maybe you're right. You *are* raising Tony, and his happiness *is* your charge. You don't have to trust what we're saying or recommending. Check it out for yourself, on your terms, so that, for Tony's sake, what we are suggesting isn't overlooked or ignored. Then we can talk about the results and we'll try to abide by the outside psychologist's judgment. Can you accept that?''

Mr. D., with evident reluctance, accepted the suggestion but delayed obtaining the independent evaluation for several months. Nevertheless, once it was completed (because it corroborated the team's finding), he accepted the idea of school-based counselling for Tony until the custody battle was concluded. He said he wouldn't go for further, outside professional help because, although it had also been recommended by "his'' psychologist, he expressed the fear that getting involved with psychiatric treatment could be used against him in court.

It had become overwhelmingly clear as the team had tried to confront Mr. D. that the expressions of concern about Tony were only rubbing salt into his custody-battle wounds. Initially, he clearly mistrusted the team's intentions and interest in Tony. It was equally clear that Mr. D. was not about to trust too many people who, he felt, might in any way influence the outcome of the custody fight. The team therefore needed to find a way to address the youngster's needs in a way that permitted the father to retain control of the situation, and not put him in the position of having to approve an action that might be used against him.

To resort to an independent evaluation is often an extremely valuable option. In this case it provided the opportunity for Mr. D.

to get a third party's point of view, which he could use or not use as he wished. The team relied on his basic desire to do what was best for the boy in the final analysis, and this reliance paid off. Had the independent evaluation minimized the team's concern, it might have been necessary to leave it at that, depending upon how Tony progressed. But that did not happen. (In fact, it seemed one of life's little ironies that Mr. D. won the custody battle for Tony because his lawyer was able to use the fact that he had followed the team's recommendation as evidence that Mr. D. was a fit parent.)

Obviously not all suspicious, defensive, or legalistic parents will be involved in so dramatic a situation as a custody battle. However, the strategies that were effective in dealing with Mr. D. will often prove useful in dealing with other such parents, regardless of their particular situation.

Effective Strategies for Dealing with Defensive Parents

The following techniques might be used effectively in encounters with defensive parents.

1. Avoid confrontations at team meetings.
2. Be willing to defer decisions, if necessary, until major conflicts have been resolved.
3. Appeal to reasonableness for the sake of the child when legalisms threaten to overwhelm the team's efforts.
4. Deal directly with the parents' mistrust or hostility. Acknowledge it; discuss it with them; try to deal with the reasons for it.
5. Acknowledge openly that the parents have an intelligent point of view. They usually do! Don't fall into the trap of thinking, and behaving as if, all the expertise resides with the school staff and the parents don't have valuable perspectives and contributions.
6. Make strategic use of independent consultation. Sometimes the corroboration of an outsider will swing the parent over. On the other hand, an outside consultant's disagreement with the team's recommendations may open the team to another perspective.
7. Therefore, when parents ask for recommendations for outside consultants (which, surprisingly, they often may, even if they are suspicious), do not succumb to the temptation to recommend outsiders willing to "play ball" with the school system. Help all outside consultants maintain their independence. Guard the integrity of the consultation procedure.
8. If a parent will agree only to part of a program rather than the complete recommendation, don't take a rigid position. A good start may be all the team can hope for immediately.

Emotionally Disturbed Parents

Perhaps the most difficult parents are those whose own emotional instability renders it almost impossible to conduct any sort of team business with them rationally and responsibly. They frequently miss meetings or, if they do attend, are unresponsive to requests to participate in team decisions. On the other hand, the inappropriate actions at team meetings of some emotionally unstable parents and their inability to follow through with their portion of the responsibilities for implementation of plans can be even more frustrating than unresponsiveness. Emotionally unstable parents can disrupt meetings with antagonistic outbursts; they may take time up with confused, meandering verbal outpourings; or they may sit passively, sullenly, despondently, seemingly oblivious to what the team decides. Such parents either may not be heard from for months, or they may make enormous demands upon staff time for constant reassurance. Their actions may represent their own behavioral cries for help.

The pathetic aspect of working with such parents is that, while one hopes to be able to effect a breakthrough for the child which may prevent the child from repeating the parents' difficulties, there is a gnawing realization that every effort may be futile. The prospects of reversing a process which already seems well entrenched can seem hopeless.

Nevertheless, the task of the team is clear. The team must realize that what is attempted at meetings may be only routine and ritual. But parents' outbursts or confused responses must nevertheless be countered with reassuring, clarifying reiterations or explanations. Even when both parents tend to be emotionally disturbed, it is rare for both of them to be unstable or irrational simultaneously. Thus, if both are at a meeting, the team can work with whichever parent appears to be the most capable and responsible at the moment. Clearly, the most effective way of involving such parents is to do most of the team's work either through prior or follow-up individual conferences with whichever staff member has the best current relationship with them. The following case study presents an example:

> Mrs. M. arrived almost at the conclusion of the team meeting about her daughter Cindy, a fifth-grader, whose pattern of frequent withdrawal from peer relationships had resulted in her feeling alienated, alone, and friendless at school. Mrs. M. apologized, saying, "I'm just so disorganized I wasn't sure when you all were meeting, but I was sure it was sometime this morning—what have I missed?" The chairperson summed up the most recent observations of Cindy and asked Mrs. M. to what extent she was aware of the youngster's apparently increasing unhappiness. The report obviously depressed Mrs. M., because she just sat, nodded, and, in a bare whisper, said she knew, but didn't know what to do about it. A moment

later she became agitated and then, angrily, talked at length about the fact that her ex-husband had abandoned them.

"He's behind six months in his alimony, too—I can't get a penny from him—I'm afraid we're going to have to move back to Florida with my mother!"

The school social worker had spent many hours in conferences with Mrs. M. since this mother and daughter had moved to the district. By tacit consensus, the meeting was quickly concluded and the social worker asked Mrs. M. if she could stay awhile and talk. Earlier in the year, the social worker had arranged a referral for family therapy for Mrs. M. and Cindy, so it seemed appropriate for her to take Mrs. M. aside for a more private discussion about the ongoing therapy.

A sad feature of cases like this is that they can make team proceedings seem so pointless and efforts so hopeless. But perhaps the point has been made about what to do under such circumstances, and what to avoid at a team meeting. It would not have been constructive to try to conduct team business as usual in the face of Mrs. M.'s agitation over her current situation. It was far more appropriate to allow the social worker to use the time to explore what was happening and possibly to reassure Mrs. M. If Mrs. M. had not already been directed toward outside professional help, it would have been appropriate to initiate whatever referral process might have seemed best. Frequently, the most effective way of responding to emotionally unstable parents during a team meeting is to draw them off into a less formal conference so that what is really troubling them may be handled more directly. If any team business has been left incomplete, it can be left to the case manager to conclude at a future time.

More aggressive, acting-out parents are, of course, not as easily drawn off into a private session. They may resent the implication that they are not in command of themselves or the situation. The alcoholic parent, who will be discussed next, often reacts in this manner.

Alcoholic Parents

The alcoholic parent is highly unpredictable and therefore extremely difficult to deal with. Many alcoholics, in order to deny their problems, often try to assure all those around them that they are capable and fully in control (when they are sober). Then, when they've been drinking, angry, caustic, and more unsociable feelings tend to emerge, mixed occasionally with obstreperous behavior—all the more difficult to cope with when it occurs at team meetings. If the parent comes to the meeting intoxicated and disrupts it with loud, boisterous, unacceptable behavior (even if the behavior is less than totally disruptive), it should *not* be the responsibility of the team to calm the parents down. The meeting should be terminated immediately. However, the parents should not be allowed to feel that they have been "thrown out," nor should they be patronized or humiliated. Every attempt should be made to help them retain their self-respect.

A meeting should never be used to exchange charges and counter-charges. It is always necessary to show a willingness to explore seriously whatever issue has been raised and to set a time for talking it over when the parent is less upset or agitated. Again, if one of the staff has been able to maintain a close relationship with the parents and appears at the moment to be trusted, that staff member may be able to try to draw the parent off and talk things over right away. In situations like these, the chances are that the parent will not be easily calmed, or will have already left. Sometimes it may even be necessary to call the police for help if the parent's agitation increases. But if the parent can be calmed down, the school principal, case manager, team contact person or staff member who knows the family best may be able to turn the situation to some advantage, as occurred in the following example.

Mrs. G. had come to a meeting called to discuss her son's bullying behavior on the playground. Peter was almost thirteen years old and in sixth grade, and was therefore larger than most of his classmates. He sometimes used his physical size to keep some of the other sixth-grade boys in line—particularly those who knew he had repeated kindergarten and had teased him about being a "retard." It was not unusual for Mrs. G., a frequently heavy drinker, to show up at school reeking with alcohol. She would verbally abuse anyone in her way on those occasions; angrily state her mind to the principal, office secretary, or anyone else within earshot; and usually storm out of the building before anyone answered her.

On the occasion of this team meeting Mrs. G. was intoxicated, but instead of displaying her usual loud, complaining manner, she sat quietly throughout most of the meeting—that is, until it was mentioned that Peter bullied other students.

"I've heard enough!" she replied. "How dare you call Peter a bully when he is only getting even for all those names the other kids call him?"

"We know about the name calling, Mrs. G.," the team chairperson said, "and we've talked to Peter and the other boys about that--that hasn't been an issue for several weeks. But Peter simply has persisted in pushing around anyone who takes his place in line, or crosses him in any way, at least as he sees it."

"That's enough! You don't care about him! Nobody around here cares about him, or has ever cared about him—you're a bunch of screw-pots, the whole lot of you!"

At this point, Mrs. G. was standing, waving her hands wildly, and obviously out of control. She started out of the room, but tripped and fell into the principal's chair (fortunately cushioned).

The school counselor had known Mrs. G. for several years and was familiar with her outbursts. He waved the rest of the team out of the room and began talking to her softly and reassuringly. Some twenty minutes later she emerged and, without glancing at any of the team members still standing around the office, mumbled something that couldn't be heard and walked out. The counselor, following her out, motioned to the others not to respond.

"She'll be okay," he said. "In fact, I got her to agree to go back to AA after she apologized. She said she was sorry about the way she blasted us, but she felt we were coming down on Peter too heavily, and I agreed we'd look into whether or not the other boys might still be giving him the business—even though they've stopped the name calling."

Although the outcome of this particular situation with Mrs. G. was successful in that one of the staff who had been at the meeting was able to talk with her, calm her down, and turn the incident into something potentially constructive, these cases do not always end happily. Sometimes the parents' emotional difficulties or alcoholism are of sufficient magnitude to interfere with all efforts to assist the child. Sometimes, however, their concern for the child may help even unstable parents to rise above their own problems and cooperate with the team's efforts, even if that cooperation takes a passive (noninterfering) rather than an active (actual assumption of responsibilities) form. Regardless of the apparent seriousness of the parents' difficulties, therefore, teams ought to employ certain strategies in dealing with them in the hope that there may be some positive outcome for the child.

Effective Strategies for Dealing with Unstable Parents

Among the techniques that might be employed with unstable parents are the following.

1. The team must work to clarify the parents' understanding of the child's situation.
2. The team must be willing to provide more than the usual reassurance for upset, despondent, or insecure parents.
3. One team member should try to establish a solid relationship and work with the parents in individual conferences to prepare for the team meetings.
4. Team meetings may be directed toward whichever of two unstable parents appears most rational at the time.
5. Never exchange angry words with parents, regardless of the provocation. Always behave professionally. However, deal firmly with alcoholic or aggressive parents, even if it means bringing a meeting to an abrupt conclusion and attempting to draw parents into an individual conference.

6. Use outside sources of assistance when appropriate or necessary (e.g., police; parents' minister; good friend of the family).

Belligerent, Angry Parents

The responses outlined above, which are appropriate to obstreperous, belligerent outbursts by alcoholic parents or parents who are emotionally unstable are notably troublesome in that the team somehow has to contend with someone who has lost control and who is known to be often out of control. Therefore, if immediate calming efforts are not successful, the idea of calling in other authorities like the police is not inappropriate, given the circumstances. It is something else entirely, however, to contend with angry outbursts from otherwise "sane" and "rational" parents. Their unexpected intense annoyance and any accompanying belligerent behavior must be taken more seriously. It must be acknowledged that there may be legitimate cause for their anger. Such outbursts, which usually come as a surprise, require the team to consider carefully and not to dismiss too quickly as inappropriate the parents' objections or complaints. It is possible that the parents' complaints are valid and that something has been overlooked, a mistake has been made, or something has happened of which the team is unaware, which may explain the parents' reactions. An experience with Mr. and Mrs. R. illustrates this point:

Clara R. was a junior in the high school program for socially and emotionally maladjusted students. She was in a regular academic program part-time and had also been assigned to a sequence of supervised on-the-job prevocational placements to help develop her confidence in preparing for and holding a job after she graduated. The team met with Mr. and Mrs. R. to review Clara's progress during the year and to plan accordingly for her senior year and graduation.

The team's recommendation the previous year for Clara's vocational program had been accepted only reluctantly by Mr. and Mrs. R. They hadn't been entirely convinced that Clara couldn't handle the regular high school program successfully and possibly go on to a junior college (and then to a regular four-year college) after graduation. The team had felt strongly that Clara's learning difficulties would prevent her from succeeding in college, and that it would be more to her advantage to develop practical work skills, which in turn might help build her self-esteem. They had persuaded the parents to accept the program for Clara.

As the meeting began, the staff had nothing but praise regarding the results of Clara's on-the-job experience and what they thought her placements had meant for her. Her employers' reports were glowing, and the staff who worked with her expressed gratification that she seemed to have done so well. Mr. R. said nothing. Mrs. R. stared at the floor.

"What's wrong?" asked the assistant principal who was the team chairperson. "You seem less pleased than we would have expected you to be."

"Less pleased? I'm here to tell you that Mrs. R. and I want Clara *out* of this program immediately. I didn't like it when she started it, and now we know it's been a big mistake."

"But why?" the vocational placement counselor asked. "I'm amazed that you'd say that. She's done so well on all her jobs."

"Have you visited her on her jobs? Did you check out who she's been working with? She came home in tears yesterday. She was molested—on one of your damn jobs—our child was molested. She could have been raped!" Mr. R. was furious and Mrs. R. was extremely upset. She began crying, "This would never have happened if we hadn't listened to you."

The chairperson quickly commented, "I'm sure we would have heard about that from Mr. Watkins [the owner of the luncheonette in which Clara had been most recently working under our counselor's supervision]. Are you sure?"

Mr. R. was standing, pointing his finger at the counselor. "You promised us she would be supervised—so much for your supervision!"

"Please tell us what happened, Mr. R.," interrupted the chairperson. "We're shocked about what you've said. What happened to Clara?"

Mr. R. described how Clara had gone to the kitchen storeroom of the luncheonette, at Mr. Watkins' request, to get some new tablemats, when the dishwasher grabbed at her and made obscene remarks about her breasts. Nothing more than that actually happened, but Mr. R. said Clara was quite shaken by the experience, had been afraid to tell the owner about it, and had cried about it all night after she described the incident to her parents.

The chairperson then made a mistake. He said, "But that could happen to anyone. Doesn't Clara have to learn how to take care of herself? She's a big girl now—and nothing really had happened, did it?"

Mr. R.'s face turned ashen, and he seemed on the verge of leaping out of his chair and attacking the speaker, had his wife not restrained him.

"Wait a minute, hold on!" The counselor was the first to react. "I do not argue," she said to the chairperson. She turned to the parents, "At the very least," she said, "let me interpret for him. I don't think he meant what he said—at least not the way it sounded. I'm shocked and sorry for Clara about what happened. I will also have to talk to the owner about it. He needs to know about his dishwasher and may decide to fire him. But that's not the most important thing. Please hear me out. I would like to talk to Clara about the whole thing. She really does have to learn how to handle situations like that, but not until we've let her know it's an upsetting experience we are concerned about and will do something about—and that we're all sorry it happened."

The parents seemed to relax.

The counselor continued, "But this is no reason for taking Clara out of the program. In fact, we probably even more now need to work with her to prepare her for the world out there."

Mr. and Mrs. R. did not withdraw Clara from the program. They found that their concern for their daughter was shared and respected, and they eventually felt satisfied that something would be done by the owner about the dishwasher. The counselor had also managed to turn the R.s away from their initial angry reaction to the chairperson's remarks. What the counselor demonstrated so well was that in situations like these, becoming defensive is extremely ill-advised. What must be done is to accept and respect the parents' anger as, at least, deserving of further exploration or investigation to see where it comes from and to determine what action may be necessary to make sure that their concern is relieved as soon as possible.

Sometimes the source of the parents' anger is not as readily discoverable as it was in our vignette. They may be upset about how a child has been handled by a teacher or other staff member without being able to specify any particular incident. Sometimes they may be unwilling to admit that they are angry about something outside the team situation, either because they themselves are not conscious of the source of their anger or because they fear retaliation against their child.

Absurd as that fear may strike responsible professionals working for children, it is a real, palpable concern of many parents, and it occurs frequently and often over relatively insignificant matters. A task of the team is to help the parents feel relaxed and confident enough that the team truly has the child's best interests as their focus to be able openly to recognize their own anger, pinpoint its source, and deal with it. This may seem a tall order for the team, but, after all, that is what this work is all about. To be frank, while problem parents and problem situations can be upsetting and frustrating, they also may be very interesting and challenging. They may turn what could be a routine and dull afternoon into a far more stimulating one. That we sometimes may relish challenge and difficulty is not something we are often encouraged to admit, but it is quite natural to get a sense of satisfaction in overcoming a tough situation.

Sometimes, however, though the parents may not be emotionally unstable, their anger still may not have a legitimate source. They may be highpowered parents who have learned to *use* anger, hostility, and belligerence effectively to intimidate and pressure staff into meeting their demands. It will not be difficult to recognize these tactics. Dealing with them is another matter. One effective way to deal with such parents is, obviously, *not* to be intimidated by their anger or to permit their demanding demeanor to influence the team decision.

It would be easy just to give in to aggressive demands, but the path of least resistance is rarely the best path for either the child or the school district. Giving in to parents' aggressive demands may mean instituting a program that the team does not fully believe in. It may, depending upon what kind of demands the parents are making, mean committing the school district to unnecessary expenses. (This obviously is not always the case, as parents in some instances may resist special education identification and balk at putting the child in a special class or similar placement. However, at other times the parents may press for an expensive outside placement, at school district expense, which is not warranted.)

Sometimes parents may press for a particular placement that is not only inappropriate (in the team's view) for the child, but that may negatively affect the other children in the class as well.

Sometimes it is not a particular class placement that is at issue, but the nature and extent of support services. The parents may demand excessive and unwarranted staff time or attention for a relatively minor problem, which may take needed attention away from other children. There is no end to the number and variety of demands that some highly assertive parents may come up with. And these parents often are people who are used to having things go their way. They may be prominent in the community or have powerful connections which they will not hesitate to use.

Resisting demands is not always easy, particularly since the team chairperson must eventually deal with higher administrators and possibly even the board of education. Boards of education frequently want the teams to keep things quiet. The typical board member does not wish to be on the receiving end of angry letters or phone calls. In small communities where board members are well known, they don't like to be stopped in stores or at cocktail parties and subjected to angry complaints. They often may attempt to appease such pressuring parents by making promises that they then rely on the staff to carry out.

We therefore do not casually toss off the advice not to be intimidated by these parents. Nevertheless, we believe that though these parents may be among our biggest professional challenges, it may be possible to deal with them effectively when the team member acting as coordinator for their child takes the trouble to build a relationship with the parents. Through this relationship we should develop the parents' respect for the staff's professional competence and integrity and make them understand that the staff will not yield to inappropriate pressure.

It is, of course, to be hoped that if a situation with pressuring parents does come to a head, the school board will eventually back its professional team rather than crumble under pressure. Though we do not wish to be thought cynical, it is our experience that school boards are more often likely to stand firm when parents are pressuring for an expensive alternative and to yield when the parents' demands are merely inappropriate rather than costly.

RESPONDING TO CHARGES OF DISCRIMINATION IN TESTING OR PLACEMENT

Many parents of children from minority racial, ethnic, or religious backgrounds are sensitive to the possibility that, in either the evaluation or placement of their children, the fact that they are from a minority background will operate to their disadvantage. The justification for some of this feeling is evident in the recent acknowledgment of the need for—and the subsequent development of—special nondiscriminatory testing procedures. Such tests and screening devices were particularly necessary for use in large urban centers where significant numbers of minority children had been found to have been disadvantaged by the frequent use of tests (often for placement purposes) standardized on the basis of populations of white children. In the reaction against discriminatory testing, many complaints were made that schools had used biased testing procedures for many decades, often to support unwarranted placements for many minority children in programs for the learning disabled, educationally disadvantaged, or retarded. In fact, it was claimed, had those children been evaluated by appropriately standardized tests, or in their native language, or had their different ethnic background or experience been taken into account, many would not have required special education placement at all, although they may have needed some remedial assistance to improve skills that had been developed to a greater degree by nonminority children.

Federal regulations now require the use of nondiscriminatory, unbiased evaluation tools and screening procedures. Furthermore, the law specifies that communications with parents for whom English is not the primary language must be in the parents' native tongue, or an interpretor must be employed at the school's expense to assure that the parents' permission for certain procedures, their awareness of what is being proposed for their child, and their opportunity for meaningful participation have been safeguarded.

Adherence to regulations and nondiscriminatory testing procedures notwithstanding, however, it is not unusual for a team to be confronted either with a direct charge of discrimination or with an allusion to that possibility, when parents from minority backgrounds already are feeling sensitive about the fact that their child has been identified as having a problem and may be wondering whether minority status has influenced the identification.

Mr. C. expressed his view at the outset that he hoped that the team would not think of his son, Robert (a fifth-grader), as "a Black child," but as "any of your lily-whiters," for the purposes of judging his needs. He wanted no one "bending over backwards" helping his son. He said he was proud of having gotten along successfully for so many years in the (predominantly white) community, and he wanted no special favors for him or for Robert. "I just want a fair shake for him—like anyone else," he said.

"Mr. C.," said the school principal, "I should think you'd know us well enough by now to know that's exactly how we do view you and will treat you." The principal smiled, but he seemed a bit uncomfortable, probably because he was anticipating Mr. C.'s objections to the team's recommendation that Robert go into a special class for retarded children, which was part of a regional program.

The meeting proceeded smoothly, however, until the psychologist reported her test results, classroom observations, and recommendation for consideration of the special class.

"Wait a minute," Mr. C. interrupted Mrs. Clark's final summary. "Are you talking about that class in Marwood? I agree that Robert needs to be in a special class, but why that one? What's wrong with the class you've got here in this school? Wait a minute—that class has got other black kids in it, right?"

It was quickly explained that the local class was for more capable, learning disabled children, and that because only a very few children in the system had been identified as educably retarded, all of them were sent to Marwood. It was also emphasized that Marwood enjoyed an excellent reputation for the quality of its regional special education programs.

"How's Robert going to feel—shipped away like that every day? I think you're selling him short. He's brighter than a lot of kids in our neighborhood. How come your tests didn't pick that up?"

"How do you mean we might be selling him short?" asked the principal.

"You know what I mean. I've read a lot about Black kids being put away in retarded classes because they've not been tested with the right tests. How do I know that's not what's happening with Robert?"

The psychologist explained that she had allowed for the fact that Robert's test scores might have been slightly depressed because of the standardization-racial factor. But she felt he still did not show the potential needed for consideration for the learning disability class. She reminded Mr. C. that she had reviewed all the data with him.

"Yes, I know, but are you sure he's really retarded?" Mr. C. wasn't being argumentative—he was really asking the team to be sure it wasn't making a mistake.

It is not unusual for *any* parent to resist the idea that his or her child is retarded. Although a parent undoubtedly may have harbored suspicions since early in the child's development, the actual identification is a hard emotional pill to swallow. A parent who feels there is even a slim chance that the school system is wrong will grasp at the possibility. As it is known that minority children have indeed been more frequently misdiagnosed and mislabeled, it is no wonder that this possibility will occur to a minority parent.

The school social worker, who was responsible for arranging for regional placements, understood the real concern in Mr. C.'s question. "What about getting another opinion on Robert?" she suggested. "Maybe we're entirely on target about his limited ability, about his persistent difficulties trying to keep up with the other kids, even after he's been retained once, and about his not being suitable for our LD class. But in this case, shouldn't we doublecheck to make sure?"

"Remember, no special treatment here; Mr. C. said so himself," the psychologist responded before anyone else had a chance to comment. "Baloney!" the social worker answered. "Mr. C. wants a fair shake, too! I don't think Robert is getting one, unless we make a special effort to make sure we're on the right track for him. Mr. C. is right. It may be even tougher for Robert, because he's Black, than it would be for other kids to handle being the one kid from his neighborhood who goes to a different school. We can't ignore what is reality for Robert—a slightly different reality than for most of our kids. Any parent is entitled to another opinion. That is decidedly not giving 'special treatment.' If the independent evaluation bears out our impression, we will have lost nothing and at least have reassured Mr. C. that we haven't overlooked anything. But if it does not, we will all be doubly glad we obtained it."

The logic of these comments and suggestions was inescapable. Even if the testing had been done with special consideration and allowances for Robert's minority background, and despite Mr. C.'s protestation that Robert should receive no more than equal attention, the real issue was the correctness of the team's evaluation and recommendation, and there was certainly no reason not to doublecheck the results since the parent was concerned. This was a case of recognizing the possible influence of the racial factors and making certain that the team was accurate in assessing those factors before making a decision which was likely to have a more-than-usual impact upon the child. It is important to be mindful not only of what the law requires when the team is making decisions about children from minority backgrounds, but also of what may affect the children's adjustment in a community in which they constitute a minority. The use of an independent evaluation to affirm or improve the team's accuracy is, once again, the most valuable option available.

Problems related to possible discrimination are not always as easy to resolve as the one in our vignette. Precisely because it *has* happened that Black children have, in some places, been mislabeled or inappropriately relegated to classes for low-functioning or retarded children, school personnel must be extra alert to be sure that such stereotyping and mislabeling does not occur. However, just as any parents who are unhappy with team decisions, or who are pressing for particular options found unacceptable to the team or too costly, may seize upon *any* evidence, however meager, of the team's error, incompetence, or malicious intent to fight the recommendation of the team, so minority parents may use an accusation of ethnic bias. Parents so embroiled in battle may convince themselves of the team's bad intentions. Similarly, minority parents may convince themselves that their child's "improper" (in their view) diagnosis or placement has been racially motivated. What happens when such an accusation is made? Obviously, any team's best defense rests upon its true innocence of the accusation, the thoroughness and professional competence of its procedures, and the soundness of the evidence upon which a decision has been made. But even when appropriate documentation exists there may be times when an accusation of bias is made. It is hard to prove a negative. It can be hard to prove that racial bias was *not* operating, for example, if parents try to use the differential disposition of two similar cases (one involving a minority child, one a child from the majority ethnic group) as evidence that the minority child was discriminated against. The strategies for dealing with such problems really go back to before the problem existed.

A school system receiving federal funds should have an affirmative action program. It should be in compliance with all aspects of civil rights legislation and regulations in its programming and employment practices and be able to show documentary evidence that it is in compliance.

And the team should, indeed, review its own functioning and question that of other teams in the school system to make absolutely sure that racial ethnic bias does *not* play a part in decision making.

The doubts expressed by Tolor (1978) and Ysseldyke (1982) about team decision making, discussed in Chapter I, included the contention that sometimes decision making is based upon factors extraneous to the child's real problem, such as appearance, sex, socioeconomic status, and the like. If their views have any validity, then ethnic bias *could* also creep insidiously into the process. It is to be assiduously guarded against, and inservice training for team members should include discussions of the ways in which test scores and other assessments, both subjective and objective, may be affected by ethnic classification, other ways in which ethnic bias may seep into decision making, and strategies for reducing the possibility of its occurring.

All this having been done, however, and in the face of a team's firm conviction that its decisions have *not* been swayed by ethnic considerations, how should a team deal with such an accusation?

In such situations, it is probably a good idea to involve higher administrators in discussions with the parents early in the confrontation, rather than waiting until the parent goes "higher up." But by dint of its evidence and its past record, the team must make every effort to convince the parent that bias was not an issue.

Sometimes, if it is feasible and not excessively costly or wildly inappropriate, it may even be wise to try out the parents' preferred solution on a trial basis to demonstrate the team's willingness to be flexible. If the child's performance clearly continues to show a need for the placement or program recommended by the team, reasonable parents are likely to be willing to examine the recommendations more objectively.

In rare instances, however, the team may be facing parents who deliberately wish to humiliate them or the school system, to bring a test case, or to use the threat of legal action as pressure. We refer here to parents who do not truly believe that prejudice has been at work, but who see the opportunity to exploit a sensitive issue to gain their own advantage. They must be dealt with as the team would deal with *any other* parents who bring, or threaten to bring, unfair pressure to bear to gain their point. The team should hold to its position and seek the support of the board of education. To do otherwise—to yield to the accusation of prejudice when the team does not customarily yield to other hostile pressure—would itself be a sort of reverse racism.

COPING WITH INARTICULATE PARENTS

Sometimes a team must meet with parents who are themselves handicapped in ability to articulate, comprehend, or communicate. Usually, such parents avoid team meetings or arrange for someone else to represent them. Helping make such arrangements is one of the first options to pursue with such parents, who may be self-conscious or embarrassed by their problems when they need to attend school functions.

Occasionally, such parents are unable to arrange representation or are too proud to accept the suggestion that they need assistance. And sometimes it is the inarticulate parent who, defensively, becomes angrily abusive and disrupts team meetings because he or she doesn't understand what is happening and is unwilling to admit it.

Some inarticulate parents may not be averse to services—they may even seek services—but they may be hostile toward appropriate procedures (as the vignette below illustrates).

Sometimes parents' difficulty in comprehending or their general distrust of the school system and its procedures may result in their rejection of needed services for their children. Under these circumstances, a school system could itself initiate due process to make sure the child receives needed services—on the technical basis of "neglect." However, few staff members, administrators, or board of education members would choose to engage in such overt adversarial relationships with parents except under extremely unusual circumstances. Such an action should be considered a very last resort and used only when all other efforts to engage the parents' cooperation have failed and when the child is being seriously damaged by the absence of the recommended program. Sometimes, when nothing will bring the parents around—and when the detriment to the child is not of overwhelming proportions—the children of these parents simply do not receive the services that could help them. In this respect, they may suffer no more than children of parents who have no trouble comprehending the team's recommendation but adamantly refuse the proffered program for any one of a number of personal reasons. At this point, rather than invoke "due process" to force a position on the parents, professionals may need to back off and accept the fact that the ultimate responsibility for this child is not theirs. As Featherstone (1980) so sensibly observes, "people disagree about the efficacy or the practicality of a particular treatment . . . . At the deepest level these are not professional or technical questions; they are human, and the buck stops with the parent" (p. 119).

This is not to say that there are never any circumstances under which a school system should invoke due process either for substantive or legal reasons. These are discussed elsewhere in this chapter. Fortunately, however, there are some effective strategies for dealing with inarticulate parents which often do succeed, as the vignette below and the subsequent discussion will illustrate. These strategies often involve utilization of third-party assistance.

> Mr. and Mrs. P., long-time residents of the area, prided themselves on their frontierlike values and down-to-earth approach to most matters. They often were absent from meetings about their children but occasionally would call the principal or some other school official to protest some rule, regulation, or "frill" which they couldn't understand or didn't feel was necessary. The calls tended to be infrequent because the P.'s were never really comfortable about sustaining a telephone conversation. Usually they would make their complaint and hang up angrily after the school official they called had a chance to make only one or two comments in response. Similarly, during town meetings, Mr. P. was known to complain occasionally about taxes being too high because of unnecessary school services, but he would not respond to questions or any requests for clarification of his statements.
>
> The P.s had two boys in school. A third—their eldest son, John— had dropped out of high school to work with his father. There were occasional newspaper reports of complaints brought against the oldest boy for drunken driving, loitering, breaking the peace, etc., but Mr. P. usually raised a fuss about the local police picking on his son, and invariably the charges were dropped or reduced to small fines.
>
> Mr. P. called the school one day to say that he had heard about the special education law which made the schools responsible to provide education for students up to age twenty-one. He said he wanted to talk about what could be done for John if he registered again at the high

school. The high school team, familiar with John's severe learning difficulties and long history of acting-out behavior, agreed to meet with Mr. P. to try to work out a vocationally oriented program, combined with remedial math and reading assistance, which might permit John to graduate within two years. Mr. P. said that both he and his wife would attend the meeting, but only he showed up.

He did not understand why John needed to be evaluated prior to being identified as a special education student. "I thought you knew Johnnie from when he was here before. He don't need to be tested any more. Besides, he never does good on those tests."

We explained again that testing had to be done. "The law requires an evaluation of his present skills to aid in developing a plan to meet his needs," the assistant principal reiterated. "John has been out of school for more than a year. We really need to have him tested."

"Why don't you just give him tutoring?"

"We can't do anything for John until he's registered and we've had a chance to evaluate him—it's the law, Mr. P." The administrator was looking somewhat exasperated.

The school psychologist tried his hand at explaining the identification procedures, but Mr. P. responded as if he hadn't heard a word. "You're supposed to see that he gets schooling until he's twenty-one. I saw it in the newspaper. All I want is the tutoring. What's so hard about that— I pay my taxes!"

The psychologist said, "We probably will be able to tutor John as you're asking us to do, but we have to see him first, talk to him, find out what kinds of jobs he might be interested in, test his reading and math so we can set up the tutoring to try to get him up to grade level, and so on— that's what the testing is all about, but it's got to be done—it's the law."

"Who do I call about that? I know people in the capital. I'll see about all this red tape. You guys are worse than the police—always red tape!"

The psychologist held up his hand. "Hold on, Mr. P. I'll give you the person to call in the state office, but let me suggest something first that may make all of this easier for you to check out. When John was arrested last month, you had a lawyer help you, didn't you? Why not have him call us about this whole business and have him check out the regulations with the department of education."

Mr. P. took the suggestion, his lawyer contacted us, and school officials explained the procedures required by law. The lawyer convinced both John and Mr. P. to cooperate. In a similar case, the parents were encouraged to contact the state education department's special education consultants as Mr. P. had indicated he planned to. However, that process created more confusion for the parents, who did not really comprehend what had been told to them, and who later accused everyone of giving them "the runaround."

The serendipitous recollection that the P.'s had sought help from a local lawyer was fortunate, because it was felt that Mr. P. would not get any further with the state officials than he had with the school personnel, and John would have been lost in the process. Fortunately,

Mr. P. had respect for the lawyer who had helped John out of police jams, and because the school and the lawyer had worked well together previously for other students whom he had represented in juvenile court, there was little difficulty working with the P.s through him, arranging for the necessary evaluations, and developing an appropriate IEP for John. If the lawyer had proven to be someone who couldn't work well with the school, Mr. P.'s direct contact with the state officials would have been unavoidable and the situation might not have been satisfactorily resolved. Still other possibilities in this case included bringing John in to explain the situation so that his father needn't have responded defensively for him. Another possibility might have been to have the high school social worker, who also knew them, meet with the P.s at their home to explain the procedures again—but under more relaxed circumstances for Mr. and Mrs. P. In any event, it was obvious that the team's efforts were doomed if the staff persisted in trying to gain Mr. P.'s cooperation through conventional approaches. Whatever the reasons, Mr. P. was not listening, or perhaps was not able to listen. Another vehicle for communication was needed. Fortunately, in this case it was available through the utilization of an attorney.

In some instances it may be advisable to seek the intervention of a third party who is not necessarily either a lawyer or an educational specialist. Parents who are known to have difficulty with communicating, as well as parents with a past history of hostility or belligerence, should be more than *informed* of their rights to have a third party present, they should be encouraged to do so. The presence of a neutral outsider may serve to temper aggressiveness on the part of hostile parents. A third party may help the parents see that situations which they interpreted negatively may not have been negatively intended by the staff. Parents who have difficulty understanding the staff or communicating their own ideas articulately may be reassured by the presence of someone they have chosen to accompany them and may use this person as a sounding board later on to help them review the meeting.

Obviously, while a third party of the parents' own personal selection may be reassuring to them, it is always possible that they may choose a person who shares their own biases (if such exist) about the staff, the program, and so forth. Or they may choose a person who is not significantly more skilled in understanding or communicating than they themselves are. In such a case, the staff may find that the presence of the third person only reinforces and exacerbates the difficulties in dealing with the parents. It is for this reason, as well as the others mentioned in our earlier discussion, that many school systems have found it useful to develop an ombudsman program. A well-run ombudsman program would not preselect a third party for the parents but would make available to them a choice of assistants. Thus, parents may still obtain the comfort and reassurance of a companion of their own choice at the meeting, while schools can be more certain of the rationality and impartiality of the third person. It may help parents to feel less as if they are in "alien" territory and open them to more thoughtful and rational consideration of staff suggestions.

WHEN SHOULD THE TEAM INITIATE DUE-PROCESS ACTION?

The stringent due-process provisions of the law exist to protect the child's right to an education regardless of whether it is the school system or the parents whose actions—or lack of them—are interfering with that right. Sometimes it is necessary for a school district itself to initiate legal action to safeguard a child's education when parents or guardians are intractable in their refusal to acknowledge the extent of their child's handicap or to consider or approve a program that the staff feels is essential. Obviously, this measure should be employed only in the most extreme circumstances when all other efforts to engage the parents' cooperation have failed, or in situations where the parents' behavior is judged by the team to be "neglectful" on the basis of their disruptive or obstructive behavior and general resistance to a special educational program which everyone, except the parents, agrees is essential for the child. There may be no other evidence of neglect or child abuse. Consequently, the due-process action itself constitutes the development of evidence in cases where the school staff perceive the parents' negative, resistive actions as constituting a danger to the child's welfare.

In the cases cited earlier in this chapter, action by the school system could have been pursued against Mr. P. But, since his son was no longer registered in the school district, there were no legal grounds for the board to initiate due-process action against him. Moreover, there was already plenty of evidence of the boy's delinquent behavior in the community to justify pursuit of charges of parental neglect more directly through the local police department, had the district wished to follow through.

In the case of Mrs. G., the alcoholic parent, a due-process action would have been appropriate if the team had felt the need to recommend another placement for Peter and she had resisted it. However, because of her recognized drinking problem, the system had recourse to direct and helpful action through Alcoholics Anonymous.

Similarly, because Mrs. M. had responded positively to a referral for family therapy, there was no need to pursue due-process action for Cindy's sake as a result of the mother's emotionally unstable behavior. It was possible to deal more directly with Mrs. M.'s own personal difficulties (as they affected Cindy) through the family therapist.

Perhaps, had Mr. D. not accepted the team's recommendation for an independent third-party evaluation of Tony's emotional upset over his parents' custody struggle, a due-process action might have forced the issue. This would have amounted to a legalistic strategy against this father's insistence on the development of an IEP without support services.

The most effective strategic use of the district's option to pursue due-process action tends to occur in situations where a vigilant, litigious parent like Mr. D. threatens to tie the team up in due-process procedures unless it yields to his point of view. When the team makes it clear that the school district may initiate such action first, this position may underscore the fact that the team views its concerns seriously and is willing to pursue those concerns as vigorously as the parent.

Sometimes the school system needs to resort to legal action not because the program or placement is in question but because there is disagreement over the extent of the district's financial responsibility. If these disputes cannot be settled amicably, a legal determination may be the only option.

Pursuing due process to determine primary financial responsibility for children who are more seriously handicapped and who need to be placed in residential programs is much more routine. It is often a mutually accepted method of resolving financial issues. In states where an alternative option for mediation or arbitration also exists, resolving financial issues with the help of a state-appointed official is much more desirable than struggling with the parent over who is responsible for costs. At times, when parents are not willing to accept cost responsibility for board and other noninstructional costs (such as therapy), the team's recommendation that the issue be resolved through mediation or other due-process action serves to emphasize the team's judgment that there is a legally valid reason for the parents to assume some cost responsibility and that the team is not just attempting to avoid school-district cost obligations without supportable grounds. Therefore, when made by the school system, the very suggestion that the issue be submitted to mediation may sometimes be enough to bring about a change in the parents' attitude toward assuming some financial responsibility.

Situations can become very tricky, however, when dealing with the needs of a severely physically handicapped child who is still not in need of residential placement. While the United States Supreme Court, in its Rowley decision (Hudson v. Rowley 1982), may have resolved the issue of providing an interpreter for a deaf child who was deriving substantial benefit from her schooling without one, it left many other issues unresolved. Is it the obligation of the school system to provide an individual aide to lift or carry a wheelchair-bound youngster? If a child with severe muscular dystrophy, cerebral palsy, or other paralysis or muscular disfunction cannot turn the pages of a book (although his or her ability to read and comprehend is unaffected by the illness), must the school system provide someone to fill the gap? These and numerous other situations often appear to pit humane sensitivity against callous concern for financial realities when the team refuses to recommend filling such needs totally at public expense.

It is tempting to resort to due-process resolution of conflicts such as these, and this certainly gets the staff off the horns of humanistic dilemma. But school boards do not often look with approbation at staffs who permit too many situations to deteriorate to the point where legal procedures are necessary. They like the staff to come up with solutions which serve the child well, satisfy the parents, and don't cost too much money! Lacking Solomon's sagacity, however, most staffs are hard put to satisfy these requirements—though they try. The staff, moreover, must, for the sake of the entire program, have a realistic awareness of the true financial constraints of the system. It is not Solomonic to jeopardize a program or severely limit other children's opportunities in order to meet the needs of one child. Yet each child deserves utmost consideration and vigorous efforts to provide what is necessary for his or her educational success.

Whether or not one personally agrees with the Supreme Court's limitation (1982) on the schools' responsibility to that of providing the opportunity for the child to derive "some" educational benefit, or whether one is of the opinion that the school system ought to do much more for the child, unquestionably this limitation of their responsibility will be relied upon increasingly by school boards bombarded with requests for costly services.

Ironically, it is the child who potentially may derive the *most* benefit who may be caught in the Supreme Court bind and for whom the staff may have to do the most inventive work. A child who is so severely handicapped that he or she requires costly special assistance or special out-of-district placement to derive *any* benefit from schooling is currently served by the mandates. It is the child whose handicap is such that he or she *can* derive some benefit without extraordinary assistance (albeit not as much as would be gained with special assistance) for whom the school system has only a limited responsibility. Thus, those handicapped children with greater potential for educational success may, in the long run, be the recipients of *fewer* public funds than those with significantly less potential.

Therefore, it will be necessary for staff to view these difficult dilemmas as opportunities to devise creative solutions—to find ingenious ways of meeting special needs. One such solution may involve the use of volunteers. More and more school systems are using volunteers in the schools to enrich the classroom experiences of all children. The concept of special education volunteers is not unknown. It may well be necessary to turn to volunteers to assist with severely physically handicapped children who can otherwise benefit from regular instruction.

In order to increase the benefit directly derived, the parents of severely handicapped children—or of any special needs children— are often extremely supportive in developing volunteer programs, from recruiting through training to placement and follow up. A school system interested in pursuing the use of volunteers would also do well to contact the National Association for School Volunteers for literature, advice, and assistance with all phases of volunteer program development.

RESOLVING STAFF DISAGREEMENTS

Chapter III emphasized that nothing is more discouraging to parents than to see staff members sharply disagreeing among themselves about evaluations, squabbling over role responsibilities, or acting confused about who should follow up the team's decisions. Previous chapters have described how some of those difficulties can be resolved by encouraging greater staff preparedness, clarifying role functions in individual conferences with staff members, and providing inservice training sessions for the whole staff, in order to increase awareness of one another's strengths and weaknesses as well as of different job functions. Already noted has been the importance for each team of specialists to learn to complement one another's professional skills and to defer to the strong points of other specialists rather than insist too stringently on credential distinctions or bicker about job delimitations relative to titles.

Chapter IV covered the leader's role relative to organizing and coordinating the staff's presentation and determining who should implement the team's decisions. It also emphasized the team leader's need to keep members "on target" and mindful of the overriding purpose of the meeting, as a means of resolving certain problems which threaten to divert attention, particularly when a guest specialist and the staff disagree. The remainder of this chapter, therefore, will elaborate upon some of those points with regard to specific kinds of intrastaff problems and will specify strategies which, experience demonstrates, may best resolve them.

DISAGREEMENTS OVER EVALUATIONS

Prior to team meetings, and sometimes, unfortunately, during meetings, disagreements may arise among the staff regarding the main cause of a child's learning difficulties. Clearly, such differences can and should be resolved prior to discussions with parents. This may be accomplished by arranging for further diagnostic testing, observation, or data collecting to verify one or another of the different sets of impressions. Most parents are likely to be pleased to hear what was done to confirm or reject the various original hypotheses, and to learn which impressions were finally agreed upon. However, it may not always be possible to resolve differences of opinion among some team members, and therefore such differences will surface at a team meeting, creating uneasiness and embarrassment unless they are handled appropriately.

Under such circumstances, provided the staff's different impressions have been developed in a professionally responsible manner and are not merely interjected speculatively, the team leader should:

1. Acknowledge openly and *underscore* the persisting differences of opinion among the specialists, even after further investigation or testing of each one's views. To underscore the differences, each member should be asked to specify the grounds for his or her opinion, using terminology that the parents can understand easily.
2. Explain to the parents the reasons that the differences in impressions are important diagnostically (i.e., tell them how those differences affect identification of the child's problem).
3. Show the relationship between the diagnostic differences and differences in expectations concerning the child's performance, including alternatives for program or service that could be recommended (i.e., tell parents how the differing impressions directly affect program components which need to be provided to help the child).
4. Acknowledge that the IEP objectives may have to be considered

temporary and the program implemented on a trial basis, pending evaluation of the child's actual performance.

5. Schedule a team meeting for progress review purposes in the fairly near future (usually in a few months), to evaluate the effectiveness of the trial placement or program.

6. Reaffirm the legitimacy of differences of opinion. Point out that while it is true that diagnostic categories are loose and therefore may create ambiguity, the ambiguity should not prevent trial planning to aid in the eventual determination of an effective program.

If these steps are followed, the differing team specialists are not likely to feel denied unless they are so far apart in their views that their program recommendations are mutually exclusive. The parents may remain somewhat worried about the remaining unresolved differences, but will often agree to a trial program if the reasons for the ambiguity are made very clear.

When the recommendations are in sharp contrast to one another and a temporary solution seems impossible or no trial program options seem immediately feasible, the best course of action is to defer the decision, pending review by a central district or regional team—which may want to do its own evaluations. A community child guidance clinic or similar agency may also be helpful in instances in which it is felt by the team that a particular program component should not be pursued without more certainty in the diagnosis. Diagnostic disagreements about whether a preschool child is retarded or suffering from persistent hearing difficulties; or whether a child has a severe handicap masked by a foreign language background, or is just experiencing difficulty because of that background; or whether a child who may possibly have an as-yet-undisclosed neurological disorder or specific learning disability should be placed in a program for children with emotional difficulties are the kinds of differences that may result in mutually exclusive sets of expectations for planning or considering programming options. These differences often may best be resolved by another interdisciplinary study by a second team. The team, of course, need not bind itself to abide by the findings of a second assessment; but if there is good communication with the staff of the outside agency, the second team's findings may be very valuable and its recommendations readily accepted.

The use of independent assessment is also advisable, as has been noted previously in Chapter III, when there are disagreements between the school staff and the parents' own consultant. However, it is often advisable, when attempting to resolve differences between the staff's and the guest specialist's impressions, first to make use of the guest consultant's skills. If, for example, a private educational psychologist has assessed a child's needs at the parents' request, it may be valuable to obtain, with the parents' permission, the actual test data, protocols, or records of the child's responses for comparison to and inclusion with the staff's findings. If parents give permission to communicate with the consultant, it may be possible to resolve any further differences by making an ally of the guest specialist in order to arrive at the most appropriate program for the child. Unless there is a hidden agenda, such as the parents' use of a private expert to pressure for a program they anticipate would be unacceptable to the school staff (in which case they are likely to block open communications with the specialist), the private consultant will probably welcome cooperation from the school to arrive at a mutually acceptable plan for the child. It is always advisable to respect and to try to work with the parents' expert consultants rather than to try to fend them off.

PROBLEMS STEMMING FROM OVERLAPPING ROLES

Despite all administrative efforts to clarify staff members' roles and functions, and despite a table of organization which specifies responsibilities and lines of authority, it is in the nature of the work of special educators that their similar skills and work methods will create overlap in functions which sometimes may become a source of conflict. Many speech-and-language-development clinicians, for example, are now trained to use some of the same assessment devices formerly considered the private domain of school psychologists, e.g., the Illinois Test of Psycho-Linguistic Abilities and the Peabody Picture Vocabulary Test. Social workers, counselors, and clinically trained school psychologists all may possess interviewing and counselling skills. Special education teachers are now trained in the administration of batteries such as the Wide Range Achievement Test and the Woodcock-Johnson Diagnostic Inventory, which formerly were administered only by reading specialists and school psychologists. Therefore, no job description is likely to clarify perfectly where one specialist's job begins and another one's job leaves off.

Some school districts make arbitrary assignments: psychologists do testing and do not confer with parents, with the latter a function delegated only to counselors or social workers. Such an arbitrary division of labor sometimes may appear to work smoothly, but it tends to create resentment and morale problems when the people in the various roles are well-rounded in their training and object to artificial job limits because they feel perfectly capable of performing broader functions.

A totally different approach is recommended. Staff members' credentials should be viewed as establishing primary areas of responsibility, but within each team formal credentials should be considered *secondary* to personal strengths and skills. For example, a speech clinician who can use screening measures for cognitive ability effectively should be encouraged not only to do the IQ screening of children referred primarily for speech or communication disorders but also to do screening of other groups of children (pre-kindergarten screening, for example) instead of reserving that task only for the psychologist. Similarly, the caseload of parents who need follow up or ongoing counselling may be split among psychologists, social workers, counselors, and administrators who have had counselling training. Among team members, job assignments may thus be distributed according to individual skills rather than on the basis of title, or according to the extent of caseload rather than on the basis of formal credentials. Then, when conflicts arise over who should perform a function, the issue may be decided on the basis of who has the time and the necessary skills rather than who has the correct title. Each staff member could then have designated caseloads; the minutes of team meetings should specify the delegation of assignments for later reference.

Finally, the implications for inservice staff training are evident. Staff members should be trained to work together as a group of professionals with individual, overlapping strengths that need to be capitalized upon and not ignored because of a lack of formal credentials. The superordinate goal is to provide the best combination of services for a child.

STAFF MEMBER INCOMPETENCE
OR INADEQUATE PERFORMANCE

Perhaps the team's greatest internal difficulty is the need to contend with staff members who have shown marked personality change, who have not kept up with current skills, or who have never possessed appropriate competence for their current role function. Tenure laws may create certain of these difficulties, and changes in role assignments sometimes create problems. For example, a teacher may have taken enough additional schooling to become certified as a specialist late in his or her career, sometimes because he or she has become bored with teaching. Possession of proper credentials may not really assure a high level of competence, but, according to certification laws, that person is unlikely to be displaced without evidence of gross incompetence.

Conversely, sometimes a person may have become certified in a specialty many years earlier but never really worked in the field. Reduction-in-force, sometimes called "riffing," may suddenly push someone into a speciality area on the basis of "paper" credentials when the individual is really not able to function at a high level of expertise. Tragically, the riffing process may sometimes result in the displacement of a highly skilled and experienced specialist by a person who possesses a much lower level of skill, and less (or no) experience in the speciality, but greater seniority in the district.

Finally, some staff members close to retirement may begin to "coast"—to ride out the last few years.

All of these situations can create circumstances where effective service to children is jeopardized. For the sake of the children, these situations must be resolved, case by case.

In some instances it may be possible to limit such a staff member's functioning to small groups of those kinds of children with whom he or she still can work effectively. Sometimes reassignment to a more compatible team or to a special project are possibilities. Occasionally, concentrated inservice training or special course work may enable a staff member to make up certain skill deficiencies, such as improving educational-diagnostic testing. However, often none of these solutions will work, and something further must be done about a difficult situation.

With the cooperation of the local teacher association, some school districts have legally worked through a competency-review procedure. Such procedures require the filing of documented complaints about the staff member and prescribed suggestions for improvement with specified means of progress review.

Also, in the interest of fairness to the individual, meetings to review professional improvement must be elaborately documented. Unfortunately, direct straightforward confrontation and counselling may be discouraged when legalistic procedures are undertaken. Yet this should be an option always available for special education administrators to use with their staffs.

The annual staff evaluations of performance or professional growth required routinely in many systems may be the best vehicle for direct confrontation. In addition, inservice training programs should be developed to establish the acceptability of regular self-evaluations by team members and to encourage group members to share reactions to one another, and to help each other actively with professional development.

CONFLICT WITHIN THE TEAM:
MEMBERS VERSUS LEADERS

Those possessing the leadership characteristics described in Chapter IV may not often need to contend with intrateam revolt. The sensitivity, awareness, knowledge, and other skills of such leaders provide the best assurance that little more than occasional disagreements will arise. But disagreements do arise, and they are usually not a function of anyone's inadequacy or incompetence. They may occur because of differing philosophies, differing views on how to use certain staff, or differences in personal style.

Team styles may vary greatly. For example, one team may generally be run in an orderly, businesslike fashion, except for what are perceived as the humorous but distracting antics of one team member. Another may basically reflect the team leader's "cavalier" attitude about many matters, especially formal procedures, except for one or more team members who want things taken "more seriously." Such stylistic differences are probably best met by simply acknowledging their existence. If anything, such differing styles probably work as checks and balances to one another.

With respect to the more discordant, inherently more disruptive issues, more direct confrontation may be necessary. For example, certain members of the team may regularly tend toward recommending placements in special education classes or programs fairly quickly, rather than following the slower, more gradual withdrawal process consistent with "least restrictive environment" policies. They may argue, with some justification, that the student is likely to experience increasing frustration until his or her school environment is totally changed. This occurs most often when working with secondary-level students with social-emotional handicaps, or when parents easily accede to a recommendation for out-placement. This kind of situation may also be further complicated by the team leader's concern over budgetary constraints—a factor which, in itself, can exacerbate intrateam conflict over legitimate child-oriented versus budget-oriented approaches.

The best strategy for dealing with such sources of conflict is to openly address them. Whatever the conflict which may lead to intrateam squabbling—whether it is a potential disagreement (on the basis of budget problems or program issues) over the advisability of placing a student out or a divergence in professional opinion based upon background or training differences—the team format should enable open reference to those differences. For example, a team leader should be able to say:

"I have a problem with what you're suggesting. It may be that Theresa *is* likely to keep on having trouble with her current schoolmates even though we move her into a 'transition' class in the same school, but I think we've got to give her a shot at that class before we send her out. Once she's placed out, the road back is tougher. Why are you pushing her so fast for placement-out? I know you usually don't like to delay what you think is inevitable, but what is the urgency with Theresa?"

or

"When I wear my administrator's hat, I'm dead set against placing anyone out. You all know that. Our budget is tight and each child we place out makes it less possible to do other things for other kids. So convince me— if you can—why do we need to move so quickly with Sandy?"

or

(To the school social worker) "You know every time I say something about behavioral management, I figure you're going to jump all over me. I also know you're usually opposed to reinforcement schedules and the like, but don't you think we ought to try that kind of an approach with Martin?"

The more that potentially conflictive issues are faced openly, the more the team may be able to confront one another directly and constructively. The more those issues remain hidden or are allowed subtly to influence the team's deliberations, the less the team is likely to be able to serve the students' best interests. It is entirely up to the team leader to initiate and maintain a receptive attitude that will permit open confrontations of this kind. And, to reemphasize an important point, one of the most critical attributes required of team leaders is the ability to listen. They must be able to listen to what is *not* being said as well as to what is, and to listen for the genuine concerns expressed by staff members who have professional differences of opinion—and then be able to reflect those differences, sometimes even before they are stated.

A social worker–administrator from a large urban school system put it this way. "Whatever the conflict situation, the most effective, problem-solving administrators seem to be the ones who convey the impression that they are willing to listen, and *do listen* to what their staff has to say."

Chapter III covered some methods of improving communications among staff members. The discussion emphasized the importance of handling problems away from actual team meetings rather than during meetings, because of the need to keep discussions and planning on target. If the team's leaders have, in fact, followed up on staff members' feelings of being overlooked, or of not being fully appreciated for their contributions, then it should not be too difficult to make appropriate reference to those concerns in subsequent team meetings. A team leader might say something like the following.

> "Last time we met, I don't think we gave Susan [the teacher] enough chance to describe what she has seen working with Billy. Why don't we start with her report this time—particularly to see what kinds of progress he's made during the past few months."

or

> "Since we last met, Joanne [the school psychologist] and I have had a chance to discuss her feeling that we really ought to get a neurological examination for Connie. I still don't agree on the need for one, but perhaps this is a good time to hear her out on what she thinks would be gained by a neurological, and then we can let the team decide."

or

> "Joe Perkins [the school guidance counselor] and I still don't see eye-to-eye on whether or not we ought to be looking for a suitable outside placement for Marty. I think we know where we stand on the whole idea of going out too quickly or prematurely, but I also think Joe may have some new information for us to consider."

An attitude of receptiveness to differing and potentially conflictive feelings or ideas has to be nurtured. Therefore, in order to convey genuine listening, which underlies receptivity, it is sometimes necessary to create the opportunity to reinforce the feeling on the part of the staff that they have been heard.

FURTHER COMMENTS ON THE ROLE OF THE CASE MANAGER OR TEAM CONTACT PERSON

Many extraordinary or unusual problem situations may best be handled by delegating certain responsibilities to the case manager or contact person. In Chapters III and IV it was noted that that person might serve as the team's spokesperson for a child—for ongoing coordination of the child's program, for follow-up contact with the child's parents, and for keeping the rest of the team aware of the child's progress on a more frequent basis than would have otherwise been possible.

In school districts where the case-manager concept is employed, case assignments are often made during the initial team meeting for IEP development, and the case manager may be written into the IEP as the child's program coordinator. Then, in addition to the role functions noted above, the case manager may act as the liaison among the staff who work directly with the child, helping bring out questions and concerns expressed by different staff members about the child's program, and enabling the team's leaders to be aware of any developing critical issues before they become serious problems. In some instances, the case manager may provide the team coordinator or chairperson with needed information or "warning" cues, so that one or the other of them can act quickly to avert a potential problem. Particularly when a regular classroom teacher has a complaint or question about a child's special education program, intervention of the case manager may bring appropriate action from the building principal before the complaint has festered.

At other times, the case manager may be able to handle the situation directly (depending upon the leader's confidence in the case manager and the amount of latitude permitted). How nice it is to hear from a case manager the following:

> "Doris [classroom teacher] was annoyed that Margie would have to miss some additional homeroom time during the next two weeks because Pete [the special education resource teacher] is making up for the session Margie lost while she did the sixth-grade screening, but I think I straightened it all out. Doris just needed to know that it wasn't likely to happen again until the spring—she seemed satisfied by what I said, but you know her, she was getting ready to raise the roof about kids missing time from homeroom before I reassured her."

For secondary-level students, the case manager system is almost a requirement. The role is frequently assigned to a guidance counselor who has close ties with special education staff, or to a special education supervisor, or to any of the special education staff whose schedules permit them to maintain contact with all of the subject teachers with whom a special education student comes into contact. Without such coordination by a staff member who knows everyone who may need information about, or suggestions on handling or responding to a particular student, the youngster might easily run into a difficult situation, aggravated by a teacher's lack of awareness of his or her special needs or problems. The case manager, therefore, can help prevent, if not entirely avoid, comments like the following:

> "If only I'd known about Jack's reading problem, I would have had him

give his report orally. No wonder he got so flustered when I insisted he read some of his material to the rest of the class."

or

"I chewed him out yesterday for not wanting to try the parallel bars. How was I supposed to know he's got some kind of a perceptual problem? I don't see where he should get special treatment anyway, but maybe I wouldn't have yelled at him in front of everyone."

or

"I don't care if he's spent six months in an institution! In my class, he's got to do his work and get it in on time, or he's had it!"

Obviously, even the best and most fleet-footed case managers can't cover the whole gamut of possible student contacts to ease the way constantly, or prevent all forms of frustration to which special education students may be subject. But at all school levels, the case manager's on-the-line, daily contact with most others who teach their students can be a tremendous value.

SUMMARY

This chapter has dealt with unusual problems that a team may have to face, including those which are parent-related and those which are staff-related. Among the principles for dealing with any or all of the problems that can occur, the following are the most important to eventual successful resolution:

1. The team leader should acknowledge the problem and deal with it directly whenever possible.
2. Outside consultation should be used advantageously, whether to satisfy parents' concerns or to resolve differences among staff.
3. A serious problem that is extraneous to the child should not be permitted to become the focus of a team meeting. A meeting should be terminated judiciously in the face of unresolvable conflict and reconvened when the issue has been otherwise reconciled.
4. Parents should be encouraged to have friends or other third parties attend the meeting with them and assist them whenever necessary.
5. The team should be sensitive to the legitimate concerns of parents, even when they arise unexpectedly or are expressed in a hostile manner.

6. The team leader should be willing to face—and deal with—problems that the team members themselves have created, due to personality clashes, real professional disagreements, or even professional incompetence.
7. The best interest of the child should always be the focus of the session and the common ground upon which disputants can meet.

7

Parents' Rights

INTRODUCTION

For handicapped children and their parents, there seems little doubt that PL 94-142, the federal Education for All Handicapped Children Act, which was signed into law on 23 November 1975, had a tremendous impact on the provision of special education services nationwide. The prohibition of discrimination against the handicapped, embodied in Section 504 of PL 93-112, the federal Rehabilitation Act of 1973, assured the rights of handicapped children and their parents to due process and procedural safeguards in educational programs. Section 504 denied federal assistance to school districts which did not comply with the federal special education mandates promulgated under PL 94-142 and its legislative prototype PL 93-380, the Education Amendment Law of 1974.

At the end of the 1970s, and specifically for fiscal years 1978 and 1979, the "Second Annual Report to Congress on the Implementation of Public Law 94-142" reflected significant gains made and some problems still to be resolved in the effective implementation of the federal statutes (Ballard 1981). Of the number of handicapped children identified in the public schools, over 94 percent, or more than four million children between the ages of three and twenty-one, were being served. Among other positive reports, it was noted that good progress had been made in school staffs' development of skills for writing individualized educational programs, and that less than one-half of one percent of parents participating in team meetings for the purpose of writing an appropriate IEP refused to give their approval to the plans proposed for their child.

On the negative side, the second annual report noted that despite the fact that increasing numbers of identified handicapped children were being served, and despite extensive inservice efforts initiated by local education agencies to prepare regular educators for work with the handicapped (which included recognition of the need to involve parents more meaningfully in the special education team process), only about one-half of all scheduled IEP meetings were attended by parents, and their roles were generally passive. Consequently, so as to improve the quality of parent participation, a number of regional parent-information centers were being initiated, and further monitoring by the Office of Special Education and Rehabilitative Services (OSERS) was planned to increase implementation of the procedural safeguard provisions of the federal statutes.

The tone of the 1980 annual report to Congress was, therefore, essentially positive. But, in addition to some of the negative factors noted above, there were also rumblings of discontent from several sources about the increasing costs of special education; too much federal control imposed upon local special education administration; too much bureaucratic red tape for accountability purposes; too much time devoted to regulatory procedures, record keeping, due-process involvement or hearings; and too little time left for direct services to handicapped children.

Consequently, the political atmosphere regarding the reduction of federal support for many social services led to close scrutiny of the costs of special education for the handicapped shortly after President Reagan took office in 1981. First, Executive Order 12291, which called for reducing taxpayers' financial burdens by reducing government paperwork and improving accountability, provided the mechanism which enabled the Reagan administration to begin to pursue reduction of federal intervention in local and state affairs. It therefore came as no surprise when Secretary of Education Terrel Bell announced the administration's intent to review several aspects of PL 94-142 as part of the movement toward reform of governmental regulations in all areas. Secretary Bell also stated the administration's expectation that all regulations would be deleted that were not actually required by statute, "particularly when they impose paperwork, fiscal or other burdens" (Klein 1981). Secretary Bell also said, "We must weigh the benefits of increased guidance to states to assure the rights of handicapped children *against the legitimate need for local flexibility in decision making*" (italics ours). But, in an effort to be reassuring, he added, "The administration remains committed to the goal of providing a free, appropriate public education for handicapped children."

At approximately the same time that Secretary Bell and others representing the Reagan administration were advocating the concept of defederalization, legislative proposals for new ways of "block-grant" funding for education (including special education programs) were already being debated in Congress, in line with the proposed spending cuts. Programs for disadvantaged children and funding for handicapped children escaped inclusion in the first round of block-grant statutes, which were passed in 1981 to consolidate several federal school aid programs, but in 1982 and 1983 the administration's efforts to restructure the funding and regulatory supports for programs for special education children were vigorously renewed and pursued. However, equally vigorous expressions of concern by a large majority of members of both houses of Congress asking the president to provide continued support for PL 94-142 programs and services to handicapped children led to the president's assertion that Congress would not be asked to repeal 94-142. The president added, however, that continued aid for the handicapped should, nevertheless, be included in a block grant that consolidated funding for the handicapped with vocational rehabilitation programs. He also indicated that some portions of PL 94-142 might need to be amended.

In addition, Congress was asked by the Justice Department to modify Section 504 of the 1973 Rehabilitation Act so as to discontinue the inclusion of references to the right to a free, appropriate provision of public education for handicapped children within the jurisdiction of civil rights legislation. In fact, a March 1982 issue of *Education of the Handicapped* reported that the Justice Department was proposing to do away with "almost the entire elementary and secondary education section of its Section 504 rules" so as to delimit the special costs of educating the handicapped. All references to a "free appropriate public education" were eliminated from the draft rule-change proposals, and there were also suggested changes that would eliminate the category of emotionally disturbed from Section 504's list of handicaps. The Justice Department official who was quoted regarding the change proposals indicated that the changes were intended to correct the misuse of the law by educators who sought funds for students inappropriately labelled emotionally disturbed as a means for school districts to obtain funds. In addition, a civil rights official was quoted as saying that the real issues of concern were not "whether or not an individual had a right to services. . . . The question is who pays for it" (*Education of the Handicapped* 10 March 1982).

Finally, it was announced that OSERS was moving ahead with proposals to deregulate PL 94-142 in order to make the law more cost-effective. It was also later made clear by OSERS officials that cost-effectiveness in the area of learning disabilities meant eliminating the provision of 94-142 services to slow-learning students who needed remediation but who were either poorly motivated or didn't have a clearly identifiable and significant learning disability. Other issues scrutinized for cost-effectiveness included the matter of the extended school year, the principle of least restrictive environment, and the regulations regarding due process, notice, challenge, and appeal.

By the late fall and winter of 1982, the various administration efforts to defederalize special education regulations appeared to be blunted, following the submission of a series of proposed changes to public hearings. Expressions of great concern and criticism of many aspects of the proposed rule changes—which had been voiced previously by congressional leaders and a number of education-for-the-handicapped advocacy groups—were joined by many thousands of parents who wrote to the Department of Education requesting withdrawal or reconsideration of the plan. The department, in response, announced that it would indeed go back to the drawing board, with parents, educators, and disability-rights advocates, before drafting any further proposals for change in the special education regulations. This move was applauded by many organizations, including the Council for Exceptional Children (CEC), the Children's Defense Fund (CDF), and the National Association of State Directors of Special Education (NASDSE). In addition, Secretary Bell stated that a new notice of proposed rule making (NPRM) would be published at the conclusion of further analytical study, which would cover the entire set of regulations and which would be subject to at least another comment period (*Education of the Handicapped* 3 Nov. 1982). Secretary Bell also indicated that the Department of Education would seriously reconsider those issues that might insure that parents would have adequate and timely information about the evaluation and placement of their children, that parents would be fully involved in educational program decisions, and that children would be evaluated by a multidisciplinary team using appropriate criteria and procedures to identify the children's disabilities (*Education of the Handicapped* 17 Nov. 1982).

Interestingly, and perhaps also in reaction to expressed public sentiment, by mid-December of 1982, in an apparent reversal of its earlier plans, the administration indicated that it had decided to continue civil rights protections specifically for handicapped schoolchildren in its draft revisions of proposed rule changes for Section 504 of the Rehabilitation Act. Any proposed education section changes, it was reported, would at least maintain a "minimum framework" for compliance by the schools (*Education of the Handicapped* 15 Dec. 1982). Fears that Section 504, long considered the most effective support base for PL 94-142, might be gutted by the administration therefore seemed at least temporarily eased.

Nevertheless, the main thrust of the Reagan administration's efforts to modify and defederalize special education regulations still could not be ignored. The specific OSERS proposals presented to Congress in the fall of 1982, though later withdrawn, still reflected the administration's intentions to bring about a gradual shift from federal to state statutory control over the provision of special education services and due-process regulations. This was entirely consistent with the overriding philosophy and intent of the administration, i.e., to cut federal spending and diminish federal control in many areas of government.

The likely or potential future impact upon state agencies and local school districts, therefore, remains clear. Each state, depending upon actual changes in federal funding and the need to comply with any eventual modifications in the federal statutes, will have to reexamine its own special education laws, regulations, and funding structure with an eye toward improving cost-efficiency and increasing local regulatory options or flexibility. Consequently, based upon the pattern of events of the early 1980s, if one were to predict or propose a course of action for the future for those state agencies and local school districts who wish to continue to provide the essential programs and services outlined under PL 94-142 for handicapped children and their parents, the following needs or considerations will probably be among those that require the greatest attention by parents and educators alike.

1. The need for parents' increased involvement in planning for the provision of appropriate special education programs and services for identified handicapped children.
2. The need for specific but flexible due-process mediation and/or optional challenge procedures to assure proper identification of needs; and the provision of appropriate and adequate programs and services without placing undue emphasis on those legalistic procedures that tend to undermine mutual trust.
3. The development of reasonable timelines to assure the prompt delivery of services, and a mutually agreed upon IEP will still probably be required, but accountability-reporting systems, and the distributed responsibility for costs among appropriate state agencies will probably vary somewhat from state to state and will therefore require considerable local attention.
4. A multidisciplinary team decision-making process will probably

continue to be required, but the actual composition of the team may increasingly become a matter of local option and availability of personnel. Safeguards assuring the consideration of potentially different points of view, including parents' views, when identifying needs or planning programs for handicapped children must be preserved.

5. Antidiscriminatory safeguards are likely to be maintained with respect to the identification of handicapped children. Effective, workable local requirements need to be developed and monitored to assure increased *understanding*, as well as informed consent, by non-English-speaking parents or guardians, regarding the provision of special education and services for their children.

6. The actual local provision of programs and services is likely to continue to be monitored by state statutes to assure that the numbers, training, and selection of special education staff are appropriate to the numbers and kinds of handicapped children to be served in each school district. But attention will need to be focused on the quality and appropriateness of preservice and inservice training for staff, and on the quality of programs provided by local districts, particularly with regard to the continued provision of adequate, important "related services."

PROBABLE EFFECTS OF EXPECTED CHANGES IN FEDERAL AND STATE LAWS

Notice, Referral, and Initial Evaluation

Prior to any proposed or eventual change, the federal regulations required state and local school districts to give parents appropriate notice that their child was being referred to a special education team for consideration of need for special services. The notice was required to specify the reasons for the referral in order for the parents or guardians to give their informed consent and to take an active part in the identification process. In addition, the district needed to obtain agreement from parents or guardians to the identification process and to the specific procedures to be used. The district was required to inform parents of their rights to refuse any or all aspects of the evaluation procedure. Furthermore, the school district was required to inform them of: the pupil-records policy, including confidentiality; their right to challenge or appeal the team's decisions; and the role they would be encouraged to play in decision making. These regulations involve large quantities of paperwork, including notice forms; referral forms; permission-for-evaluation forms; a variety of summary statements regarding due-process rights and records policies; and a myriad of other forms, including the written IEP developed by the team for the actual provision of services. If the parents were not actively involved, particularly at decision-making stages in this process, still other documentation was necessary to show that the school district had made a reasonable effort to involve them.

It is not surprising, therefore, that during the early 1980s, proposals to modify some of these often cumbersome and time-consuming notice, accountability, and due-process procedures did not exactly fall upon deaf ears. During the fall of 1981, the commissioner asked for and received considerable advice and comment from state Department of Education officials who, in turn, had compiled their information from meetings with special educators in the field and special education advocacy groups. At approximately the same time, OSERS circulated a briefing paper (U.S. 1981) which included both discussion and alternative proposals to resolve certain issues and concerns about existing regulatory requirements.

The briefing paper actually specified sixteen topics for consideration and summarized the issues of concern as they were brought to the attention of OSERS through public comment, litigation, problems in (state) plan approval, complaints from the field, difficulties in enforcement, paperwork demands, and so forth (U.S. 1981, 12). Additional information was derived from reports by the Council of Chief State School Officers, the Education Advocates Coalition, and the Congressional "Oversight" Hearings, which were a prior series of presentations on PL 94-142 successes and shortcomings to the Congress by OSERS and former Office of Special Education officials.

With regard to the issue of parents' rights in connection with initial notice, referral, and evaluation or identification, the briefing paper underscored the following areas of concern, in which the regulations were more stringent than the statutes governing them:

1. Regulations require specific actions regarding the notification of parents about special education team meetings, including what to do about holding meetings when parents will not or cannot attend, but the statutes governing the regulations do not mandate such actions.
2. Assuring parent advocate participation in the identification process is provided in regulations, but not required by statute.
3. The statutes set no timelines with regard to the period between the

determination of a child's need for special education or related services and the call for an IEP meeting. The regulations state that that period of time shall not exceed thirty days.

The discussion section of the briefing paper pointed up the expressed need for streamlining the team process, diminishing the number of people participating in team decision making, and reducing the burdensome paperwork involved. However, it was also emphasized that according to a study conducted for OSERS, "although there are still complaints about paperwork and time burdens, these factors are perceived as less burdensome over time as benefits are derived by children and staff from the process" (U.S. 1982, 52).

Considering the kinds and sources of most common complaints cited, it seemed probable that of the various options described in the briefing paper for the resolution of these concerns there would be an eventual revocation of those federal regulations that imposed administrative burdens where administrative action was not clearly mandated by statute. Indeed, what still seems likely would be a gradual shift from requiring state and local school-district compliance with federal regulations to establishing guidelines, suggestions, and recommendations which each state might use for the development of its own regulations to protect parents' rights.

The implications of the briefing paper, therefore, seem clear. The federal government is likely to continue to assure that parents have certain rights. It would also most likely want to retain those portions of the regulations that provide clarification for program administration and compliance by states and local school districts. But the government will probably tend to leave the specifics regarding how, when, and where those rights might be safeguarded up to state and local regulation—possibly by gradually dismantling *some* of the uniform regulatory procedures governing notice, referral, evaluation, and the development of IEPs, with which states and local school districts have had to comply. Among the most controversial of Secretary Bell's 1982 regulatory change proposals, for example, was one which would modify the requirement of notice and parental consent prior to evaluation or initial placement.

The prospects for the future, therefore, seem clear regarding this area of parent involvement. Despite some anticipated variation from state to state, and possibly from school district to school district within a state, parents' basic rights to receive notice of and to take part in their child's identification and program planning for special education or related services are likely to continue to be assured. But the specific methods and overall responsibility for implementing appropriate procedures and thereby assuring those rights may very well be shifted to each state's legislature, court decisions, and the continued maintenance of lobbying power by parent advocacy groups. It may, therefore, increasingly be left to the school district's available staff to implement the state's standards for initial parent involvement in the identification and planning stages. Some *musts* would be pursued, but there could be a shift to what a school district *wants* to do rather than is compelled to do, to encourage active parent involvement.

The implications for the special education team regarding evaluation and identification also seem evident. What a team must do for a particular child or the child's parents will vary from locale to locale. What it will wish to do, or *should* do, to assure the most thorough assessment of the child's needs, is increasingly likely to become a function of the team leaders' and members' values and professionalism.

In many states the team will be less constrained to pursue formal notice to parents about the referral of their child, although the evaluation process itself will undoubtedly still require informed consent. Fewer details of the evaluation process may be required to be specified for parent approval. The team, in many states, will also probably find less paperwork required for accountability or recording purposes, and there will undoubtedly be greater flexibility in making arrangements for meetings—including a reduced need to pursue parents who are reluctant or unwilling to attend them. This diminished statutory responsibility, which might tend to reinforce the team's neglect of many parents, leads us to urge even more strenuously the pursuit of active parent involvement. A genuine spirit of parent-school cooperation, which, in turn, can only enhance the long-range benefits to the children we serve, is more likely to occur when parents and the team are brought together because they wish to be than because they are required to be.

Provided the team leadership does not abuse the greater flexibility afforded by statutory modifications by choosing to avoid or ignore difficult or reluctant parents, the team approach may actually be enhanced by the elimination of mandates which tend to reinforce adversary relationships and cumbersome compliance requirements. Parents, in fact, may come to feel that their presence is actually desired rather than merely tolerated, when it is sought by the team rather than imposed by law. What a boon to professionalism! What an opportunity to be able to convey to parents that the team's interest in getting them involved and in obtaining their informed consent for evaluation procedures is genuine, because their participation is considered valuable rather than merely legally required. The opening comments at a pre-evaluation team meeting could even go something like this:

"You are probably aware, Mr. and Mrs. V., that special ed. regulations in this state are somewhat different from those in the state you've come from. But while those differences do permit us to do some things without your written consent, we want to make sure you know what we're about, why we may want to use certain evaluation procedures, and when we will be reviewing our findings with you so that you can help make some decisions about your son."

or

"Mr. J., our state regulations don't necessarily require that we inform you about the specifics of why your daughter was referred to us, and, as you know, we also do not legally need your approval of our evaluation procedures, but we *want* you to know exactly why Sheila was referred and we also want you to know how we expect to evaluate the questions raised by her teachers so that you can help us decide what needs to be done to help her."

What parent can resist such an invitation? A few, probably, who already perceive the school staff as the enemy for one reason or another, but most will welcome the proposed invitation; and their concerns about rights, statutes, and regulations may be appropriately laid to rest. In the final analysis, we remain special educators, primarily interested in helping children, not lawyers vigilant about statutory procedures.

IEP Approval and Implementation

Many of the same conclusions regarding the impact of any eventual statutory changes upon parents' rights and team procedures in connection with notice, referral, and identification apply to this area as well. The 1981 briefing paper outlined specific reported concerns regarding:

1. Unilateral placements of children in private or public schools out of district or out of state by parents who then seek public school financial support.
2. The requirement that personnel necessary to implement programs and services be "qualified" rather than simply "adequately prepared and trained."
3. The requirement that the IEP must be "in effect" for services to be provided or must be implemented within a certain time limit following the IEP meeting even though federal statute does not set such timelines.
4. The requirement that parents have a copy of the IEP provided by the public agency (not in statute).
5. The requirement that parents be notified of IEP meetings and that

specific actions must be taken when parents will not or cannot attend, when the statutes do not require such actions.

The briefing paper also discussed comments from the field regarding the legal status of IEPs and the length, format, and minimal requirements for IEPs. It was noted that interviews with local education agency (LEA) personnel and reviews of IEPs disclosed that the requirements for IEP content and meeting participation that had been imposed upon local educational agencies far exceeded federal regulatory requirements.

Again, the implications of any eventual change may be broad and sweeping. Along with parents' rights to notice and involvement, their rights to have records of decisions or copies of plans determined by the team, to expect certain actions to be taken during prescribed timelines, or to be able to hold school officials accountable for IEP implementation may all gradually revert to state statutory provision, guided rather than mandated by federal law.

The long-range implications for the local special education team, similar to what was discussed regarding initial notice, referral, and evaluation, seem evident. More is likely to be left to local option and professional judgment than will be imposed—as parents have come to expect—as a matter of legal requirement. There will probably also be substantial variation from state to state. Therefore, special educators will have a "mandate" imposed more by conscience or compliance with professional dictates than by federal or state laws. It would seem to follow that when a decision is to be made about a child's program or services, the direct, active involvement of parents in that process will better assure the success of what has been recommended than when the parents or the child's guardian are allowed to be passive bystanders or, worse, are purposefully denied awareness and involvement. Parent involvement does not guarantee that a child will be better prepared for a special program and motivated to take full advantage of services. However, without the parents' active support, sanction, and encouragement, a child may become easily confused, upset, or wary about why he or she has been singled out for special attention. Confronting the child's concerns about being or seeming different and overcoming those concerns as they affect the child's motivation often require a spirit of close home-school cooperation. Change in the regulations should *not* alter that objective!

Procedural Safeguards and Due-Process Challenges

With regard to due process procedures, the briefing report highlighted the following areas of concern:

1. While regulations allowed either the parents or the school district (LEA) to initiate a due-process hearing, the federal statutes did not provide for the LEA to initiate such a hearing.
2. Timelines for the arrangement of hearings and extensions or time exceptions, including considerations about scheduling at the convenience of the parents, were not specified in the statutes.
3. Certain specifics in the regulations regarding state review of LEA decisions—such as requiring the state-appointed hearing officer to examine the entire record and giving the hearing officer the discretion to allow oral or written arguments—were not delineated in the statutes.
4. The regulation permitting exclusion of evidence not offered at least five days before the hearing was not included in the statutes, nor did the statutes specify the regulatory rights of parents to have their child present, or to open the hearing to the public.
5. Paperwork demands were often substantial, since parents could file complaints on practically any matters affecting the education of a handicapped child; and subsequent administrative activities, imposed by due-process procedures, had an impact on program efforts because of the time required for staff to participate.
6. Enforcement difficulties arose when timelines were affected by vacation periods or when a hearing officer's impartiality was questioned.

The briefing paper also discussed the variety of communications received from the field on the topics of relaxation or revocation of timelines, and regarding whether the department should endorse mediation as an alternative to the more formal and burdensome hearings. It was also noted that parents and advocates generally recommended no changes in the regulations, while school officials complained that the regulations went too far beyond the statutes.

Apart from the consideration that existing regulations might simply be amended to eliminate portions not specifically required by statute, the main thrust of the options which would be likely to receive most serious consideration in regulation-change proposals seems to center on three points. First, the qualifications and duties of the "impartial hearing officer" need to be clarified. Second, mediation or other prehearing efforts to curb the number and length of due-process hearings might be sanctioned or given official status. And finally, the issue of more consistent, workable timelines needs to be resolved. Another proposed option for serious consideration is to revoke all burdensome, hard-to-enforce requirements not directly derived from statute and to provide guidelines, or to leave those matters to state and local school-district discretion.

The implications for the future regarding parents' rights in due-process matters again seem clear, particularly as possible federal funding changes add impetus to the need to reduce the administrative burdens and costs of compliance. These matters are very likely to be left increasingly to state and local discretion, and it is also very likely that state governments will in turn encourage more in the way of prehearing or mediation options (sanctioned by the federal government), which have been generally found to be less costly, less time consuming, and frequently more humane. Indeed, if mediation procedures continue to produce the positive results they have shown in states like Connecticut which include mediation as an alternative regulatory procedure, parent advocacy groups, who are likely to protest federal deregulation in this area, may find that the protection of parents' rights has been enhanced rather than diminished. The reason for this effect is that the adversarial relationship between schools and parents, which tends to be reinforced by formal hearing procedures, is discouraged by successful mediation. Mediation is a process of arriving at a compromise which acknowledges the validity of at least some portion of the grievances expressed by both parties, thus leaving both feeling like "winners." On the other hand, a formal hearing, by its adversarial nature, tends generally to create both a winner and a loser.

The probable implications for the special education team are extremely interesting, to say the least. If the potential threat of an adversarial cold war in the courtroom atmosphere of a formal hearing is significantly reduced, the members of the team, including the parents, may very well choose to develop and pursue more mediational mechanisms of their own design when significant disagreements arise. The resort to outside independent evaluations undertaken at school expense is one such mechanism we have recommended in earlier chapters. Other similar mechanisms, which are far less formal than LEA administrative or state-level hearings, can also be developed. These include such concepts as an ombudsman (discussed in Chapter VIII), a parent-assistors program, or a local grievance review panel which includes parent-advocate representatives along with local school personnel not directly involved with the case in question. But whatever mechanism is adopted to resolve major disagreements, the team will be able to signify at the outset, when differences of opinion are still relatively minor, that parents will have greater access to other resources to help resolve potential conflicts without having to escalate matters precipitously.

In no way has it seemed that the availability of locally developed mediation mechanisms diminishes the parents' right later to challenge team decisions or to retract prior agreements. In fact, mediation options will probably be increasingly employed as their effectiveness is more widely recognized. In addition, parents frequently have tended to yield rather than pursue their rights through state-level hearings once they have learned about all the formal procedures involved. They are often dissuaded from pursuing their rights by the possibility of a broader disclosure of their personal affairs and concerns, and they become discouraged by the prospect of legal entanglements and related legal costs. In addition, parents soon learn that formal hearings can result in a delay in any desired program change for their child, or that the child might have to stay in an undesirable transitional "home-bound" situation until matters are finally resolved. Children, caught in the middle in these situations, are in an unfortunate position, and some have in fact been known to blame themselves or otherwise hold themselves accountable for having created "so much fuss." Alternative mediation processes, therefore, may actually make it easier for parents to pursue their rights while avoiding the disadvantages of formal hearings.

PARENTS' RIGHTS VIA FORMAL HEARINGS

Parents will probably, for some time, continue to have the right to a local hearing or an administrative review by the local School Board of their grievances. If they are still aggrieved after the review, they may appeal the local hearing outcome, according to prescribed timelines and with the recommended aid of legal counsel. Such appeals result in a state-appointed hearing officer's review, and ultimately parents can appeal further to the civil court system. Mediation—currently available in some states, and probably eventually to become available in all— is another state-level due-process option which can be mutually requested by parents and school officials and may precede a request for a formal hearing without waiving the eventual right to a hearing.

The pursuit of state-level due-process options (in the absence of prehearing or other available local mediation options) may, however, cost more than money and more than aggravating time delays because of the added possibility of disruptive or upsetting effects on the child. The following illustration may best illustrate what we mean.

Six months after the conclusion of the state-level hearing called by Mr. and Mrs. Z., which had resulted in a decision against them—that the public schools would *not* have to pay for Margo's noneducational boarding expenses incurred during the previous year in a private, residential school— the district special education team was called together to consider the possibility that Margo, now age ten, might return to a special education program within our school district. The formal hearing had been a tense, upsetting experience for the staff as well as for Mr. and Mrs. Z., because considerable testimony had to be given to ascertain whether the primary reason for her placement in a program for emotionally maladjusted children was really the school's inability to provide a suitable special educational program for her, or whether the primary reason was the parents' difficulties in their relationship with her. The testimony at the hearing eventually focused upon Mr. Z.'s history of personal psychiatric difficulties and the fact that he had been in intensive outpatient treatment when Margo was a preschooler. There had also been statements made by school staff that Mrs. Z. might not have been attentive enough to Margo's needs because she seemed preoccupied, perhaps about her husband's emotional instability, and, therefore, unable to do what she had been advised because she was fearful that Margo's difficulties during her first two years in school might upset him too much.

The Z.s had, with the help of legal counsel, vehemently denied that any of their family difficulties had anything to do with Margo's frustrating school experience, but the hearing officer decided that the need for residential placement was primarily due to family issues and not a result of the school's inability to provide an appropriate program of special education. The consideration of Margo's possible return to the public schools, therefore, arose partly because the Z.s could not afford to pay for the youngster's residential noninstructional costs. But it had also been suggested by the private school staff that Margo had made sufficient gains during her year and a half in their program to warrant consideration of return to the public schools.

Unfortunately, it became quickly evident at the teem meeting that the scars remaining from the exchange of testimony at the hearing were not completely healed.

"I don't want Margo assigned to Mrs. Parkinson's class again if we can avoid it," announced Mrs. Z. "I guess I haven't yet been able to get over what she said about me at the hearing."

"It was difficult for all of us to have to say what we thought about the reasons for Margo needing to be in a residential program," I responded, as chairman of the team meeting. "But we're here today to try to determine which program will make the most sense for Margo. Besides, didn't your lawyer prepare you for the kind of testimony you might have to listen to at the hearing?"

"Well, yes, he did warn us that you might see everything as related to my husband's problems, but it hurt me nevertheless to hear Mrs. Parkinson say I didn't care about Margo."

"But she really didn't say anything like that—she said you were probably too worried about Mr. Z. to tell him what was happening about Margo in school."

"That really doesn't matter anymore—I just don't want to have to deal with her as Margo's teacher—and from what she said about me, I would imagine the feeling is mutual."

In the situation described above, it took quite a while to assure Mrs. Z. of Mrs. Parkinson's professionalism and willingness to work again with her and to have Margo back in her special class. Indeed, for some time after Margo returned to class the following fall, the relationship between Mrs. Z. and Mrs. Parkinson remained quite strained despite Mrs. Parkinson's efforts to regain the Z.s confidence. Clearly, they were no longer in the mutually perceived adversarial positions which the hearing had temporarily reinforced, but neither did they ever completely return to the trusting relationship they had once shared—a fact which may not have proved detrimental for Margo once she returned to Mrs. Parkinson's class, but which probably limited Mrs. Parkinson's effectiveness in her communications to the parents about the child's readjustment.

The imposition of due-process courtroom procedures upon parent-school relationships may indeed be an absolute necessity to protect the rights of handicapped children and their parents. But, as this situation may suggest, there are sometimes hidden, insurmountable costs which need to be assessed before formal actions are pursued. The same holds true when school officials wish to pursue a neglect charge or to initiate a due-process procedure themselves, in order to try to force a course of action the child's parents have been unwilling to consider. Such adversary procedures should be considered only as an absolute last recourse. In our experience, rarely does anyone emerge from formal hearings unscathed. And, as seems clearly the case with Mrs. Z., some wounds in personal relationships never completely heal.

There is still another disadvantage for both staff and parents in going to formal hearings, before they are absolutely necessary, to protect a parent's, a child's, or the school's rights. When there is the slightest expectation that a formal hearing may be anticipated, or when the school staff or parents have been contemplating the possibility of an eventual hearing, that cognitive mindset tends to inhibit what might otherwise be a helpful confrontation. For example, we recently interviewed a special-class teacher who confided that he says nothing anymore that might be possibly antagonizing in a team meeting or conference, particularly with the parents of emotionally disturbed students. "If I do," he added, "they might listen and follow through on what we then get down to, but they may also retaliate with a hearing. I don't need hearings! I've got enough aggravation and enough already to keep me busy with these kids!"

Teachers, support personnel, and even school administrators generally have not been trained in special education law, nor, as human-service-oriented professionals, are they particularly comfortable with formal, courtroom-like proceedings. Giving accurate testimony at hearings and struggling with the constraints of crossexamination strategies while trying to make a point are not activities in which school officials excel, or in which they take any particular delight. The huge amounts of time and paperwork consumed by such activities are especially burdensome. Once experienced, such hearings may become easier to prepare for, but they seem no less onerous to the school staff involved. Consequently, the determination to avoid hearings at all costs becomes a potentially self-defeating and inhibiting obstacle to more open and honest confrontation with parents—when, indeed, it may in the long run be extremely helpful for the parents to be confronted. Hopefully, the trend toward increased use of prehearing and other local mediation mechanisms will diminish such unhelpful predispositions. In that connection, again, what may be risked from the parents' point of view by deregulation of federal authority may be gained in closer, more straightforward working relationships with school personnel.

THE ROLE OF PARENT ADVOCACY ORGANIZATIONS

Despite the feeling sometimes expressed by school officials that parent support or advocacy groups may inadvertently encourage parents' hostility toward the schools, there is no question about the important role that local, state, and national parent advocacy groups have played in the past (for example, in supporting the lobbying efforts which originally brought PL 94-142 into existence, and in obtaining the retraction of Secretary Bell's 1982 change proposals). Furthermore, there is little question that such groups will continue to play a major role regarding the extent to which PL 94-142 is or is not defederalized. They will also have a particularly important role in determining how to assure that there will be appropriate local and state follow-up efforts to develop and implement continued due-process safeguards, regulations, and procedures.

As a result of proposed legislative changes, a number of parent support organizations—whose membership had dwindled since the late 1970s, when most states began to comply with federal law—have enjoyed a resurgence of parent interest and involvement. This has occurred since 1981, when the Reagan administration first announced its intent to defederalize education for the handicapped. The administration's initial efforts to reduce budgets and block-grant funds for the handicapped were significantly diminished by the lobbying efforts of the Council for Exceptional Children in conjunction with a number of parent advocacy groups, such as the National Association for Children with Learning Disabilities and its state subsidiaries.

In 1982, the National Council on the Handicapped also urged further legislative-watch and lobbying efforts to block cuts in funding and changes in laws affecting the handicapped. The purpose of this fourteen-member council was to advise the Department of Education on matters pertaining to disabled individuals, including vocational rehabilitation as well as education for the handicapped. Such organizations have also taken as a main purpose the support of continued implementation of Section 504 of the Rehabilitation Act of 1973 to protect the civil rights of the handicapped, and of PL 94-142 to assure the continued provision of a free and appropriate education for handicapped children (*Education of the Handicapped* 24 March 1982). Still other organizations, like the American Council on Rural Special Education (ACRES), were developed to make people more aware of the inequities of special education in geographically isolated rural communities that would result from proposed federal budget cutbacks. And others, such as the American Coalition of Citizens with Disabilities, the Ten State Coalition of State Advisory Councils, and the Children's Defense Fund also reacted strongly to proposals that they felt might weaken the rights of the disabled. Similarly, in January 1982, an organization of parent support and lobbying groups—the Ohio Coalition for the Education of Handicapped Children, initially including parents from Ohio, Indiana, and Illinois—was organized with membership extended to all parents around the nation to coordinate legislative efforts in opposition to moves toward deregulation and budget cuts.

The importance of coordination of opposition to defederalization had become increasingly evident. The parent advocacy groups, the large numbers of legislators supporting education for the handicapped, the increased numbers of school officials who sought some—but not major—legislative change, and the OSERS officials who were involved in proposing change all expressed the wish to continue to safeguard the rights of the handicapped and to support only those changes in federal regulations that might benefit the handicapped. Most of the combined groups' objectives were mutually shared, but there also were apparent differences. The goal of the various coalitions, therefore, clearly became one of pursuing common aims despite their differences, so that conflicting special interests were not allowed to diminish the impact of the concerns shared by all. By mid-December of 1982, the more than 20,000 letters and comments received by the Department of Education on the special education regulations change proposals were ample testimony of the success of such organized efforts.

It is hoped that parent advocacy groups on both the state and national levels will maintain that same perspective as they carve out their future roles. Parent support groups, working together with school officials and legislators who have the welfare of handicapped children at heart, must recognize the need to continue to coordinate their efforts and reconcile their differences if they wish to remain effective. For example, parent advocates who opposed any and all proposals for change in the PL 94-142 federal statutes may have to gradually accept the idea of the need for *some* forms of deregulation as prescribed by OSERS and educators or administrators in the field. Then, parent advocates and support groups will need to pool their efforts to assure appropriate state-level compliance with and implementation of any amended federal statutes. Finally, at local school district levels, the cooperation of parent support groups and school-district special educators will be absolutely necessary to see to it that handicapped children continue to receive the program services they need. Any actions on the part of either special education school officials or parent support groups that tend to antagonize one another's interests will be ruinous —just as the adversarial stance taken by school officials or parents within a special education team tends mostly to hurt the child.

In many places, close cooperative working relationships have developed between parent advocacy groups for children with learning disabilities and/or mentally retarded youngsters, and state-level or local school district special educators. Their spirit of cooperation has evolved, despite some obvious differences regarding special interests, because of their major mutual goals. For example, when school officials meet with representatives of parent advocacy organizations, it soon becomes evident that the advocacy group tends to encourage parents to pursue their existing rights vigorously and even try to extend those rights or interpret them more broadly so that all programs and "full services" continue to be provided at no cost to parents. While they may find it difficult to accept full-cost responsibility in principle, school officials are clearly more interested in obtaining a more equitable, shared interagency cost distribution of responsibilities for programs, or in delimiting the jurisdiction of the public schools regarding what constitutes "appropriate" special education. There is, therefore, much potential for conflict. The events of 1981 and 1982, however, brought the more important and overriding issue of special education survival to the fore. Representatives of local school districts, parent advocacy organizations, and state officials suddenly found their need for one another more compelling than usual.

Therefore, as any form of defederalization progresses, an important dual role for parent advocacy groups like CACLD (Connecticut), MACLD (Missouri), NJACLD (New Jersey), the Iowa and Wyoming Associations for Retarded Citizens, the Illinois Alliance for Exceptional Children and Adults, and many others operating primarily at regional or local school district levels, is likely to appear. Such organizations will continue to serve the purpose of disseminating information and providing opportunities for parents to learn more about how to get the most for their handicapped children from the schools. However, they will also have to resume the active process of joining with local and state school officials, and with other local special-education-oriented organizations, to see to it that state government and local school districts remain responsive to handicapped children's needs.

Parent organizations in several states, including Connecticut and Massachusetts, were able to bring sufficient pressure to develop effective special education statutes at the state level well before federal PL 94-142 was enacted. Special educators, school officials, and state government officials worked closely together with parent groups, resolved their differences, lobbied together, and forged the kinds of beneficial programs that made good sense for handicapped children. The state statutes reportedly served among the models that were used in writing PL 94-142. Consequently, while defederalization has raised justified concern about diminished federal spending for special education and a shift back to state control, it also has reinforced the possibility of reduction of the adversary relationship between schools and parents which was unfortunately nurtured by PL 94-142's due-process emphasis, and a return to the kind of local and state-level cooperation that produced many sound, effective state statutes. This return of cooperation is essential not only for those states which previously enjoyed such cooperation but also for those states in which such cooperation was previously lacking.

ABUSE OR MISUSE
OF SPECIAL EDUCATION REGULATIONS

It is unfortunate but sometimes true that the very laws and regulations that have been sought for the protection of handicapped children's rights may also be employed to the children's disadvantage. Indeed, just as parents sometimes accuse the schools of using certain regulations to delay or otherwise avoid providing needed services for their children, the schools sometimes protest what they perceive as parents hiding behind certain due-process regulations to avoid acknowledging what is needed to help their child. Neither the parents nor the schools are, therefore, immune from the charge that they may undermine the intent of special education requirements and procedures to foster some particular gain which may be of little benefit to—and may actually harm—the child. The parents' or school staff members' motives may not always be clear, and the negative impact of their actions upon the child may be inadvertent. But, apart from the use of regulations for pressuring or strategic purposes—where the intent of helping a child is still the primary motivation—we are aware of a few general ways whereby regulations tend to be used as the means to achieve unhelpful ends. Let us explore them as they apply both to parents and to school officials to see what, if anything, can be done to counter their effects.

Abuse by Schools

School officials or staff, because of time pressures, personal biases, staff shortages, budgetary limitations, or political reasons, may sometimes purposefully minimize or evade certain special-education-related responsibilities. The intent is most certainly not to harm children, nor is there likely to be any serious interest in ignoring the needs of any group of handicapped children. The reasons often given for such actions tend to be expressed more in terms of the feeling that the handicapped child is already getting more attention than "regular" children, or that too much is being spent on children whose potential contributions to society are limited, or that exceptional children are overprotected by the law to the regular child's disadvantage, or that parents are often interested in obtaining all they can get at public school expense regardless of what their child actually needs.

There are many variations on these themes, but they tend to result in two unhelpful courses of action. One is for the school system to keep the general public as uninformed as possible (within the context of the law) about what may be available for handicapped children. The other is to use regulations, procedures, meetings, criteria for eligibility, and the like as delaying tactics or as red tape to discourage parents' pursuit of services their child needs and may be entitled to.

Some of the counter strategies which need to be employed by parents and parent advocacy groups are obvious. State and local implementation or regulations, whether or not the need exists to comply with federal statutes, must be monitored in such a way that the schools are appropriately pressured to make full public disclosure of their special education programs, identification procedures, and available related or support services. The public schools' methods of disclosure or distribution of information must also be clearly identified and routinely checked for effectiveness by parent groups to assure that school plans affecting special education programs or services are adequately communicated to the public.

Regulation misuse by the schools is a bit more complex and, therefore, more difficult to contend with, since it is likely that only certain parents may be affected, on an individual rather than a group basis.

Therefore, patterns of obfuscation and delay may be hard to discern, but if a school system routinely appears to use regulations and procedures for delaying or blocking action regarding the provision of services to needful children, a parent advocate organization can address the issue as a broader matter. Unfortunately, individual parents, with a more personal and justified concern, are at a distinct disadvantage when they feel they are being sidestepped or sidetracked for some reason difficult to identify.

Such parents need to be encouraged to seek appropriate assistance. Parent organizations can and should assist them and should communicate, through their organizational publicity, the availability of such assistance. Again, improved cooperation between schools and parent groups can be realized when school system staff are also active members of the parent advocacy organizations and can assist the parent groups with categorical information about consultant services, availability of resources, knowledge or background information about school procedures, eligibility criteria for different programs, and so forth. In several states, for example, school officials are encouraged to serve on parent group advisory boards or in other governing capacities. The Council for Exceptional Children certainly encourages such parent-professional interaction, particularly in their local and regional chapters.

Another strategy which parents can employ directly, and one which is certainly a disarming tactic when it occurs at a team meeting, is for parents to express concern when confronted with delay or red tape and ask what they can do or whom they can speak to in order to expedite matters for the team. Parents do not generally perceive themselves as the team members who should initiate anything. They therefore are often overlooked as the agents who can affect change regarding a local policy, budgetary problem, or placement matter. In fact, the school staff may consciously choose not to reveal to the parents the inner workings of the system because they have learned to expect resistance or even bigger headaches, rather than assistance. The following example may illustrate this point:

> Toward the end of the school year, the M.s called for a meeting with their special education team—called the Committee on the Handicapped, or COH, in their region—for the purpose of considering an out-of-district regional placement for their daughter, Thea. As the meeting drew to a close, the M.s began expressing their feeling of hopelessness that the school staff's efforts to maintain Thea in a local self-contained class were doomed to further frustration and failure.
>
> The staff at first seemed to agree, but then there were several comments made by the school principal, who was thinking about the system's overexpended tuition budget, about the fact that it was getting close to the end of the school year and that a few recent program changes had not

yet been implemented effectively. The staff began to echo the principal's views, until Mr. M. finally, feeling exasperated, blurted out, "If you really cared about Thea, you would move her now. What's the point in waiting? If we're willing to have her to go the Burbank regional program, why are you all dragging your feet? We visited Burbank, we like it for her, and we're sorry she didn't make it in Mrs. Sunday's class, but we'd hate to see her struggle for another couple of months if she doesn't have to."

"It's not that, Mr. M.," responded the principal, who was acting as team chairman. "It takes time to make all the arrangements to transfer a child to a regional school, and by the time we're done with the arrangements we'd be within three or four weeks of the end òf school. We might as well plan what we have to for next September and try some of the things we said we would with Thea in the two-month period during which we still have her here." The other staff members nodded their heads. They were listening to more than one message, and were not about to fight their principal over a matter of two months—besides, they were not of the opinion that the delay would be particularly harmful for Thea.

Mrs. M. pleaded, "Can't something be done about the time needed for all those arrangements? Couldn't I help you with the transportation? In fact, I would be willing to drive her there in the morning, and we could arrange to have her picked up at the end of the day, so that those arrangements needn't hold us up."

Mr. M. added, "And if the costs are any problem, well—I can't afford much, but I'd be willing to pay part of the tuition for the next two months. I know you are usually short in your budget at this end of the year."

"You make it difficult for us to say no," the principal said, totally disarmed, and perceptibly relieved. "Let me see what I can do, that is— if everyone here agrees with what you're suggesting."

With a shared sense of relief, everyone seemed to breathe more easily, and they quickly found ways to move Thea to the regional program within a week's time. The M.s' open, concerned expression of willingness to do whatever needed to be done overcame the hidden source of the team's resistance; and their willingness to sacrifice their own time and money won the day. Too frequently, due-process and mediation procedures are required to encourage such cooperation, and then sometimes nothing is resolved until a formal hearing decides the issue for both sides—while the child waits! The local (rather than state-level) mediation or "ombudsman" option we discussed earlier might be called effectively into play in similar situations, when parents are not as immediately willing as the M.s were to volunteer whatever they can.

Abuse by Parents

The often-heard complaint about parents hiding behind regulations to avoid acknowledging their own responsibility regarding their child's problem or difficulties has some validity, particularly with respect to the defensive parents of emotionally and socially maladjusted children. Such parents are extremely difficult to work with because their resistance, defensiveness, or uncooperative attitude usually arises because they feel threatened with potentially overwhelming guilt.

Such feelings must be eased before they can work cooperatively *with anyone.* If the team tries to impose cooperation on such parents, the parents may perceive the team as antagonists and respond in kind. Any trust which has previously been developed tends to become strained and often lost under such circumstances. Consequently, it is not surprising when parents back off and fight the team tooth and nail rather than admit any implied personal failure or incompetency as parents. When such circumstances arise, both sides tend to become entrenched in their positions as points of difference become further intensified. In the absence, therefore, of some form of arbitration to block the further escalation of those differences, or when it is not possible for significant intervention to help ease the parents' concerns, it is not uncommon for such parents to withdraw entirely or to pursue unilateral legal action.

It takes considerable patience, professional sensitivity, and endurance to avoid perpetuating this adversarial state of affairs, as the following illustration suggests.

> The D.s, parents of an extremely unassertive, often fantasy-preoccupied and withdrawn ten-year-old child, had had many conferences with the school psychologist over a two-year period to try to get at the reasons for their son's poor school performance and reticent behavior. They had noticed and had expressed some concern about his quietness at home as well, but each time outside professional counseling had been suggested to try to remedy matters, the D.s had balked at the idea for one reason or another—frequently citing financial difficulties as their main reason for not seeking help. They also said that they were sure that Andy would eventually "grow out of it," because Mr. D. remembered having had similar problems when he was a child.
>
> Andy was, however, showing no signs of outgrowing his difficulties and was recommended for retention in fourth grade because he was falling so far behind everyone else. After the third in a series of evaluations by the staff, which tended once again to underscore the child's apparent unhappiness, and following a pre-team conference with the psychologist to review the findings in detail, the parents came to the annual team meeting in June to review everyone's recommendations, consider the retention issue, and develop a plan for the next school year. As the meeting progressed, the teachers' reports and other specialists' observations, along with the psychologist's test results, seemed to be building toward the undeniable impression that Andy was in deep trouble, becoming increasingly frustrated about his own sense of failure, and beginning to withdraw even more into silly, inappropriate behavior. Mrs. D. stared down at the floor, and Mr. D. seemed to react to each report's conclusion. Unfortunately, at one point, someone commented that it was

too bad that the D.s hadn't followed the suggestion made some time ago that they seek outside professional help.

Mr. D. slammed his fist on the conference table. "There you go again," he exploded, "like it's all our fault—that we're some kind of monstrous parents who need to get our heads screwed on straight by some shrink who doesn't know us from Adam! Forget it! I don't have the money to fork over to some guy who's going to meddle in our personal affairs just to get all of you off the hook. I've had it."

The room grew quiet. Mrs. D. still stared down at the floor.

Mr. D. regained his composure, sat back, and looked around the room, coldly eyeing each person as if he or she were a distant cannon. After what seemed like an endless silence, he continued, "I've come to the sad conclusion that none of you really know or understand Andy— that you're doing a number on us, blaming us for his problems in school, making a big deal out of his being a quiet kid, and now you want to keep him back—well, we think you're all wet!"

"Mr. D.," the psychologist began to protest, "no one is blaming you and your wife for Andy's problems. But he seems unhappy—doesn't he to you? We're only trying to help—" He never finished. Mr. D. was standing, and as he reached to help his wife up, he angrily interrupted, "We neither need nor want your help. We have our legal rights in all this and I'm going to insist upon them. We will call you. Do not call us!" he yelled back as they walked stiffly out of the conference room.

The situation with the D.s did not develop into a formal due-process hearing, as the remaining team members might have predicted when the D.s walked out. The D.s rescinded permission for further testing, insisted that Andy be promoted to fifth grade, refused to have anything further to do with an IEP for the following year, and practically hung up on any-one who tried to call them. The team's leaders fortunately decided not to press matters further until the middle of the next school year, when the D.s themselves called the psychologist to confer again about Andy. Andy had not done too badly at the beginning of the school year. However, after the review of the previous year's work had been concluded early in the fall, he did "absolutely nothing."

The psychologist met with the D.s alone in a meeting called at their request. He listened, offering no comment or suggestions, while Mr. and Mrs. D. described, with evident pain, that they had come round to our conclusion that Andy was indeed unhappy and in need of outside help. Mr. D. apologized for his angry outbursts at the June meeting. He added that he had even thought of asking for a hearing with our school board to complain about our efforts to push them into psychiatric treatment, but that he had finally calmed down and decided to see what the fall would bring. He said he still didn't feel that he and his wife were "such rotten parents," but that they agreed that something had to be done.

It never became entirely clear why the D.s had been so resistive to the recommendation for outside professional help. The team learned little more than the fact that it had been extremely difficult for Mr. D. to accept the need for outside help and that he remained somewhat aloof and barely cooperative throughout the course of Andy's treatment. But Andy improved sufficiently in his school work to get by until his junior-high years, when the family moved away and contact with the family was lost.

The D.s did not actually pursue the legal recourse they implicitly threatened when they walked out of the team meeting. Instead, after briefly contemplating a board of education hearing to express their annoyance over the way they felt the team had treated them, they chose to withdraw their child from his program of special education services, rescinded permission for further evaluation, rejected the IEP, and, in essence, pulled back behind their rights to refuse further special educational consideration—until it was clear to them some months later that they were only hurting their child and could no longer deny the validity of the team's expressed concerns.

Another set of parents might have persisted in pursuing their due-process rights if they had insisted on a course of action for their child other than the one recommended by the team. Such maneuvering to force a point of view against team advice is not at all uncommon and serves to bolster the parents' denial of what really needs to be done—especially when their lawyer is brought in to represent their position. In such circumstances, the team members feel increasingly helpless because of the adversarial-reinforcing quality of due-process procedures, which make it harder and harder for people to talk with one another as soon as the mediation stage has passed.

With the D.s, their own subsequent experience with their son's unhappiness led them to back away from denial and from the use of their rights to block further assistance. When the team is patient and can afford to wait a while, provided that the child's status doesn't deteriorate too much in the interim, parents like the D.s sometimes do come around to accept what they couldn't contend with earlier. If, however, such parents more aggressively pursue legal due-process action, the only hope is that they can be persuaded to consider state-level mediation or some other, more local form of arbitration, which in some states has proven remarkably effective. In Connecticut, for example, where state-level mediators are carefully selected and trained to counsel both sides toward some form of compromise solution, an agreement-success rate as high as 77 percent has been realized. Statistics like those certainly support and reinforce this direction for the future, possibly with even greater utilization of local resources.

Another form of parental misuse or abuse of regulations, though usually less serious in terms of the direct effects upon children, is even more difficult to contend with than the use of regulations and due-process rights to help deny their own responsibilities. We refer to the parents who have felt angry, annoyed, or hurt over a long period of time. They are often aggrieved over something concerning their child that may have happened years earlier and that they have never for-gotten. Then, in connection with a current incident involving their child, they reopen the past, even though the current staff may have had little, if anything, to do with it. In such circumstances, it becomes quickly evident that little can be done about the present situation until the old conflicts have been somehow resolved. And, when that cannot be readily accomplished, pleas to stick to the present issue may never be adequately addressed. Such parents often respond initially more to the point of their old grievances than to what is current—as is the case with Mrs. S.

"I want to see and receive copies of all of Debbie's records," Mrs. S. announced at the mini-team meeting called to discuss Debbie's re-referral for acting-out, clowning antics. Debbie, now an eighth-grade student at our junior high school, had frequently been disciplined for rude, disruptive behavior, and it was obvious to the school administration that the usual disciplinary efforts were no longer effective. Debbie had also had a history, in the early primary grades, of a specific learning disability, which she seemed to have overcome successfully with supplementary tutoring assistance. A search of her records showed no special educational involvement beyond third grade.

"I insist that you give me a copy of all the notes and reports you have in Debbie's files before we go any further," continued Mrs. S. "I knew this would happen!"

The school social worker, who had made the initial contact with Mrs. S. about Debbie, was startled by the mother's anger. She had known only that Debbie had had special help once before, but nothing in the records explained Mrs. S.'s insistence upon reviewing them. "Why," she asked, "do Debbie's records seem to mean so much to you?"

"I want to see what they said about her, *and about us.*" Mrs. S. was obviously annoyed by the social worker's question. "Isn't it all in there?" she asked.

"Isn't what in there?" asked the social worker innocently.

"I can't believe you don't know what was said about me when Debbie was in third grade—that I was a neglectful or negligent mother, or something like that—I'm sure it's all in there and I want to see what was said!" Mrs. S. demanded.

Recognizing the need to satisfy Mrs. S.'s insistence on reviewing the records before anything else could begin to happen, the social worker did not persist long in trying to talk the parent out of her urgent demand. She concluded the mini-team meeting temporarily, rescheduled it for the following week, and obtained the records for the purpose of reviewing them with Mrs. S. right then and there.

Mrs. S. picked out a summary report on a conference held in third grade by the speech clinician who had been working with Debbie on verbal expressive problems and listening skills. The conference report made no reference to negligence, but mentioned only that it had been difficult to arrange a follow-up session because Mrs. S. claimed that she was too busy to come in and had broken several previously arranged appointments.

Mrs. S. waved the conference report under the social worker's gaze. "Here it is—she made me sound like I was neglecting Debbie. When I spoke to her over the phone, she was absolutely insulting. She said if I cared at all about Debbie I would have been able to come in for my appointment—she had no right to say that to me."

The social worker briefly explored with Mrs. S. what the reasons were for the old series of missed appointments. She wisely did not challenge Mrs. S.'s account or try to defend the speech clinician, but indicated that she would have the conference report modified to eliminate the references to the missed appointments since such information was no longer relevant. In fact, later that same day, she sent a copy of the modified report to Mrs. S. for her approval. The following week, the postponed conference on Debbie's current difficulties was concluded with a considerably more cooperative Mrs. S. in attendance. The day had been saved by the social worker's alert response to Mrs. S.'s needs, and by her remedial action regarding the old, unresolved wound which more current concerns had reopened.

The team was fortunate in this case that the social worker quickly resolved the mother's grievance before trying to reengage her cooperation. In other experiences, we were not so fortunate; and in a few, the need for immediate action in a current problem situation could not be addressed effectively because an old wound could not be healed. In one in particular, the parents' grievances ultimately took months of records-challenge procedures and hearings because of the parents intense need to "set the records straight" and purge them of incriminating intimations.

These are a few examples of how specific legal rights, official procedures, due-process regulations, and other legislative mechanisms are sometimes misused or abused by both schools and parents, despite the intent of those legalisms to safeguard or protect children. Unfortunately, statutory procedures requiring strict compliance can usually also readily be misapplied to satisfy some other purpose. Again, the only recourse we have in overcoming such misadventures is to appeal to our superordinate goal—the shared concern all members of the team, including the parents, have for the child in question. In the final analysis, the real issue of parents' rights derives from safeguarding the rights of their children. The school's rights, similarly, derive from the need to provide adequately for what will most help children learn. We all sometimes need simply to remind one another of those basic overriding objectives when laws, statutes, regulations, and procedures tend to get in our way.

SUMMARY

This chapter has covered the present and future implications of, and reactions to, the federal laws and regulations that mandate the education of the handicapped, specify parents' rights, and provide due process to insure those rights. The following seems likely:

1. Parents will continue to be involved in decision making by virtue of legal requirements to include them.
2. There is a need to review the burdensome, legalistic bureaucratic procedures which undermine trust between schools and parents.
3. Specific methods and overall responsibility for implementing appropriate procedures are likely to be shifted to state legislatures, courts, and parent lobbying groups, with the possible emergence of greater flexibility in applying special education laws.

Any long-range changes will require greater efforts on the part of professionals to implement the *spirit* of the special education laws. The utilization of prehearing mediation is likely to increase, a development we regard as less costly, less time consuming, and ultimately more likely to serve children's needs than the pursuit of the more legalistic formal hearing procedures. Mediation tends to diminish the adversarial nature of relations between schools and families, whereas adversarial relations may be encouraged by due-process regulations. Mediation is the process of arriving at a compromise in which both sides concur, while the outcome of a hearing results in a "winner" and a "loser." Clearly, then, mediation is preferable.

While we concede that due-process courtroom procedures may be inevitable under certain circumstances where all efforts toward compromise fail (or in instances where there is neglect on the part of the parents), we advocate that school personnel exhaust all efforts to avoid such procedures. We believe that rarely does the school/family relationship emerge unscathed. Moreover, the process itself may seriously delay implementation of needed programs for children.

Parent advocate groups nationwide have played an important role in bringing about and supporting education for handicapped children and will undoubtedly continue to do so. School personnel and aroused parents can be powerful allies in assuring that the needs of handicapped children continue to be well served and that special education regulations are not misused or abused either by parents or school systems.

8

Training School Staff for Working in Teams

INTRODUCTION

Chapters III and IV covered some of the theoretical and practical issues that special education teams must handle in order to function more efficiently and effectively. They cited studies by Pfeiffer (1980) and Yoshida et al. (1978) reporting some of the problems often confronting multidisciplinary teams. Our discussion of those studies dealt with what we perceived as the source of some of those problems and some methods for resolving them, based upon communications and leadership principles derived from the literature on group dynamics. Our purpose in this chapter is to consider some of the implications of those studies and others for graduate school professional preparation and for on-the-job school system training programs designed for personnel who participate on special education teams.

To begin with, the research literature suggests that there are some important differences between hypothetical expectations about the sources of problems and the specific concerns reported by those actually working on teams. For example, Pfeiffer (1981), after having directly questioned school personnel representing forty multidisciplinary teams in four urban, northeastern school systems, noted some striking differences between what had been expected *might* be the "recurring problems" faced by intraprofessional teams, and the actual comments made by urban school personnel. The "insiders," reported Pfeiffer, were much less concerned than expected over such issues as

179

lack of clarity in role definition, insufficient team-member influence over team decisions, scarcity of inservice training opportunities, inappropriateness of referrals made to teams, or rigidity of team procedures. They did express some expected concerns over procedural matters, e.g., knowledge of due-process or legal procedures and, as anticipated, they expressed concern about the lack of involvement of parents and regular classroom teachers and the need for more organized sharing of diagnostic information.

But, clearly, the issues that most concerned those who were polled were practical issues. They were troubled over their difficulty in determining whether a problem is of sufficient magnitude as to require special education. For example, how, diagnostically, can it be determined, they wondered, whether a particular youngster is actually "learning disabled," or "merely" a slow learner? These categories are not clearcut, and they involve the need to discover *why* a child's learning is not progressing at an acceptable pace. Has the child been turned off motivationally? Is the child hampered by a deprived economic or cultural background? Does the child have a marginal perceptual handicap? Is a child easily distractible, and hence not learning, because of preoccupation with emotional problems or because of a slight neurological dysfunction?

In addition to their diagnostic difficulties, team members also cited as problems the fact that there were fiscal restraints on certain program options and the general lack of sufficient program options to choose among. Many also complained about the lack of time and opportunity for following up the team's program or placement decisions.

The discrepancy between the anticipated problems and the actual problems reported by team members has implications for training of staff, both at the graduate-school and inservice level. Both types of training, to be effective, most certainly need to address the problems that practitioners in the field consider to be the most pressing difficulties. However, it is also important to address the issues raised by theoreticians in the field and to help the practitioners on the line to recognize that some of these issues may be causing, or exacerbating, the problems that concern them most directly and acutely.

Pfeiffer's (1981) findings led him to suggest the use of a more consistent and systematic Assessment Intervention Follow-Through (AIF) procedure to aid in training team members and to improve the team's efficiency. Such an AIF procedure, Pfeiffer felt, would enable team members to focus on diagnostic decisions, increase each member's sense of involvement in decision making, increase participation by parents and "regular" educators, and encourage follow up of children's progress. The provision of such a system, Pfeiffer asserted, would offset the tendency of the team to become preoccupied with the labeling of children, and might free some of the members from unnecessary involvement in certain routine procedures.

Although Pfeiffer did not specify the elements of the AIF, he earlier (1980) had recommended the establishment of "a clear and formalized structure—for all aspects of the team's functioning," including procedures for the review of referrals; the collection, rating, and analysis of data; the recording of team meetings; adherence to due-process requirements and communications with non-team persons and agencies. The purpose of the system, clearly, was to structure the team's functioning and its division of responsibilities so as to integrate assessment and remediation.

It seems apparent to us that the utilization of a case manager, as we have previously discussed, or a team contact person (whom Pfeiffer also suggests as a parent advocate) would clearly be helpful in the development of an effective AIF system. We will also elaborate upon training strategies designed to increase the kind of team-member participation suggested by Pfeiffer, but first let us consider at least one other systems approach to viewing and resolving the problems confronting special education teams.

Butler and Maher (1981) describe a "family-systems" approach to understanding and working more effectively within the "Special Service Team." They particularly direct their recommendations for team conflict resolution to school psychologists, who—according to Yoshida et al. (1978)—generally see themselves as active team participants, most often in team leadership roles. The family-systems model was employed because, according to the authors, the team is somewhat analogous to a family which often meets to make joint decisions. Like a family, the team also has to contend with the existence of role conflicts, ambiguity about role expectations, and within-system stresses (such as the need for compliance with legal requirements versus immediate practical pressures) which sometimes interfere with the most effective response to a child's needs. Butler and Maher also describe team circumstances, again analogous to family crises, where two team members in conflict with each other may "triangulate" or involve another team member in an effort to reduce tension between them. In addition, they describe the sharing of responsibility among team members, as opposed to making some members too dependent while others become "over-functioning." Such a situation is analogous to the family in which a parent assumes too much responsibility for children, thereby increasing the children's dependency, instead of allowing the children to gain a sense of self-assurance through doing more for themselves.

The family-systems approach places a great deal of emphasis upon preservice and inservice training for all team members, including those who perform more than one role, such as the teacher-administrator or social worker–supervisor. Exploration of role expectations, clarification of areas of overlap in role responsibilities, and development of time-management and priority-setting skills constitute the content of the training sessions. Role-playing, problem-solving and decision-making exercises, along with intergroup negotiating, are used as the training methods for developing increased self-awareness and awareness of others' team functions. Furthermore, peer discussion of one another's expectations, "boundary-role" responsibilities, and discussion of conflict between real and unreal aspirations, are also encouraged, to increase team members' awareness of any irrational personal belief systems which may impair their efficiency and interfere with constructive team participation. Furthermore, the authors recommend special training sessions for team leaders to help them reduce role-overload conflicts created by their excessive or ambiguous demands on team members. Finally, all team members are exposed to training in the recognition and avoidance of "triangulation" or alignment maneuvers, especially when new members join the team or old members leave.

This family-systems approach to understanding and resolving team conflicts has considerable merit, particularly when one or more staff members skillfully can employ its family counseling concepts. The terminology is easily translatable—e.g., "alignment" for "triangling" —but care must be exercised so as not to distract staff with theory and terminology when more direct approaches may exist for the development of increased self-awareness. Otherwise, employing the family-systems model for training purposes can be extremely effective. The primary objective is to focus upon individual team members' expectations of themselves in addition to their expectations of others as the team is brought together to meet its responsibilities.

Whichever training model a school district may adopt, local school systems also have access to state guidelines for special education, personnel development, and inservice training. Such guidelines must be developed by each state, in compliance with PL 94-142, for regular as well as special educators, and models are available for the assessment of training priorities. One such model, developed by Gable, Pecheone, and Gillung (1981), may be used to determine training needs in a given school district by using a specified questionnaire to identify staff competencies and any discrepancies between staff members' views of their present and desired levels of skills. This SENAP (Special Education Needs Assessment Priorities) model then permits comparison between teacher-perceived needs within a school system and the consensus ratings of special education professionals regarding the relative importance of specific competencies involved in teaching handicapped children. Consequently, the inservice training needs of a given school system can be prioritized, taking into account what "experts" might *theoretically* consider important for all special services personnel, and what *practically and realistically* are the expressed needs of a local school district.

Let us turn now to a more comprehensive consideration of what may generally be agreed to be among the most commonly cited training objectives for team members and leaders.

TRAINING OBJECTIVES FOR TEAM MEMBERS AND LEADERS

It is expected that all team members will have adequate and appropriate skills in their respective disciplines. However, it is apparent, through reviewing the literature and through analyzing the problems peculiar to teams, that, in addition, team members need also to possess the competencies and personal characteristics enumerated below, to help them cope with—or, better, to avoid—some of the typical problems facing teams. The development of these attributes, therefore, should be among the major objectives of inservice training programs. Furthermore, graduate schools preparing professionals who will function as members of multidisciplinary teams would do well, also, to emphasize the importance of these personal attributes as well as those having to do with more technical expertise.

ATTRIBUTES OF EFFECTIVE TEAM MEMBERS

Commitment to cooperative, interdisciplinary team work, including shared responsibility with parents and other staff members. This commitment must necessarily include awareness of one's own professional skills, acceptance of one's limitations, and awareness of the scope of one's job responsibilities in relation to others' job descriptions. Such a commitment would include support for *increasing* participation by parents and other educators where appropriate, rather than the mere tolerance of their presence. It requires a thorough understanding of the local special education programs, services, and options as well as a willingness, when necessary, to act as a team spokesperson to inform other staff, parents, and members of the community about such programs.

Awareness of the dynamics of communication systems as they affect problem solving and decision making. This awareness should be accompanied by the willingness to consider others' points of view, as well as the courage to assert one's own professional opinions even when they differ from the majority.

Willingness to express professional opinions and observations in clear, jargon-free language that can be understood by parents and other laypeople as well as by professional colleagues in different disciplines. Such a willingness suggests that the communicator wants people to understand; that the objective of the report is not to hedge or to obfuscate, but to be clear and not to show off the educator's status and knowledge as an expert through the use of technical terminology, but to help others to know and to understand.

This simple attribute seems so self-evident as barely to need assertion. Yet case reports are filled with incomprehensible language, and discussions at team meetings can sometimes deteriorate into what almost seems like a competition to see which "expert" can be most technical and most obscure. We are hoping that these things occur not because these colleagues are *unable* to communicate in clear direct English but because they have never been required to do so, and have fallen into the trap of expressing their ideas in high-sounding technical jargon and complicated language comprehensible only to persons with similar training and background (if it is, indeed, truly comprehensible even to them!).

It is not surprising that special educators fall into this trap. All educators do—even teachers. The most superficial glance at most professional journals yields evidence to suggest that editors of these journals and learned professors do not discourage this type of language, and may even reject simple writing as being of less intellectual depth. But special educators working on teams have more of a responsibility than others to avoid murky noncommunication. The well-being of their clients (the children) depends upon their being able to make other educators and parents understand what they are talking about. Abstract and difficult language does not necessarily contain (and certainly does not *convey*) more or deeper meaning than plain talk!

Possession of a thorough knowledge of federal, state, and local regulations. This would include specific emphasis on parents' and children's rights, limits of school systems' responsibilities, and understanding of procedures to be followed with respect to notification, requests for review, placement decisions, due-process challenges, and so forth.

Commitment to nondiscriminatory evaluation methods and the need for ongoing program evaluation.

An awareness of different leadership and decision making models. This is an important attribute for participants as well as team leaders, for it would include a willingness on the part of participants to operate within the model employed in the district even if the particular model is not the one the participant would personally prefer.

IMPLICATIONS FOR STUDENT OR STAFF SELECTION

Before we consider how to train graduate students or school staff members, we need to consider how to select candidates for programs, and how to select employees for the jobs that will place them on teams.

Until recently, both in the selection of candidates for graduate school training programs and in the selection of special education support staff in the schools, insufficient attention appears to have been paid to an individual's potential for functioning as an effective team member. In the public schools the primary focus in hiring staff has traditionally been on individual teaching, diagnostic, or casework-related skills. Graduate programs tended to seek out students with academic promise and records of solid achievement. In recent years, however, both school systems and universities have begun to place importance on the possession of broader program-evaluation, consultative, and group-process-oriented skills, as well. This has been particularly true with respect to the selection and training of school psychologists (Maher and Kratochwill 1980; Losen and Diament 1978; Berlin 1977; Bardon 1981).

Of late, both graduate schools, in the admission process, and school systems, in the hiring process, have been more apt to seek people who, in addition to their basic competencies, can demonstrate personal flexibility and resourcefulness, and who appear to have the potential for multidimensional functioning. This is important because staff members find themselves needing to function sometimes as program developers, sometimes as coordinators, sometimes as diagnosticians, and almost always as problem solvers. The need for these additional assets has not displaced the demand for other skills. On the contrary, in each specialty area—e.g., speech and language development, social work, school psychology, learning disabilities teaching—the professional literature still recognizes the need for more and improved technical diagnostic, preventive, evaluative, and prescriptive skills. All professional training programs must and will obviously continue to emphasize those characteristics to be able to meet primary service needs.

The implications to be drawn from the list of desirable personal attributes outlined above are clear. It is imperative to select and train people to be as "process-oriented," with regard to the development of effective small-group problem-solving communication and leadership skills, as they are "product-oriented," with regard to diagnostic and remediation skills. For one thing, the continually increasing involvement of parents in the determination of special programs and services for their children requires of the professionals almost as much ability to *communicate* findings as to be accurate in the determination of those findings. In the past, universities' demands for communication skills in human services tended to be focused on report writing. The major objective was to interpret data correctly; the second objective was to be able to write clear, concise reports for record-keeping and referral purposes. This writing skill is still important and should not be underplayed. However, an additional focus in communication must now be added. Professionals must be able to use the data from testing, ratings, evaluations, observations, and the like directly for the purpose of reporting to and consulting with parents and other specialists, who then need to concur, as a team, in making program decisions. The specific skills needed therefore now include the ability to translate technical terminology across professional disciplines into written and oral language understandable to less sophisticated laypersons and to colleagues trained in other disciplines.

And, as we have asserted earlier, those writing professional communications must not only be able to communicate clearly but must be *willing* to do so! Our bias in favor of elimination of technical jargon is evident by now. Yet we must admit that not all of our colleagues concur.

Practitioners in many fields defend technical "jargon" as a useful shortcut in communicating with colleagues who understand the code words and cryptic references and have accepted new, or specialized, definitions for words which may have a different meaning for laypeople.

It is probably impossible to get jargon completely out of any field, particularly one which is rounded and bounded by government regulations and definitions written in the incomprehensible language of the federal register. Even the government, however, has been making some attempt to rewrite rules and regulations in simple, understandable English. (An apocryphal story concerns the Department of the Interior's contest to reduce a lengthy set of regulations governing national parks and forests to a simple, concise, and understandable form. The story goes that the winner of this Clear English contest was the writer who condensed the 10,000-word code to seven words; "Don't mess with the bushes and trees!")

While not advocating such drastic terseness, we believe that in the field of human services it is particularly important that our writings communicate rather than obfuscate. We are dealing not only with colleagues possessing specified knowledge but with other professionals whose noncomprehension of our jargon may interfere with their ability to cooperate with us in programs for children, and with parents who may be intimidated or angered by what they consider an overly technical way of talking about their children.

In addition to being able to write clearly about one's findings, a professional also needs to adopt a flexible perspective about his or her findings. One cannot and should not consider one's own findings and decisions about those findings absolute. There must be a willingness to consider, if not to debate, alternative points of view and different frames of reference. It is necessary, therefore, to seek students and staff who are comfortable with group decision making, and who, while able to assert their own points of view with ease, also demonstrate receptivity to others' viewpoints. They must be capable of resisting absolute diagnostic methods. They must avoid the "fictional finality" or self-fulfilling prophecy inherent in certain special education labels. Among the absolutist "myths" to be avoided, for example, is the concept of any absolute value of any particular diagnostic category or of the absolute application of a diagnostic tool, such as the Gesell Developmental Scales, the Illinois Test of Psycholinguistic Abilities (ITPA), or the Bender Gestalt Visual-Motor Test.

Team members must be able to weigh their own findings and their own evidence in the context of the findings of other members of the team. One must resist the too-easy trap of assuming about a child, "he or she did thus on the ____ scale and so must be (label)." One of the values of having a team rather than one individual practitioner develop a diagnosis and a plan for a child lies in the team's ability to temper the effect of any one diagnostic finding and to utilize a wholistic approach to the child. The members of the team must be willing to consider their pet diagnostic devices as only one in a whole arsenal of tools available to help determine the best course of action for a child. While monitoring their own tendencies toward absolutism, team members similarly must be able to resist any definitive pronouncements made by other specialists, when these pronouncements appear to be substantiated by only one particular diagnostic dogma.

While these skills in communicating clearly and listening to others, and the ability comfortably to challenge authority may seem to be functions of hard-to-change personality characteristics, the professional attributes we are recommending *can* be developed through training and through effective and appropriate on-the-job supervision.

Graduate school trainers particularly need to reinforce their students' abilities to listen to others and, where appropriate, to assert themselves in group problem-solving situations. This may possibly be accomplished through the use of leaderless group discussion techniques and other group dynamics training methods which encourage openness, listening, learning to hear what others are saying, and assertiveness. It is anticipated that administrators charged with the responsibility of hiring school staff will seek evidence of those traits in candidates for positions.

School systems, however, need not necessarily limit their hiring to people already totally skilled in team functioning. On the contrary, having chosen staff members with evidence of these attributes, and who—it is hoped—have already had some training in team functioning in graduate school, pupil personnel administrators have the responsibility to reinforce these skills in their staff members. They may do this by demonstrating that they value this method of functioning and by continuing to provide training opportunities for the strengthening of these interpersonal skills. Ongoing training in communication skills is as important in the special education area as ongoing curriculum skill training is to a social studies or math teacher. (One might also say that communication skills are as important as curriculum skills for the subject-matter teacher as well, but that is the topic for a different book!)

To provide training, an administrator need not feel that he or she must do it all alone. The regular utilization of professional consultants to conduct workshops with staff is as important a part of continuing professional development as is one-to-one supervision and group meetings held to assess needs, share new techniques, discuss new professional developments, and engage in mutual problem solving.

It has become increasingly apparent that effective supervision emphasizes self-evaluation, mutual goal setting by staff members and supervisor, and development of strategies for improving skills as well as for assessing improvement. This direction in supervision meshes well with the foregoing comments on professional development and inservice training. A staff member's increasing communication and group-functioning skills should be as important a part of professional evaluation as his or her specific professional abilities.

Improvement in these areas should be considered as legitimate a professional development goal as learning to use a new diagnostic tool or refining a method of teaching reading. If inservice "credits" are given for attendance at workshops to accomplish the latter, so should they be given for participation in personal growth activities. Moreover, inservice opportunities such as these should be offered not only to special services personnel but to teachers as well.

The first and most obvious reason, for our purposes, is to enhance ability to participate in the team process, as regular classroom teachers frequently do participate. However, the skills we have enumerated are likely to improve all-around classroom performance as well, whether the teacher instructs special education students exclusively or is a "mainstream" teacher with only occasional contact with special needs students.

In graduate school and inservice training programs, there is also a need to develop more of an awareness of the importance of taking an active part in special education program development and evaluation. Pfeiffer's (1981) findings note that one of the main sources of complaint reported by school staff who are active members of the special education team is the lack of sufficient program options or alternatives for the school staff to consider. Part of this lack, of course, is related to the broader issue of budgetary constraints and subsequent program limitations. But part of the difficulty lies in the staff's inability or unwillingness to evaluate, and possibly change, already existing, traditionally reinforced program alternatives. Graduate training programs must, therefore, seek those students who are comfortable with and show promise for the development of program-evaluation skills, e.g., use of systems-analysis procedures for program and needs assessment, observational methods, efficiency rating techniques, and the measurement of those factors that aid or dissuade openness within a particular unit. Individuals who possess some of those skills may, when they are hired by a school, be further encouraged through appropriate supervision and inservice training on the job to use these skills effectively.

Finally, and perhaps the most important professional trait of all, is a multidiscipline-oriented, team-focused attitude which, in broad terms, not only includes the willingness to work with others but to seek actively to involve others in decision making instead of trying to take all responsibilities upon oneself. A high degree of tolerance for relinquishing control to others is characteristic of such individuals. At the very least, the individual must demonstrate the ability to acknowledge that mutual decisions are more compelling and, probably in the long run, more efficient than decisions made by a single team member or imposed by a leader.

It is, of course, desirable that most, if not all, graduate school candidates will already possess this important attitudinal attribute when they are accepted into a training program. But for those who do not, this professional approach can be developed through training. Attitudes about one's work, and about appropriate professional relationship to colleagues in other disciplines, are frequently acquired during graduate school and supervised field experiences. Most often the encouragement of such an orientation is a function of the prevailing philosophy of the training institution.

The most desirable candidates for a school-district staff position should already be able to demonstrate such a team-oriented attitude. The main focus of further inservice training would, therefore, be to help new staff members implement effective team procedures, or to learn ways to encourage other team members to maintain a constructive group-process orientation in the face of the countless daily pressures which tend to reinforce more authoritarian and expedient procedures.

MEETING TRAINING NEEDS OF SCHOOL STAFF

Several areas of team performance which can be improved through inservice training have already been discussed. Chapter III covers the dynamics of small-group communication and problem solving. It also includes reference to developing training sessions using demonstrations of problem-solving effectiveness relative to different ways of sharing (or withholding) important information. Chapter IV similarly refers to the development of inservice training involving the exploration of different leadership styles. Training exercises can be specifically designed for use in inservice sessions, so that following some practice or warm-up in role playing, there should be ample material to increase training participants' awareness of the kinds of problems that block communication among team members. Similarly, the sessions can promote experimentation with the various leadership styles which may stimulate more or less active participation by team members and affect their sense of meaningful involvement.

There are, however, some additional areas of team member functioning relative to training objectives which deserve consideration. They arise from the fact that graduate schools have not yet been able to catch up with some of the practical issues—resulting from recent varying interpretations of the special education laws—that confront special education personnel working in the field.

One area which cuts across professional disciplines but is, nevertheless, sometimes neglected, is the broad issue of child or parent advocacy versus the question of what is the legitimate jurisdiction of the public schools. This issue is not often included in course curricula, probably because graduate schools have not yet been made aware of a sufficient number of school situations relative to this point to appreciate the need for delimiting what is expected of the public schools and public school staff. For example, one must have experienced the variety of pressures and demands upon one's limited time in order to temper the idealism of child advocacy with practical awareness. One must also recognize what is feasible, what may and may not be reasonably accomplishable for a given child, where and how the regulations designed to protect parents' and children's rights are sometimes abused or manipulated so that real protection is undermined, and under what circumstances the regulations themselves actually diminish the provision of service that they were intended to facilitate.

In light of Pfeiffer's (1981) findings, the translation of regulations into what constitutes a public school's obligations, and an awareness of what those obligations may create in the form of budgetary conflicts, are certainly appropriate subject matter for inservice discussions, or for consciousness raising regarding why certain desirable program options may be unavailable. Practical school experience is also necessary to understand the complexity of the relationship between special education and "mainstream" programs, or between special and regular education in general. Graduate students usually have not yet sufficiently experienced bureaucratic realities to appreciate these complexities and are, therefore, often inclined to write off practical considerations too quickly in favor of the principle of advocacy. The school staff, however, *must* know more about the system in which they are employed, what the conflicts are, what overriding issues are affecting decisions to be made, and what practical means are available to work constructively and productively within the system. An increased awareness of such issues through appropriate inservice training will help staff to work effectively and avoid the "burn out" that can otherwise come with disillusionment.

Therefore, some inservice sessions should be devoted to increasing the staff's general awareness of the school system as a structured system, or, as Butler and Maher (1981) suggest, a "family system," which, in terms of team functioning, reinforces certain familylike modes of communication, a sense of alignment, individual feelings of self-worth, and the like.

Another practical inservice training area, already discussed in some detail in Chapter II, has to do with the staff's preparation for, and greater understanding of, legal due-process challenge procedures. Most graduate training programs have still not quite caught up with the fact that students need preparation in how to respond during quasi-legal, if not actual, courtroomlike proceedings. For example, they need to know how to give testimony about the quality of programs or service, and how to testify about a child's behavior, the child's potential for learning, his or her degree of disturbance, the observed extent of disruptive behavior, the child's actual response to individualized help and need for peer support, the appropriateness of the present instructional program, and so on. In fact, staff members are sometimes asked to testify regarding the relative frequency of certain of their observations in attempts to establish more objectively the child's needs for "appropriate" special education services. Graduate programs need, therefore, to prepare students better for that kind of precision in behavioral observation, which may be of greater legal than diagnostic value.

The countless judgments made, explored, questioned, crossexamined, and verified during due-process proceedings are, consequently, often totally different in nature from the judgments staff specialists have been trained to make or are used to making. The "probability" notions about behavior and learning, which so many professionals are comfortable with, are inadequate for the kinds of judgments that hearing officers, lawyers, and judges demand. Staff members, therefore, tend often to be overwhelmed by the nature of the questioning employed to pin down concretely the issues that they, from their direct experience with children, tend to see as highly relative and variable. And, unless they are more adequately prepared and trained, staff specialists may be easily shaken and demoralized under such circumstances.

It has been our experience that inservice, courtroomlike role playing is excellent preparation for due-process mediation or hearings. It provides the opportunity to experiment with unfamiliar roles and to examine one's reaction to them. It also provides the backdrop for greater in-depth exploration of the justifications and limitations inherent in the judicial process, as applied to school matters. Again, without such preparation, staff members are often confused, overwhelmed, and sometimes angered by the courtroomlike questions they find they *must* respond to—under oath. The following illustration perhaps best describes how staff members tend to react to the hearing process.

A teacher was interviewed shortly after her two-hour testimony and crossexamination at a state-level hearing. She was emotionally drained by the experience but anxious to talk about it. She was then a junior high school special education resource teacher who had worked with emotionally and socially handicapped children for several years, and was highly regarded as the most active member of the junior high school special education team.

> "I never thought it would be anything like this. I'm exhausted, but I also feel agitated, as if I'm expecting still another question from the lawyer who crossexamined·me. What I couldn't understand was why no one

would ask anything directly. I also felt that when I finally answered their questions, I had a million qualifications to add, but no one was interested, and I felt like I'd been roped into saying something I really didn't mean. It was all terribly, terribly frustrating. I'd like to go somewhere and just sleep it off, but the whole thing disturbs me every time I think about it. They really don't want to know the truth—they just want answers!"

The explanation that had been given to the teacher immediately following the hearing by the school board's attorney was obviously unsatisfying. She had been told that the hearing officer, like a judge, was oriented toward slowly and deliberately collecting information that was intended to help arrive at "the truth" from among the varying points of view being asserted. When reminded of the lawyer's explanation, the teacher again dismissed that interpretation of the judicial process saying, "I can't function that way"—and walked away. It should be noted, however, that the teacher eventually became a star "roleplayer" in subsequent inservice training sessions which were designed to prepare the staff better for testifying at hearings. Not surprisingly, she became particularly adept at roleplay which involved mimicking the lawyer's efforts to pin down the teacher who was called to testify about her student's behavior in class.

One other area that needs to be encouraged as a focal point for inservice training, and one which is also pertinent for graduate school preparation, is the development of consultative parent conference skills. Losen and Diament (1978) established both the need and the rationale for developing a "coworker" orientation when discussing childrens' problems with their parents. The approach recommended is appropriate for all special education team members who wish to improve their parent contacts. The ways of overcoming parent resistance or one's own defensive reactions, the timing of interpretations of data, the anticipation of questions or concerns, and the development of trust and mutual respect are all deemed subject to training. They constitute skills that can always be improved, particularly during inservice sessions which permit the staff to share experiences and roleplay challenging or unusual circumstances. In fact, we have found that the best training occurs during those sessions when team members are encouraged to elaborate upon actual parent conference experiences that they consider failures, and that they expect will continue to prove frustrating. When this occurs, the staff can roleplay situations that are realistic for them, and hence more meaningful to their work situation. Again, the overall objective critical to facilitating change is the development of a more consultative approach—which is sometimes in marked contrast to the staff member's customary, more authoritative, and sometimes authoritarian, approach.

DEVELOPING AN IN-SERVICE TRAINING PROGRAM

A school system developing an inservice training program for team participants may use several different approaches, depending on the specific objective being emphasized. Considering the severe limitations on staff members' time, an administrator developing a training program would be wise to focus on one particular objective for a period of time rather than trying to do everything at once. This approach helps limit the amount of time a staff member is asked to spend in inservice training. In an ideal situation, training sessions and activities would take place during "release" time rather than infringing on staff members' personal or professional time. Training should be considered sufficiently important that a school district is willing to free staff members to attend sessions—or to pay them if they attend on their own time.

In places and periods when school enrollments are dropping, more emphasis may be placed on training for all staff members. This is because, as enrollment declines and staff members are laid off, the remaining staff are frequently older. While they have the advantage of experience, they sometimes may lack the fresh approach and enthusiasm of younger members. It may have been many years since they were trained. They may not be familiar with the latest tools or methods and may benefit from the stimulation of inservice training. In these situations, school systems may be more willing to commit funds for this purpose, while in places or at times when enrollment is increasing and staff sizes growing, there may be less interest by school administration in spending money on inservice training.

Though few school systems have the financial resources for elaborate training programs during school time, administrators should not underestimate the interest and professional dedication of their staff members. If supervisors make it clear that they consider training important—and if they provide training opportunities that are sufficiently stimulating, where staff members feel that they are truly increasing their skills—participation by staff members in voluntary training programs may be surprisingly high. Approaches to training should be sufficiently varied to keep staff coming back for more. If, for example, the object of a session is to review existing program options and local, state, and federal regulations, the individual chosen as a presenter should not only be knowledgeable, but an effective speaker as well. The speaker should pepper the presentation with examples, and case citations, so that regulations, program options, and due-process procedures are seen as related to real children and real parents, rather than being presented as a dry litany of facts. Staff members should learn how *their* students, *their* classrooms, *their* clients are specifically affected by all the dry, dusty, and boring rules.

Every training session should provide the opportunity for questions and comments by the participants, and feedback should be requested regularly so that those planning the training activities may learn what worked and what didn't work, from the participants' perspective.

One of the attributes enumerated earlier in the chapter, which serves as an objective of training, is the development of a willingness to serve as spokesperson for the team and for the special education programs and opportunities. This is an important goal which should not be difficult to achieve. Educators are not normally characterized by reticence. Usually they love to talk about "their kids," and "their programs." A school system should capitalize on staff members' natural proclivities by bringing in consultants to teach them how to be effective in "getting out the good word" about the program. School newsletters, PTA bulletins, and suburban newspapers, for example, are often packed with newsy items about the "regular" program. Children's achievements are highlighted, excellent teachers are the subjects of feature stories, curricular innovations are written up in articles avidly read by parents and community members, and students' sports exploits, as well as their dramatic and musical performances, are reported with regularity.

No less should be true of the special education program! Its students' achievements should be touted, its dedicated personnel praised, and its unique curricular and extracurricular components should be the subject of discussions and articles. Public relations is not a term to be despised! Public support of education—regular as well as special—is dependent on public interest in and knowledge of those programs and on the public's sense of ownership of the programs. "Regular" educators have known this for years. The National School Public Relations Association is a flourishing organization. Special educators should get on this bandwagon. They should have contact with PR experts who will help them become effective spokespersons for their programs. Good PR efforts are self-sustaining. As staff members begin to receive positive reactions to their communications, they will become more and more interested in telling the special education story.

A school, or an entire school system, wishing to adopt as a primary objective the more effective functioning of interdisciplinary teams might consider an inservice training program over a one- or two-year period, available to all staff members on a voluntary basis, with certain sessions particularly recommended for special education staff and all regular team members. Schools that already have ongoing general inservice programs, and that cannot devote a total program to

SUGGESTED PROGRAM

Topic	Method(s)	Target Staff Members
Implications of changing statutes	Expert lecture/ question and answer	All
Survey of special education options within school, district, and region	Presentation and discussion using a knowledgeable staff person	All
More effective communication*	Workshop/ role playing	All
Parent conferencing skills*	Workshop/ role playing	All
Practical limitations of child advocacy; limits of responsibilities of public schools	Expert lecture/ question and answer	All
Changing roles of various specialists*	Discussion	Special education and support staff
Identification of learning disabilities	Workshop	Special education and support staff
Limitations of the mainstream for certain handicap categories	Expert lecture/ question and answer	Special education personnel
Conflict resolution among team members*	Workshop/ role play	Special education personnel
Dealing with emotionally disturbed parents as team members	Workshop/ role play	All regular team members; school administrators
Testifying in court	Lecture followed by role play. School board attorney should be involved.	All
Reporting findings and opinions at Team Meetings, including what records to bring, etc.	Discussion	All
Follow up and evaluation of students' progress	Discussion	Regular team members and administrators.
Spreading the word: how to engender support through positive PR.	Workshop sessions with PR experts	All

*Probably would require more than one session.

this objective, may wish to select from among the suggested topics and approaches, offering workshops in those areas where the need is greatest. Some of the topics suggested, notably those having to do with communications and PR skills, will undoubtedly be useful to staff members in their general functioning and not just in their roles as members of teams.

There are several ways to broaden the appeal of these inservice sessions. The sessions on special education laws could be combined with sessions on other legal issues in education that school people must deal with (e.g., confidentiality, students' rights, relationships with police, rights of noncustodial parents, copyright problems, and the like). The session on parent-conferencing skills could be expanded to include conferences unrelated to special education; the workshop on conflict resolution in teams could conceivably be broadened to include general problem solving and conflict resolution. The administrator responsible for inservice program development, while broadening the topics to create more general interest, should be careful not to make them so diffuse that the objective of improving team functioning is lost.

ANTICIPATED TRENDS
AND THEIR IMPLICATIONS
FOR GRADUATE SCHOOL TRAINING

As noted in Chapter VII, there appears to be decreasing concern that federal and state supported special education services and programs, particularly for most of those developed under PL 94-142, are in serious jeopardy. During the summer of 1981 and spring of 1982, Congress seemed to respond favorably to the lobbying efforts of the Council for Exceptional Children (CEC) and other parent advocacy groups by much less cutting of federal funding for handicapped children than had been feared. CEC and other special education supporters were further encouraged by legislative action in 1981 to forestall the inclusion of special education regulations and funding under "block grant" proposals. Those proposals seemed intended to decontrol federal-level monitoring of special education regulations and to provide more state-level and local latitude in their implementation—with, of course, a commensurate shift to variable local financial support (or lack of it) for special education programs in the schools. It was generally acknowledged, however, especially by school officials, that too much federal monitoring, too ardent pursuit of uniformity in accountability measures, and a broader interpretation than had been originally intended by Congress of the term "full service" for handicapped children were producing greater costs for educating the handicapped than had been anticipated. It was also conceded that rising special education costs due to federal regulations (or the interpretation of those regulations) were draining funds from regular education in many local communities, and that adverse reaction to such diversion of funds was heightened by the fact that many communities had already experienced substantial reductions in regular programs and staff.

Nevertheless, in 1982 Congress again turned away from budget cuts and other dramatic proposals that were considered harmful to special education interests. Instead, by the fall of 1982, efforts were directed toward developing specific deregulation proposals which would, in effect, eliminate costly and inefficient federal monitoring but retain the substance of protection for the handicapped advanced under PL 94-142. The definition of "appropriate free education" for the handicapped, the breadth of support services considered to be justifiably within the jurisdiction of the public schools, the practical extent of parents' and schools' due-process rights, and the need for less burdensome bureaucratic accountability systems were among the issues addressed by the proposed regulations, with the clear intent of relegating greater authority concerning those matters to the states and to local school districts.

This review and reassessment of special education on the national level led many professional educational disciplines to reexamine their own roles, particularly as each discipline had a stake in the future of special education program evaluation and development. Speech clinicians, for example—originally thought of as working only with children with specific speech difficulties or articulation problems—notably expanded their sphere of operations to include the whole range of "communication" disorders. They argued that communication disorders which often stemmed from mental factors, were clearly and justifiably within their jurisdiction and that limiting themselves to defects resulting from auditory or expressive impairments was unnecessarily restrictive. Many of them, consequently, no longer refer to themselves as "speech" therapists, or "speech" teachers, but now call themselves "speech, hearing, and language development clinicians." They intend, therefore, to be perceived increasingly as team members who are to be consulted regarding the whole area of language and communication development skills, both diagnostically and prescriptively. They no longer wish to be perceived as the team's specialists who are concerned only with evaluating and correcting children's speech.

If this new, expanded view of that role prevails, the training implications for speech clinicians in graduate programs and for inservice staff purposes are evident. First, the acceptance by other disciplines of the expanded role for speech, hearing, and language personnel has been and remains far from automatic. Regular school staff and school administrators are probably even less willing to too quickly accede to speech clinicians' broader view of their roles and team functions. Therefore, the speech clinician who successfully develops his or her role along the broader "communication skills" or language-development lines must be able to demonstrate the knowledge and awareness of early childhood development and the expertise regarding theories or principles of language acquisition which formerly were viewed as primarily within the scope of a school psychologist's training. Subsequently, appropriate inservice training for all school staff may be able to focus upon the acceptance of speech clinicians as experts in language development, for assessment of the broader communication skills affecting a child's school performance, or for their consultant role in developing preschool and "English as a second language" programs systemwide. But their graduate or professional training must already have prepared them for the areas of expertise and the broader team functions they wish to pursue.

School social workers have also begun to expand their roles and functions to include more than traditional family "casework." Once identified as the school team specialists who were most knowledgeable about community-school-parent interrelationships, and who consequently primarily played the role of liaison or coordinator in situations calling for interagency cooperation, school social workers were not otherwise considered to be involved in a child's actual instructional program. In many school systems they are now adopting a broader function. School social workers are also being trained, and need to be trained further, for greater involvement with instructional program development, for the administration and coordination of special education programs and services, and for a more significant parent advocacy role as federal deregulation has its expected impact. Again, appropriate inservice training can be developed to gain increased staff acceptance for social workers in such expanded roles, but the provision of sufficient graduate training appropriate to those roles must precede such acceptance.

School psychologists—once relegated to psychoeducational diagnostic testing as their primary and, in some instances, sole function— are now similarly far more interested in pursuing broader consultative relationships to parents, teachers, and administrators. They perceive the range of their activities as clearly continuing to involve their traditional testing of an individual child's personal and instructional needs, but they wish to expand their role to include consultation regarding program development, program evaluation, and direct teacher and parent training.

The "Proceedings of the Spring Hill Symposium" (Ysseldyke and Weinberg 1981) compiles the views on the future of school psychologists as expressed by some of the field's most highly regarded contemporary practitioners and graduate school trainers.

While in no way denigrating the traditional testing role, still seen as a major contribution of psychologists in the schools, these experts agreed that psychologists should not be confined to that role. Many, in fact, were concerned lest the emphasis on diagnostic categorization of the handicapped reinforced by PL 94-142 regulations might tend to divert an inordinate portion of psychologists' time to testing, thereby reducing other significant contributions. They also saw some need for psychologists to help other professionals understand and make more effective use of test and measurement concepts.

Trachtman (1981), for example, specified that school psychologists should *share* more of their skills with school colleagues. He believes they should also help regular teachers to learn observation and behavior-rating techniques and assist special education teachers in developing parent-consultant skills. In a sense, one might say he sees psychologists playing a key role in the inservice training of other staff members—a position with which we concur.

Trachtman and Bardon (1981) also urged psychologists to adopt a more politically active role, sharing concerns with parents and allying themselves with parent advocacy associations. They argued that if parents understood that many psychologists view *them* as their primary clients, the parents, in turn, might be more willing to support the expansion of the role of the psychologists into a wider variety of school activities, including the development of primary prevention programs which otherwise might be expected to receive little community and budgetary support. Bardon, reflecting on a group discussion he was reporting, argued that not enough psychologists are involved in or even aware of the political processes that affect public policy formation. He stated that "public policy formulation should be part of the education and training in school psychology" (p. 306).

In general, Trachtman also urged school psychologists to develop their role as "change-agents," by highlighting their consultant and program-evaluation functions, and by taking an active role in program planning, particularly in light of PL 94-142 requirements that students be placed in the least restrictive environment which may be determined by the team to meet their identified needs. On the other hand, others like Vensel (1981) concurred with Trachtman's recommendation regarding the importance of psychologists' roles in program evaluation but cautioned against school psychologists becoming so broadly functioning that they lose their primary identity as psychologists and fade entirely into special education. And finally, Grimes (1981) emphasized a systematic approach to developing acceptance of school psychologists in their broader roles, advising psychologists to forge their colleagues' expectations of what they can do by actively demonstrating new services, so that the recipients of the services can have experience with what they have to offer.

These conceptions, by the leading trainers of psychologists, of the new and expanded roles for school psychologists may have broad implications for graduate training programs. Graduate school program developers still need to bear in mind Lambert's observation that "one quality that differentiates the professional from the technician is that— the professional knows the reason for a practice whereas the technician knows only how to practice" (1981, 204). Consequently, according to Lambert, in training the school psychologist, his or her professional identity will be enhanced by the development of his or her role and specific functions within a consistent conceptual model or theoretical frame of reference. In addition, graduate school trainers heeding Grimes's advice would teach psychologists to demonstrate to their teaching colleagues in the schools the practical value of research to help solve commonly encountered school problems. In that way, they would be developing a climate of support for further research.

Trachtman sees the need to train psychologists as consultants who perform the role of "enabler-protector" and who can then open the door to researchers who need real subjects to test certain hypotheses about factors affecting learning or other school performance. At the same time, the researchers themselves can be sensitized to the problems the schools need to have researched and to the specific difficulties schools encounter when permitting research and experimentation. The psychologist thus might perform the dual function of facilitating research and protecting students and teachers from unwarranted intrusions upon their time.

Finally, in summing up the discussion about training objectives and views of the future of special service professionals' roles and functions in the school, we must emphasize one important point: graduate school training programs and inservice training efforts must not lose sight of how psychologists and other members of the special education teams are presently viewed by their regular education colleagues, their administrators, and the community. In other words, before becoming too preoccupied with future directions, it is necessary to make sure that the time is right for change, and that the need for change is both mutually understood and desired. Otherwise, special education specialists will find themselves urging new and broader roles for themselves at a time when some of their colleagues, members of school boards, and school administrators are not even sure they want to continue what is now required for exceptional and handicapped students. Chapter IX will expand upon this idea as it pertains to the school board's views about meeting the needs of special education students under PL 94-142 mandates. We will particularly explore factors affecting board concerns about special education at a time when many school districts are being forced to close schools, contend with rising inflation, and otherwise cope with declining enrollments. Apart from the boards' concerns, however, it is clear that school administrators, having to reduce staff in many regular instructional areas, are often resentful that federal regulations tend to protect special service personnel and budgets. The regular classroom teachers, asked to tolerate more "problem" children in the mainstreamed programs so as to demonstrate adherence to the concept of "least restrictive environment," are often similarly resentful. In their perception, special education children seem to benefit disproportionately from their umbrella of special protection and consideration, which, teachers feel, almost makes it unfair for the non-special-education children.

Furthermore, with reference to special service staff and special educators wanting to expand their roles for the future, the resistance of regular educators to too much change too quickly is likely to keep special education personnel mindful of all that *still* needs to be done to gain or maintain acceptance of the role and functions currently claimed by school psychologists and the special services teams. Graduate students and new staff still need to be prepared for working with colleagues who may neither fully understand nor appreciate their special educational role and functions. Therefore, they will continue to have to prove themselves to such colleagues, and demonstrate that they can be of value in meeting children's needs in their present roles, before they can pursue new or broader directions. They will also need to demonstrate that providing effective service and programs for special education children will have a positive impact on all children. If they cannot demonstrate the practical value of their services, all questions of identity, broader functions, new directions, more effective interdisciplinary collaboration, and so forth are likely to be irrelevant. In other words, graduate school and inservice training programs must emphasize the point that one must begin by meeting the primary expectations of one's colleagues. Once those primary expectations have been successfully met, modifications, broadening, and new directions may have a chance of successfully being introduced.

SUMMARY

This chapter covered the training of staff for working in teams, including graduate school preparation and on-the-job, inservice training. It is our contention that appropriate preparation can help alleviate the real problems cited by professionals, including diagnostic difficulties, determining when a special education designation is appropriate, and coping with realistic constraints on program and service options. Appropriate preparation also may diminish many procedural difficulties in team functioning and improve staff relationships and morale even when these procedural difficulties have not been specifically perceived as problems.

While it is obvious that team members should have appropriate professional skills relative to their own area of functioning, training for team participation should also focus on eliciting the following personal attributes, among others, which contribute to effective team functioning:

1. Commitment to the process
2. Awareness of the dynamics of communications
3. Ability and willingness to use jargon-free language
4. Knowledge of federal, state, and local regulations
5. Willingness not only to listen, but also to give thoughtful consideration to divergent opinions.

Selection of students for graduate training and of candidates for school positions which will require them to participate on interdisciplinary teams should be based on applicants' possession of these characteristics—or on their potential to develop them and willingness to do so—as well as on their professional expertise and experience.

Even after careful selection procedures, a school system should invest time and resources in inservice training (in process skills) for special education personnel. Improvement in these areas by special education personnel should be regarded as just as professionally desirable and necessary as mainstream teachers' improvement in classroom-management or curriculum skills.

Graduate schools should reinforce a multidisciplinary approach to decision making and deemphasize unilateral diagnostic or placement responsibility. In addition, professionals should direct attention to issues of child/parent advocacy versus public responsibility, either through inclusion of these topics in graduate courses or through inservice discussion and clarification at the local school level.

Staff should receive training, at some level, in the legal challenge procedure to avoid situations where, upon being called to testify in hearings, they may become demoralized by the unexpected black-and-white legalistic approaches, at variance with reasoned professional judgments which deal in shades of gray.

Development of parent conferencing skills should also be stressed, either by inclusion in graduate training or through inservice opportunities. School systems should provide release time for inservice training if possible. However, provision of meaningful training opportunities on a voluntary basis may result in a surprisingly significant participation rate. School systems may profitably offer much of the training process in communication skills to their whole staff, not just to the pupil personnel specialists and special education staff. These skills improve classroom performance and relationships between teachers and parents.

As special education vies with mainstream education for its share of financial and other resources, it will be important—and should not be too difficult—to demonstrate that improvement of service and programs for special education children will have a positive impact on mainstream children as well.

9

Relations with School Boards

The special education team, like every other group within a school system, is subject, ultimately, to the jurisdiction of the board of education. While boards of education in some large cities may be appointed, salaried education experts, by and large—especially in smaller cities and suburbs and in rural regions—boards are run by elected, nonsalaried members. Their educational expertise and knowledge may be widely disparate, and their motivation for serving in their demanding, time-consuming positions may be as different as their comparative educational sophistication.

One can only conjecture about how boards of education would respond to the special education mandates in an economic and social climate in which funds were readily available and schools expanding. But today, under the circumstances prevailing in many parts of the country where school enrollments may be shrinking, schools consolidating, and resources diminishing, boards do not readily commit to special education expenses.

In many places, boards may be struggling to wring educational dollars from populations whose average age is increasing. As a result, in some towns and cities the percentage of families with children in school may be decreasing, and the older families may not assign to education as high a priority as formerly. Therefore, boards of education may not look with pleasure upon the prospect of having to allocate a higher and higher percentage of their hard-to-come-by funds to pupils with special needs. Even in cities and towns with growing school populations, funds and resources do not always increase at a rate appropriate to the growth in school population.

No one even peripherally familiar with the school budget process in a period of enrollment decline is unaware of the tough fiscal questions that school boards and administrators must answer—such as "Why doesn't the school budget go down when the school population drops?" and "Why does the per-pupil cost of education continue to climb so rapidly?" The answers demand a degree of fiscal sophistication not always present among taxpayers. Thus, explanations of how inflationary price hikes and normal staff salary increases may cancel out any gains from declines in enrollment go unheeded. Explanations about the mathematical effect of dividing fixed costs among fewer pupils (i.e., the tendency to increase per-pupil costs even if overall budget expenditures do not rise) may fall on uncomprehending ears. And explanations of how reduction-in-force on the basis of seniority (which is practiced in many districts) results in a higher paid staff, per pupil, often meet skeptical, if not outright incredulous, responses.

Under such circumstances, boards of education may find themselves struggling to provide basic facilities, classrooms, texts, and teachers; special programs to serve handicapped children often assume a lower priority.

The needs of children who require special education compete with all other educational needs, while educational funds seem to be drying up. Therefore, in recent years special educators have become aware of a budgetary backlash that finds many board members (as well as educators and parents) wary, if not resentful, over what some consider "disproportionate" expenditures for children with special needs, expenditures which detract from the education of so-called "normal" children. Boards of education are elected by and represent the interests of the citizenry as a whole. When they feel that rigid interpretations of special education laws require them to provide extraordinary services at unusually high cost, they often grow resentful and sometimes refuse, thus instigating a fight in court.

Some boards, while not yet ready to openly resist complying with special education mandates (which they may see as imposed without sufficient funds to support them) at least are asking for evidence that the costly special education they *are* providing is effective. They are looking for evidence of some ultimate benefit not only to the children served, but also—by increasing the self-sufficiency of handicapped people—to society as a whole. Similarly, while there may, somewhere, still be boards of education that accept without demurral a team's recommendations for costly services or for payment of extremely high tuition for out-of-district placements, more and more boards are balking—to the point of challenging—the high cost of special education.

One can see the difficulties this stance can pose without passing judgment as to whether a board's search for less costly alternatives is justified.

It is within this context, however, that teams are operating, and the administrative team leaders must also be aware that their child-advocacy stance may not be viewed with unalloyed support by their superiors, who deal more closely with the board of education. These superiors—assistant superintendents and superintendents—are more specifically and personally responsible for carrying out the directives and wishes of the board. They are more vulnerable to criticism or censure from the board if they expend special education funds too "liberally," particularly when the board may be besieged by parents of other children who are demanding services and programs for the "normal" youngsters.

The difficulty encountered by high-level administration often is that the board members may be reluctant to directly express negative attitudes toward special education expenditures lest they present a less humane image than they wish to convey publicly. Therefore, they may communicate their desires to hold down special education spending indirectly through suggestions, comments, expressions of displeasure, and the like at executive meetings, but they rarely express themselves directly through overt statements or official actions. The special education administrator sometimes may even be kept in the dark about the Board's attitude by the superintendent, who also may prefer not to have to deal directly with the cost issues. The superintendent may pass the buck downward by subtly communicating his or her wish that the special education team not bring in costly proposals. No one wants to be the villain who refuses service to a child. It gets the superintendent and the board "off the hook" if the team falls into line and brings in supportable recommendations. However, special education administrators should try not to allow themselves to remain in this defensive and ambiguous position. They should develop strategies for working with the higher-level administrators and the board of education which will be effective in promoting a child-advocacy position and overcoming board resistance to special education spending, be that resistance open or covert.

EDUCATING BOARD MEMBERS

As a first step, the special education team leaders should be involved in educating the board of education about special education from a legal and a philosophical/educational perspective. It is not enough for team leaders to keep themselves abreast of changes in state and federal laws and regulations and to be cognizant of the outcomes of significant court cases and challenges. It is important to keep the board of education informed as well. An administrator needing to defend an expensive decision, or explain to the board why a parent has requested a formal review or mediation or has employed a lawyer and is formally challenging a team decision is in a stronger position for having "educated" the board of education about the intricacies of the process, possibly through regularly scheduled, ongoing informal reviews.

The special education administrator may also be able to find a strong ally in the school board attorney. However, special educators may often need to update the attorneys themselves, for rare is the attorney (except in large city systems) whose sole employer is the school board. More frequently, a school board attorney has the board as one of several clients, and unless the attorney is a school law specialist and works for boards of education exclusively, the chances are that the lawyer will need to be updated by the special educator. Many lawyers, however, welcome this liaison. By updating the attorney, the special education administrator helps the lawyer do the job to the satisfaction of the client school board. And the board may often be more willing to hear about special education laws from an attorney than from one of its own administrators. It may put more credence in the attorney's briefing, little knowing the true source of the attorney's information. This is sometimes hard for the special education administrator to swallow, but it is a common fact of dealing with school boards. It is better, therefore, for special education administrators to be aware of this attitude on the part of school boards and make constructive use of the attorney than to try to ignore the attorney because they feel (often justifiably) that they know more about the latest special education laws than the lawyer does.

The briefings on the latest legalisms can profitably be combined with a periodic review about placements that have *not* been challenged. Better still, these reviews may be tied in with an annual or biannual report to the board on the progress of children receiving special educational services. Since annual reviews of individual children are required under the law, information about the progress of special education children is as readily available as, say, achievement test data on non-special-education children.

While it is probably not necessary to give specific reports about individual children, it is not out of line; and it is certainly desirable to review with the board, in more general terms, the progress of these children. The board is usually interested in hearing about progress of "average" children and listens avidly to achievement test data and reports about SAT scores and college acceptances. If the board is not equally interested in learning of the progress of special education children, it is up to the special education administrators to encourage this interest. It is certainly to be hoped that the overall picture will be one of at least moderate success, so the board may be helped to develop pride in "its" accomplishments for these children and an understanding of how the many dollars spent and services provided "pay off."

At a board meeting focusing on the broad achievements of the program rather than the problem aspects of placement, the special education administrators can begin to educate the board about two other aspects. They can begin to communicate to the board the complexity and delicacy of some of the placement decisions. They should take the opportunity to review some of the problems that may have been *averted* by the work of the placement team. If a board gets decisions only, or problems only, it will have no context for appreciating the sensitivity of the work of the team and no awareness of the many ways in which the team may save the board from bigger headaches. A discussion of this nature will naturally lead to discussion of hypothetical problems that commonly occur and that the board may indeed have to face at one time or another. Thus, the board is prepared to deal with problems or challenges that do occur, and it recognizes that the team has been the source of more positive benefit to the board than of problems.

At briefing meetings, in addition to keeping the board up to date on current laws and regulations, the special education administrators, with the help of the school board attorneys, should also remind the board of the degree to which the parents of special education children must legally be involved in decision making.

ENLISTING THE AID OF PARENTS

Special education administrators may find that the parents of handicapped children are themselves powerful allies in helping to educate board of education members. They may work as individuals, lobbying board members they know personally, or operate within organizations dedicated to the purpose of achieving services for these children. And board members, being human—as well as political—creatures, are vulnerable to parental lobbying. These parents may be willing to meet with the board in public meetings or in individual private sessions to discuss how the program in general has benefitted their children and how the special education expenditures can be justified in terms of developing self-sufficiency in their children, thus reducing the potential financial burden to society in the future.

As it looks for evidence of the benefits of special services, a board may wish the administration to do a follow-up study of some of the graduates of its special programs to determine how these youngsters are faring after they are no longer the responsibility of the public schools. If the idea does not arise from the board, it is probably worthwhile for the special education personnel to initiate it. A study will be useful from two perspectives. First, such a study is likely to further reinforce the board's interest in the students and to create a sense of "ownership" of these programs. Second, the study will undoubtedly help the staff identify areas where changes in program or procedures might be effective.

Follow-up studies may be extremely simple or very elaborate, but it is probably a good idea to start off simple. Some of the difficulties in obtaining returns to follow-up studies of graduates are familiar to most educators; obtaining returns from special education students who are out of school may present even greater—but not insurmountable—challenges, and the returns are worth going after. In one western Connecticut district, the Special Education Department used the services of a college-student intern to do a simple follow up of its graduates, getting most of the responses through telephone interviews with the students, or in some cases (particularly if the students were retarded) with their parents. Among the questions asked were: Is the student living independently of his or her parents? Is the student employed? If so, is the position one that is satisfying to the student? Does it have growth potential or is it a dead-end position? Did the student go on for any further education? This particular study also asked for students' opinions about how helpful various components of the special education program had been.

Obviously there are limitations to these studies. Foremost among them is the fact that it is impossible to provide a control group of students who needed, but did not receive, special education, since all those who require it must legally receive it. Another limitation is that some questions are more or less appropriate and the answers more or less significant, depending on the nature and degree of the respondents' handicaps. These limitations notwithstanding, follow-up studies are valuable because they permit us to compare outcomes with our expectations for students.

In the absence of control groups, the department may establish certain criteria of success for the program. For example, the criteria for "program success" for learning-disabled students with normal to high intelligence may be their ability to successfully pursue continued education and/or their ability to hold jobs commensurate with their ability or to increase job skills. Program success for retarded students or for emotionally disturbed students might be measured by different criteria, but criteria for all groups should be related to the goals of the special programs and the goals (viewed on a general rather than individual basis) of the IEPs.

In designing a study, it is advisable to keep the number of questions to a minimum, to encourage returns if the study is done by mail, or to keep telephoning time manageable if the study is done by phone. It is also advisable to use different questions for different special education categories, although this may not work well if the size of the sample is small.

Less ambitious than a follow-up study of graduates may be a study of students still in the system who have received special education but who are no longer receiving services or whose services have been reduced to a minimum.

It is not sufficient to brief a board once or to make one "grand" report and assume that enough has been done. The board is dealing continually with the "regular" programs and therefore has its knowledge continually reinforced and its interest constantly rekindled. Moreover, since board members themselves were once students (and probably there were no special education programs when they went to school), they are comfortable with the regular program and consider themselves knowledgeable about it. But they may feel unfamiliar, and hence uncomfortable, with the concept of special education. So repeated discussions are necessary. Furthermore, the composition of an elected board may change every two to four years. Just when a board has become sophisticated about special education, a new board may sweep in, the majority of whose members are back at square one!

The special education administrator should not be discouraged by the need to rehash material previously covered in depth. After all, the board's business *is* education. Therefore, the new board should be considered analogous to a new group of students who need to be taught the material as if it were brand new. If the special education administrator has been successful as a teacher, each outgoing board member increases by one the size of the general public that is informed about and supportive of special education—the old ripple effect of education. The new board is a new class—a new challenge!

The special education administrator may help in meeting the challenge if the previous board has been brought to the point of support for special education where it adopted a philosophy—or policy statement—affirming that support and declaring its intention of meeting the needs of all children adequately and appropriately. Such a policy statement is more than window dressing. It puts special education alongside the regular program and is tangible evidence of the board's philosophy. The special education administrator should suggest such a written policy, which can be part of the board's regular policy handbook and/or serve as the introduction to a special education handbook. Regardless of where it appears, a written policy is a continuing commitment that binds a board even as its membership fluctuates.

A board thus carefully nurtured and guided by its special education staff will probably be less prone than others to "second guess" its placement team. Even though that may still happen, it is likely to occur less often if the board is well informed and has had chances to develop confidence in its special education personnel.

Although the special education team procedures are tied to legal requirements, its decisions are still normally subject to the approval of the board of education. As a rule, a board will be unlikely to question a decision about services that utilize existing district personnel. Decisions on behalf of individuals requiring additional personnel, whether as therapists, aides, tutors, interpreters, or others, are more vulnerable to close scrutiny and to possible rejection by the Board of Education. Decisions involving out-of-district placement, either in a day or residential setting (which can unfailingly be relied on to require a substantial outlay of funds for tuition and/or transportation) are the most apt to be questioned by the board, and in some instances it may refuse to approve the decision. Other decisions that boards are prone to question are those providing services such as summer school or special programs during school vacations. While most school children may suffer no permanent regressive effects from extended vacations (the usual over-the-summer forgetting that is dealt with through September review), special education children may regress considerably when their education is interrupted by a lengthy hiatus. In some instances, therefore, the planning team may arrive at the decision that summer or vacation programs are essential for educational reasons. And, if they are deemed *essential*, the team will probably also recommend that they be provided at board expense.

WHEN THE BOARD SAYS "NO"

What happens when a board balks at implementing a decision that the team has recommended?

Teams may be considered quasilegal bodies, in that the law requires that decisions about special education children be made by them. The legally conferred authority of the team may, at this point, come into conflict with the authority of the board of education, whose approval is necessary in most states and municipalities for the expenditure of funds for education. Regardless of other intricacies of board-municipality-taxpayer relationships, it is wise to avoid a situation where the board is in conflict with its own team. A healthy relationship between the board and the special education department, nurtured by efforts to keep the board informed about special education and cognizant of the legal ramifications, reduces the likelihood of conflict, but the team must still make extra attempts to avoid a standoff. The special education administrator's relationships with the board and the superintendent will probably serve to provide a tip-off as to when the board is apt to take an adamant position against a pending team decision.

As asserted in earlier chapters, teams making decisions about children, while having the welfare of the child as the first priority, need also to be reality-oriented and to know what is financially possible within the district. A team that has worked successfully with the superintendent and is aware of the financial status of the system is less likely to bring in a plan that the board will not approve. While the welfare of the child has a high priority, the team needs to consider other priorities as well, among them the health of the entire program and the extent to which recommending an exceedingly costly solution for one individual may jeopardize programs and services for other children or damage the delicate relationship between the board and the team.

However, when confrontations or conflict between team and board do occur there are several subsequent steps that may be pursued to resolve issues. If the board of education feels that it cannot approve a recommendation on the basis of excessive cost to the district, it should ask the team and the superintendent to renegotiate with the parents to determine whether there can be a mutually acceptable, less expensive alternative. Parents may be tractable, because often they themselves may wish to avoid legal confrontations and court fights which may delay the child's placement while being waged and which, even if won, can leave a residue of bitterness that can impede the child's progress. Because the possibility of a balky board always exists, it is wise for the team member who documents the specific recommendation and the reasoning that led to it and explains the alternatives that were considered, to do so in language that does not completely close the door on other alternatives.

This should not be seen as a recommendation for the team to "weasel" in its written recommendation. Rather, it is an acknowledgment of fallibility. No group of human beings, not even a special education team operating at peak efficiency, is utterly infallible; moreover, it is rare in human situations for there to be only *one* solution to a problem, or only *one* acceptable program for a child. Litigation is costly and damaging to the child as well as to the system. It is harmful to the child because it tends to damage the relationship between the family and the school system, and this relationship—important enough for non-special-education children—is even more critical for special education children. Therefore, litigation is to be avoided if it is possible to do so within the context of professional integrity and honest concern for child advocacy.

Sometimes the board may come into conflict with a team recommendation, not because it rejects that decision on the basis of cost but because the decision is challenged by the parents, and the board has some sympathy with the parents—or wants to avoid a fight. When the special education team makes a recommendation not in full accord with the wishes of the parents, the parents may, as the first step in exercising their due-process rights, request an administrative review by the board of education. This segment of due process is all very high-sounding and legalistic, but in effect it may be nothing but a formality. This is particularly true when the board has already supported a team's decision for placement. The board then would not be conducting a review of a decision still pending but of a decision that has already been made and approved. And a decision that has been made and approved has been approved by the board itself. Therefore, the board would, in effect, be conducting a review of its own decision. One need not be a cynic to discern that such a review would rarely result in the board's finding *for* the parents and against "itself."

However, in actual practice the concept of administrative review is not totally ineffectual from the parents' standpoint, especially when the team's decision has not yet been reviewed by the board or the team's decision concerns other than a placement-out issue. For example, when parents are unhappy with a team decision and are indicating that they will exercise due-process rights and request a review, the team may bring its decision to the board for approval with that information, and share both sides of the issue with the board. Some boards may back the team totally, particularly in situations they perceive as precedent-setting and opening the door to a deluge of requests. But if the circumstances are not such as to make the board feel it necessary to dig in, the board may ask the special education administrators to probe further, examine more closely, and try to come up with a compromise that will avoid legal entanglements that are excessively demanding of staff time and of money better spent on direct services to children.

To be completely blunt, sometimes a board may be reluctant to "take on" a parent because the parent may be seen as part of a member's political constituency. In smaller districts where board members are elected directly, they often see themselves as parent advocates and ombudsmen—or they may have made promises to behave that way during their election campaigns. But whatever the board's motivation, sometimes team members find themselves in a situation where the board, while not wishing to accede completely to the parents, may still wish to avoid a confrontation with parents and may throw the problem back in the lap of the team.

USING AN OMBUDSMAN

It is at this juncture that cautious and compassionate relationships with parents are paramount. A school system may wish to use an ombudsman or "parent assister" at this point. Such an ombudsman ideally should be a person knowledgeable about child development, about special education, and about the law, and one who has no direct relationship with either the board of education or the parents. He or she should also be someone aware of the financial constraints under which the board operates, but able to temper such concerns with an understanding of the parents' point of view. Such a neutral outsider might actually act somewhat in the nature of a mediator but would not be functioning in a legal capacity.

How can a team find such a paragon when one is needed? Probably nowhere, unless the school system had the forethought to anticipate the need. There are probably several people in any community who would be willing to volunteer their services in this capacity and it may be productive for a special education department to recruit volunteers and to train them in advance of need. As noted in Chapter VII, a fully developed ombudsman or parent-assister program might be useful even before the confrontation point is reached, as many parents might feel more comfortable in team meetings leading up to a decision if accompanied by a knowledgeable but neutral outsider.

The challenge to a system interested in developing such a resource is to devise the training program so that it provides what is needed while maintaining the neutrality of the ombudsmen. This can probably best be done by involving the parents of special education children who have "been through the system" in the development of the program and the actual training; this was done in Greenwich, Connecticut. Providing such training will assure that the ombudsmen see the programs from the parents' as well as the professionals' points of view and will maintain the credibility of the ombudsmen with the parents.

BUDGET IMPLICATIONS

A school budget is, at its most effective, a management tool that is a close estimate of how the board will allocate its funds for a year. There are many ways to develop a budget, but whether one is an advocate of zero-based budgeting or of budgeting based upon an anticipated continuation and expansion of usual costs, there are commonly accepted and effective ways of estimating most costs.

Staffing costs can be calculated with an acceptable degree of accuracy based upon projected enrollment, existing scales, and understanding of turnover experience, etc. Material costs are estimated using different formulae; the costs of running a building can be estimated using past experience, etc. Obviously, no school budget is totally prepared for every emergency, but experience can even suggest how much to allocate to a fund for emergency repairs. Unfortunately, however, special education costs are much less predictable because of out-of-district placements which may not be anticipated and which may involve very large sums of money, no matter what "caps" may be placed on the costs.

If a child moves into a district and requires extraordinary services or placement in an expensive out-of-district program, this can cost as much as $20,000 or more. Several such unexpected expenses can very nearly "break" a school budget. Many outside placements, moreover, may be court-ordered or may be associated with hospitalization or institutionalization of a child in places where the educational component (if that is all the school board is ordered to pay) may be extremely high.

In some school districts, the out-of-district costs are estimated each year and included in the budget. In lucky years, the estimates come close to reality. In disastrous years, costs may far exceed the estimates. Under those circumstances, the school board has but two viable options: swallow the excess costs and find the money in the "regular" education budget, or return to the body controlling finances and ask for additional funds. The former solution is clearly undesirable. It may penalize the regular education program and lead to increasing hostility on the part of staff and parents toward the special education component, which may be seen as eating up an unfair and disproportionate share of the limited funds available for schools. But the second solution can be difficult as well, unless the board of education has clearly established with the agency controlling municipal funds that this portion of the special education budget is highly unpredictable and that there may be a need to request additional funds beyond those officially allocated to education.

Such a request can lead to unpleasant political fallout and can even negatively affect the way the school system's overall budget request is viewed the following year. Anyone—school staff member, board of education member, or interested citizen—who has during the past few years followed the bumpy course of school budget requests from initial recommendation to final approval can attest to the stark reality of this view.

Putting "caps" on the amount of money a school district may spend on special educational services either for one child or for the whole program, based on a proportion of its entire budget, is a solution some states may find appealing. This procedure could save a considerable sum of money for a locality. But the power of aroused parents or children with special needs is a force to be reckoned with. Pressure by parent groups is unlikely to abate, regardless of the changes in the law or in the method of funding which undoubtedly will be proposed or enacted in the next decade.

Therefore, it may be time for the costs of placing youngsters in out-of-district placements or the unusual special education costs that may occur within the district to be handled apart from the regular education budget. It may be time for society at large to assume its responsibility for meeting these children's educational needs as it does the needs of other youngsters.

The cost of schooling children with special needs, thereby helping them to become self-sufficient members of society—to the good of society as a whole—should possibly be seen as a general social service cost rather than strictly as an educational cost. If a community accepted this view, or if a school board could persuade its financing agency to accept this view, then the special education costs resulting from planning-team decisions might not necessarily be included in the school budget at all. Rather, the board of education and the municipal finance agency might agree that the school board will request funds to cover these specific costs as they arise rather than try to estimate them and include them in the school budget. Ultimately, the money comes out of the same "pockets." But handling the funds in a different way could reduce much of the hostility within the school system toward the "expensive" children and programs.

To support this approach is not to advocate "open-ended budgeting," a method which would be fiscally sloppy and reduce true accountability and would probably be rejected by any astute city or town fiscal authority. The school officials would certainly need to develop a projection for anticipated costs based upon known cases and past experience of how many new cases tend to arise during the year either as result of new students moving into the district or of new identification of students already in the district. The money could be appropriated to the municipality's general fund, however, rather than to the board of education and be earmarked for this purpose. In some municipalities it may be more appropriate to set up a separate fund. The appropriation would be made with the understanding that if the caseload proved larger than usual the municipality would provide the additional funds needed. Thus, the regular educational programs would not need to be squeezed. In a year when the caseload happened to be lower than anticipated the municipality would be the "winner," because it would end the year with a surplus in that account.

This method is similar to the situation in some states that have separate special education mill levies. A separate levy may meet the costs of special education without impinging on regular education funds. However, by putting the costs into sharper focus and assigning a particular segment of the tax bill to these costs, the method could serve, again, to pit the handicapped against the "normal" and escalate antagonism. Pitting handicapped against normal is even more to be avoided than pitting agency against agency. Moreover, as Featherstone (1980, 36) indicates, "parents and other community members may disagree about priorities" for the handicapped. She quotes a parent of a handicapped child reporting a neighbor's remark, "You know, Barbara, you're pretty lucky to have Luke picked up in a cab every day, with the government paying for it." What this woman was saying, according to Featherstone, was "My taxes are paying for your taxi-cabs and I resent it."

Funding special education from state resources rather than local district funds protects districts against interagency conflicts and probably minimizes interparent hostility by blurring the source of funds which pay for special services. However, this approach removes a measure of local control over special education, and parents of handicapped children may feel it is more desirable to be closer to the source that determines the level and nature of expenditures for their children's education. They may feel it is easier to lobby school board members whom they may know personally than to deal with the state bureaucracy, although the success of parent advocacy for special education on the national level certainly suggests their ability to deal with state officialdom as well.

The conflict, if it can be so termed, over whether a school system should bear all responsibility toward handicapped children or whether their education should be considered the responsibility of the municipality has its echoes in conflicts between boards of education and other state agencies and certainly between the states and the federal government.

Customarily, problems arise—and often wind up in court—over "related services" and who should pay for them. Winds of change may blow for many years, but this much appears certain: related services to handicapped children which are necessary to permit them to profit from education will, increasingly, be paid for by public agencies. It is up to the special education team to educate the board of education about the *need* for these services, while at the same time zealously guarding against pressure by other agencies to shunt their legal responsibilities onto the educational agency. The team members and special education administrators need to spend some time keeping up with changes in regulations and court interpretations while they walk this legalistic tightrope.

NEXUS QUESTIONS

Similarly, questions of "nexus" often plague boards of education and special education teams. These issues will probably remain thorny, particularly if the divorce rate continues to increase and joint custody arrangements proliferate. One cannot truly fault parents who, through complicated custodial arrangements, have a possible connection with more than one school system and therefore try to get the system they perceive as having better special educational services to assume responsibility for their children's education. And divorce/custody situations, tough as they may be, are not the only source of nexus problems. On these issues, the special education team *must* function as board of education loyalists, stalwartly guarding against any improper assignment of cost responsibility for children for whom other towns should be responsible. But beyond being alert to the problems of nexus, the special educators should turn responsibility for legal determination over to the school board attorney, for two important reasons. The most obvious, of course, is that the educators are not legal experts and cannot defend the board in these matters. The second is that the educators should avoid adversarial relationships on nexus issues with parents with whom—assuming nexus *is* established—they may be working in an educational partnership.

Ideally, the parents, the schools, and the various social and civic agencies should be partners. As Assistant Secretary for Education Jean Tufts put it in a 1982 speech before the Association for Children with Learning Disabilities, "In the corporate metaphor, I will talk of the profits of this venture. 'Profit' means the effective and humanitarian education, training and rehabilitation of learning disabled children, youth and adults. . . . Our efficiency in using all of our resources towards this profit will be the mark by which future historians will judge us."

SUMMARY

In this chapter we have dealt with the relationship of the special education team to the board of education, noting that, during times of decreasing enrollment and diminishing resources for education, boards do not readily commit funds to special education. With resources spread thinner, yet with growing public concern about the overall results of education—for all students—dollars for special education may become harder and harder to extract. Special education personnel and parents of children with special needs must have effective strategies for addressing this phenomenon.

The high-minded, professional, child-advocacy position may not always receive strong support, and special education staff and administrators may be pulled in different directions by parents, direct superiors, board members, and school superintendents. Therefore, special education administrators need to assume responsibility for educating board members about special education mandates and about children's needs. They should attempt to develop the board's interest in special education and its pride in the success of special education programs. Handicapped children's achievements should be highlighted with the same frequency as the accomplishments of other students.

The board should see newspaper reports of special students' activities and accomplishments, receive regular reports of their standardized test results (as they do the test results of mainstream children), and be given follow-up data on the impact of special education on children's future education and careers. In this way, the board may develop a sense of ownership of the special education program.

The special education staff may be able to form an effective alliance with the school board attorney, who can help brief the board on laws and regulations. Similarly, the parents of handicapped children are often well organized, vocal, energetic, and effective lobbyists for special education programs.

The special education staff should be prepared to deal with situations where the board of education will not concur in a team recommendation. Compromise, rather than confrontation, should be sought with boards of education as with parents. Even a capable well-functioning team should be able to acknowledge that its recommendation is not necessarily the only possible alternative. Options should be kept open so that acceptable alternatives may be developed to avoid adversarial relationships and damaging litigation.

A school system may find that utilization of an ombudsman to resolve differences is effective and helps keep differences from escalating.

Special education budgets, particularly the portion allocated to outside placements, can be volatile and vulnerable. School systems and teams should seek budgeting procedures that reduce hostility toward "expensive to educate" children.

Special education teams and administrators can develop strategies for directing the energy of the system and the community toward effective rehabilitation of children with special needs, for they, just as surely as their more fortunate sisters and brothers, are the nation's most precious resource.

References

Armer, B., and Thomas, B. K. "Attitudes Toward Interdisciplinary Collaboration in Pupil-Personnel Service Teams." *Journal of School Psychology* 16 (1978): 167-76.

Asch, S. E. *Social Psychology.* New York: Prentice-Hall, 1952.

Ballard, J. *Second Insight—PL 94-142 Report sent to Lawmakers, The Council for Exceptional Children.* Government Report, Vol. 12, no. 1, Jan. 1981.

Bardon, J. "A Personalized Account of the Development and Status of School Psychology." *Journal of School Psychology* 19 (1981): 199-210.

Bardon, J. "Small Group Synthesis, Group C." *The School Psychology Review* 10, no. 1 (1981): 297-306.

Berlin, I. N. "Preventive Aspects of Mental Health Consultation to Schools." In *School Consultation*, ed. J. Meyers, R. Martin, and I. Hyman, 211-21. Springfield, IL: Charles C. Thomas, 1977.

Borgatta, E. F.; Couch, A. S.; and Bales, R. F. "Some Findings Relevant to the Great Man Theory of Leadership." In *Small Groups: Studies in Social Interaction*, ed. P. Hare, E. F. Borgatta, and R. F. Bales, 568-74. New York: Alfred A. Knopf, 1962.

Brown, D.; Wyne, M. D.; Blackburn, J. E.; and Powell, W. C. *Consultation—Strategy for Improving Education.* Boston: Allyn and Bacon, 1979.

Butler, A. S., and Maher, C. A. "Conflict and Special Service Teams: Perspectives and Suggestions for School Psychologists." *Journal of School Psychology* 19 (1981): 62-70.

Education of the Handicapped 8, no. 5 (10 March 1982): 1-3. Arlington, VA: Capitol Publications.

Education of the Handicapped 8, no. 6 (24 March 1982): 9-10. Arlington, VA: Capitol Publications.

Education of the Handicapped 8, no. 22 (3 November 1982): 1-2. Arlington, VA: Capitol Publications.

Education of the Handicapped 8, no. 23 (17 November 1982): 4. Arlington, VA: Capitol Publications.

Education of the Handicapped 8, no. 25 (15 December 1982): 3. Arlington, VA: Capitol Publications.

Featherstone, H. *A Difference in the Family.* New York: Basic Books, 1980.

Gable, R. K.; Pecheone, R. L.; and Gillung, T. B. "A Needs Assessment Model For Establishing Personnel Training Priorities." *Teacher Education and Special Education (TEASE)* 4, no. 4 (1981): 8-14.

Gibb, C. A. "The Principles and Traits of Leadership." Chap. 24 in *Handbook of Social Psychology*, ed. G. Lindzey, Vol. II. Reading, MA: Addison-Wesley, 1954.

Gilmore, G. "School Psychologist-Parent Contact: An Alternative Model." *Psychology in the Schools* 11 (1974): 170-173.

Grimes, J. "Shaping the Future of School Psychology." *The School Psychology Review* 10, no. 2 (1981): 206-231.

Hare, P.; Borgata, E. F.; and Bales, R. F. *Small Groups: Studies in Social Interaction.* New York: Alfred A. Knopf, 1962.

Hudson Board of Education v. Amy Rowley, U. S. Supreme Court 80-1002, *U.S. Law Week*, 20 June 1982.

Klein, S. "Secretary Bell—On Education for the Disabled." *The Exceptional Parent* 2, no. 4 (Aug. 1981): 9-10.

Lambert, N. "School Psychology Training for the Decades Ahead." *The School Psychology Review* 10, no. 2 (1981): 194-205.

Lindzey, G., and Aronson, E., eds. *Handbook of Social Psychology.* Vol. 4, Chap. 31. Reading, MA: Addison-Wesley, 1969.

Losen, S., and Diament, B. *Parent Conferences in the Schools.* Boston: Allyn and Bacon, 1978.

Maeroff, G. *Don't Blame the Kids: The Trouble with America's Public Schools.* New York: McGraw-Hill, 1982.

Maher, C. A., and Kratochwill, T. R. "Principles and Procedures of Program Evaluation." *School Psychology Monograph* 4, no. 1 (1980): 1-23.

Pfeiffer, S. I. "The School Based Interprofessional Team: Recurring Problems and Some Possible Solutions." *Journal of School Psychology* 18, no. 4 (1980): 388-394.

Pfeiffer, S. I. "The Problems Facing Multidisciplinary Teams: As Perceived by Team Members." *Psychology in the Schools* 18 (1981): 330-333.

Schleifer, M. "Parents and the IEP." *The Exceptional Parent* 9, no. 4 (August 1979): 10-13.

Shaw, M. E. "Some Effects of Unequal Distribution of Information Upon Group Performance in Various Communication Nets." *Journal of Abnormal Social Psychology* 49 (1954): 547-553.

Sherif, M. and Sherif, C. *An Outline of Social Psychology.* New York: Harper and Bros., 1956.

Tolor, A. "Assessment myths and Current Fads." *Psychology in the Schools* 15 (1978): 205-209.

Trachtman, G. M. "On Such A Full Sea." *The School Psychology Review* 10, no. 2 (1981): 138-181.

Trachtman, G. M. "Pupils, Parents, Privacy and the School Psychologist." *American Psychologist* 27 (1972): 37-45.

U. S. Department of Education. The Office of Special Education. *Briefing Paper: Initial Review of Regulations.* Washington, D.C., 1 Sept. 1981.

Vensel, D. "Assuming the Responsibility for the Future of School Psychology." *The School Psychology Review* 10, no. 2 (1981): 182-193.

Watras, J. "IEP's Are Not the Answer." *Educational Leadership* 39, no. 2 (Nov. 1981): 143.

White, R., and Lippitt, R. "Leader Behavior and Member Reaction in Three Social Climates." In *Group Dynamics*, ed. D. Cartwright, and A. Zander, 527-553. New York: Row Peterson, 1960.

Whyte, W. F. *Street Corner Society.* Chicago: University of Chicago Press, 1955.

Yoshida, R. K.; Fenton, K. S.; Maxwell, J. P.; and Kaufman, N. J. "Ripple Effect: Communication of Planning Team Decisions to Program Implementation." *Journal of School Psychology* 16 (1978): 178-183.

Ysseldyke, J. E., and Mirkin, P. K. "The Use of Assessment Information to Plan Instructional Intervention." In *The Handbook of School Psychology*, ed. C. R. Reynolds, and T. B. Gutkin, 395-409. New York: John Wiley & Sons, 1982.

Ysseldyke, J. E., and Weinberg, R. A., eds. "The Future of Psychology in the Schools: Proceedings of the Spring Hill Symposium." *The School Psychology Review* 10, no. 2 (1981): 116-120.

Index